Praise for

WHAT JUST HAPPENED

"A spirited testimony to hard times. . . . Related with appealing candor. . . . The narrative is freshest when the author hews closest to his own life: the childhood illness that left him immunocompromised; the consolations of smoking weed, listening to music . . . and especially his tender remembrance of his grandmother, the minimalist artist Anne Truitt. His radiant portrait of Truitt shines as a transcendent ending to his chronicle of a dark year."
                                        —*Kirkus Reviews*

"When it became clear in March 2020 that the coronavirus was more than an annoying temporary disruption, some writers took to keeping COVID diaries. We're fortunate that one as gifted and insightful as Los Angeles–based novelist and critic Charles Finch chose to preserve his recollections in the eloquent, fierce *What Just Happened: Notes on a Long Year*. . . . Finch is a keen political observer whose takedowns of the Trump administration's almost willfully incompetent leadership are both savage and, at times, savagely funny."
                                 —*BookPage* (starred review)

"Finch's precise and stunning day-by-day chronicle of the COVID-19 pandemic brings back all the shock and bewilderment, fear and outrage, grim humor and stark revelations. . . . [Finch] is nimbly incisive, scathing, and hilarious; his political analysis keen and prescient."
                                            —*Booklist*

"[A] perceptive chronicle of [Finch's] experience of the Covid-19 pandemic. . . . Readers will feel an intimate familiarity with the bewilderment that imbues his early observations, as he laments not being able to make certain foods because of scarcity issues. . . . Even at its darkest, this serves as a moving testament to the resilience of humanity."   —*Publishers Weekly*

Charles Finch

WHAT JUST HAPPENED

Charles Finch is a book critic and essayist as well as the author of fifteen novels. He is a regular contributor to *The New York Times* and the *Chicago Tribune* and the recipient of the 2017 Nona Balakian Citation for Excellence in Reviewing from the National Book Critics Circle. He lives in Los Angeles.

WHAT
JUST
HAPPENED

WHAT
JUST
HAPPENED

Charles Finch

VINTAGE BOOKS

A DIVISION OF PENGUIN RANDOM HOUSE LLC

NEW YORK

FIRST VINTAGE BOOKS EDITION 2023

Copyright © 2021 by Charles Finch
Preface copyright © 2023 by Charles Finch

All rights reserved. Published in the United States
by Vintage Books, a division of Penguin Random House LLC,
New York, and distributed in Canada by Penguin Random House
Canada Limited, Toronto. Originally published in hardcover
in the United States by Alfred A. Knopf, a division of Penguin
Random House LLC, New York, in 2021.

Vintage and colophon are registered
trademarks of Penguin Random House LLC.

Grateful acknowledgment is made to Penguin Books for permission
to reprint an excerpt from "A Wife Explains Why She Likes Country"
from *Hidden Stuff* by Barbara Ras, copyright © 2006 by Barbara Ras.
Reprinted by permission of Penguin Books, an imprint of Penguin
Publishing Group, a division of Penguin Random House LLC.
All rights reserved.

The Library of Congress has cataloged the Knopf edition as follows:
Names: Finch, Charles (Charles B.), author.
Title: What just happened / Charles Finch.
Description: First edition. | New York : Alfred A. Knopf, 2021.
Identifiers: LCCN 2021014661 (print) | LCCN 2021014662 (ebook)
Subjects: LCSH: Finch, Charles (Charles B.)—Diaries. |
  Two thousand twenty, A.D.—Social aspects—United States. |
  GSAFD: Essays.
Classification: LCC PS3606.I526 W47 2021 (print) | LCC PS3606.I526 (ebook) |
  DDC 814/.6 B—dc23
LC record available at https://lccn.loc.gov/2021014661
LC ebook record available at https://lccn.loc.gov/2021014662

Vintage Books Trade Paperback ISBN: 978-0-593-47020-6
eBook ISBN: 978-0-593-31908-6

Author photograph © Abigail R. Collins
Book design by Cassandra J. Pappas

vintagebooks.com

Printed in the United States of America
10 9 8 7 6 5 4 3 2 1

For Alexander, Annabel, and Emily,
with my endless love

PREFACE TO THE VINTAGE BOOKS EDITION (2023)

But really—what just happened? Here in America we had problems, of course, but we had generally been shielded from the mass disruptions that befell other nations, the war, famine, and contagion. Then, in early 2020, there were a few dim rumors of a new disease until suddenly, without enough warning, everyone had to go inside for a year, and the texture of life was instantly, radically different. It turned out that this virus, whatever Donald Trump's tantrums to the contrary might have suggested, was like all others in obeying no border laws.

The quarantine asked the question of who we actually were. Briefly released from the grip of hypercapitalism, people started baking, planting flowers, taking long walks while listening to Fleetwood Mac. It was both peaceful and terrifying. It seemed as if the order of things was in a state of disintegration—at least, until the notion dawned on us, crystallized in the exhilarated fury of the George Floyd protests, that perhaps out of this moment we might reconstitute ourselves in a new way.

From the very first day, I felt an urgency to write about it. When you're a teenage writer, there's a period when the words rush out of you effortlessly. That sensation came back to me in 2020. Which is not to say that this book was an outpouring, exactly. In fact, during May and June of the year, I was working on something different, a task I had to finish. But in every unused minute of the day, my mind was afire with ideas for this book: worries, anecdotes, songs, memories. In the fall, when I finally had time to write it, I gathered these notes and the words just started to come. It took a huge amount of effort after that to shape them into what this book became. It was brutal, lonely, soul-scouring work. But it mattered to me in a way that writing hadn't since I was sixteen.

Maybe your pandemic was like mine, a wending, halting, and finally incomplete journey of self-realization; maybe not. What I do know is that those of us who were alive then will be talking about it for the rest of our lives. In some ways, we haven't even started yet. For a while many readers of this book would tell me, "I didn't think I was ready to read about 2020 yet, but . . ." Only more recently have people *wanted* to start thinking about covid. As I write this, there's a trend on social media of 2020 nostalgia. Living room dances to "Savage," sourdough starters, Zoom reunions, ringing bells from a fire escape to say hello to your neighbors each night. Now the most frequent questions I get are not why I'd want to write about the pandemic but about what happened to a certain friend in the book, or what I think now about something I'd written then, in retrospect. Some people write me just to say what their own year was like. I rarely respond, I'm ashamed to admit. I think maybe I don't want to write about 2020 ever again, after the demented concentration it took to get it down on paper while it was happening. Still, I think about it all the time. If you see me, feel free to ask.

2020

MARCH

March 11

There's an emotional chill in the streets today for the first time. People are suddenly thinking and planning, which are not always part of the normal duties of life. You can see it in their expressions. Coronavirus has been a story for a month or so, but only in the last ten days has it seemed like an immediate problem, and not until today did it seem much more alarming than the various deadly flus that have been arriving here by bird and swine (is swine just pigs?) since my childhood.

It now seems inevitable that in certain places where the virus is spreading, people will have to quarantine for a week or two. I tell my mom I think it will be okay. That doesn't completely reflect what my friend Nathan, a doctor in New York, has been saying, but it at least sort of does. The best news of the past few days was his confirmation that the virus doesn't seem to affect children, really the first thing you would wish for in a pandemic. But nearly everything else is an educated guess. We still don't know how you get it. According to Rush Limbaugh, it's "like the common cold" and "all of this panic is just not warranted," so presumably we're fucked.

However serious it ends up, the virus is already politicized. A reporter asks GOP senator Jim Inhofe of Oklahoma, who's a sprightly 85, what precautions he's taking about this illness, which is reportedly particularly deadly for the old, and he replies "Want to shake hands?"

March 12

I drove just to take a drive today. No traffic anywhere. In *Los Angeles*.

A consensus is firming up hour by hour, and it seems more likely that we will all have to lock in for a few weeks to slow the spread of this new virus, not just people with symptoms. On the first of the month it would have been an unthinkable suggestion. But the directives to work remotely are cascading down—people guiltily excited for a week or two at home—and in big cities, stores and restaurants are closed, with cheerful signs in their windows that they'll reopen as soon as it's safe. For better or worse, retail gives our world its texture. When it's gone you feel it.

Most museums around the world closed today too, and this evening, in the actual midst of games I think, the NBA suspended its season, which was maybe the biggest jolt yet. It came after the 7′1″ Rudy Gobert (who made the not especially well-received covid joke of touching every microphone at a press conference a couple days ago) tested positive. Tom Hanks has also tested positive, and there's an online feeling of dread on his behalf.

Since Trump won, we've congratulated ourselves on our luck that he hasn't had to face a crisis. This is how bad he is with things going okay! people would say and chuckle. Well, here we go. So far he's lurching around in search of an alibi, his focus mostly on minimizing the threat of the virus, for what seems like a strange emotional tangle of personal and political reasons. Almost every day he says some variation of the phrase "It will go away," which is how children think about bad stuff, down to refusing to say the bad word out loud. But it's worked on us, to some degree—we were asleep. In part that's probably because even in the most liberal mind, if you could strip every veneer of politeness away, there was a sense that the virus was happening in China, where stuff sort of always seems to be happening. Their economy is expanding so quickly that we've learned it fires off these kinds of externalities at random, besides which they have egregiously limited freedom of the press, so news about the virus has often seemed uncertain.

But now "the whole of Italy is closed," as a headline making its way around Twitter from the *Corriere della Sera* says, and no one sensible thinks coronavirus is a regional problem anymore. The Italian lockdowns are the most severe restriction on movement in a western democracy since World War II, apparently. (Anyway, as Nathan said, if we're comparing countries, by the time China was at this stage of their outbreak—20 deaths—they had already built two new hospitals. We can't even test people yet.) On the news from Italy, the number has suddenly shot up: as many as 20,000 people may die in America, a number so big it's laced with a certain grim comedy for those of us who can reach deep into the mists of autocrat time, six days ago, and remember when Trump refused to let a few hundred people get off the cruise ship *Grand Princess*. "I don't need to have the numbers double because of one ship that wasn't our fault," as he said.

There are long sections of shelving at the grocery store that are empty; enough sauerkraut and maraschino cherries left to feed an army on the march, but no milk, no bread, no meat, and only the most homely non-perishable items (I pass a lone can that says **Unsalted Asparagus Spears,** in glum resignation to its contents).

If you've spent your life wandering like a docile cow through supermarket aisles stocked with an array of food that would humble an ancient emperor, it's not a good feeling. "Will we see canned peas again?" That's a terrifying question to ask your friends even 80% in jest. And people are terrified. That's the main thing. Everyone seems so scared.

I think I was naively sure that something would judder into motion in our creaky old government—some lifelong bureaucrat on the fifth floor of an overflow office in Alexandria would get an unusual fax from a colleague at the CDC about the numbers in Wuhan, the city in China where this new, fifth strain of coronavirus seems to have originated, and at that moment a long chain of rote superpower stuff would develop, labs unmothballed, production lines whipping into life. America is such an enormous enterprise that up until this moment it's still seemed that even if our government has been starved down to its bones by Republicans and big business (except the military, of course, grotesquely fattened up by profiteers) it would have some reflexive memory of capability lurking in it, which would be triggered and creak meaningfully forward while the meaningless theater of Trump played out overhead. Maybe it will still happen.

March 13

Locked in. The shelf-stable foods I ordered last week have started to arrive, today lentils and oats. I contemplate them and feel like a farmer in the Baltics receiving state rations.

Sarah Palin has been revealed as Bear Mask on *The Masked Singer*.

March 15

A day of rain among days of rain, eaves dripping hard, adding to the sense of strangeness and interiority these numb hours already have. I love the rain, and having grown up on the east coast I miss it. You can be inside and rain makes you more inside. At around six I put on a soft sweatshirt and go out into our tiny high-hedged yard, which is just big enough for a few chairs and tables and a single small tree. I sit in a wooden armchair with a green cushion and carefully roll and light a joint, an indulgence on a Sunday, but to hell with it, there's a virus. I listen to Fleetwood Mac on my headphones and sip iced coffee and feel my body soften away from its anxieties. Beneath the gray sky, the stout California trees, swaying in the wind, look suddenly both greener and less sure of themselves. Everything feels sad and witchy and possible.

I debate making spaghetti for dinner, my favorite food, but it's one of the things that's scarcest on the shelves. (Only lasagna noodles last time I went to Albertson's.) Finally, with a reckless feeling, I go inside and make it anyway, adding butter, pepper, salt, and cheap parmesan cheese, and eat it extremely hot, with unbecoming intensity and great happiness.

I text woozily with my friend Ben, who's been ordering cans of beans since mid-February. I couldn't understand why everyone wasn't doing it, he says.

Ordering beans? I write back, and realize that I'm pretty stoned.

No, getting ready!

I tell him, ah, of course, no, he'd been right (one of the most depressing things you can tell a best friend) and we talk over what's unavailable and what we have on hand. Both here and in New York there are no household cleaners, bottled water, granola bars, pasta, canned goods, rice, soap, lighters, or rubbing alcohol, and above all no hand sanitizer, soap, or toilet paper, or really any paper goods now, though you might occasionally still see a pack of fancy party napkins, whereas the last hand sanitizer went off the shelves two days ago. We've both still found a picked-over but normal selection of fruits and vegetables. (A lot of food for religious festivals is HIGHLY available. If you've been looking to stock up on matzoh and want to filigree it with a spicy Cinco de Mayo dip, your moment has come.) Both Ben and I—we were roommates for four years in college, after all—have been reading in depth about the supply chain. We agree that it sounds as if it's wobbling but safe, this might be the worst moment. But having the conversation, an alarm that had been going off in a distant part of my mind falls quiet. Unbidden, Ben says I'll probably be able to find pasta in a week or two. It just might not be my favorite kind.

I admit to him I wasn't worried enough about the virus until we were asking Nathan questions a few days ago in our group chat (the same five of us have been on it since 2005, including Ben and Nathan, and we write back and forth intermittently throughout the day, previously on e-mail, now mostly on Slack). *What's the first date on the calendar that we'll wake up and not think about corona for an entire day? May 12th?* I asked Nathan.

He wrote back, *That's when it'll be peak corona, dude.*

What? This is not the peak?

To that, Nathan, who's generally unflappable—an emergency room doctor in New York—wrote back, *Charlie, it hasn't started yet.*

Before going, I tell Ben to stay safe—not perfunctorily. New York is the center of the virus in America right now and Nathan's stories about the ER at his hospital there are getting worse.

_____

One thing he says: every day he sees new ER patients who should technically be dead. A normal blood oxygen level is about 99%, he explained to us, it's not great to see anything below a level of 95%, and you admit a patient automatically when they're at 91% or lower. At 85% there's usually imminent danger, and if they're not already there that's when he pages the lung specialists.

Or that's the standard he's worked by. Now he goes to the hospital and sees patients, many of them day laborers passed on to him from the flooded hospitals in Queens, who say, sitting up and to all appearances okay, though taking off oxygen masks to speak, "Hey, doc, finally, can I get out of here yet?"

Nathan says he checks the chart again to confirm what he'd read a moment before—that the blood oxygen level of the person in front of him is at something like, say, 70%, maybe 72%, either way a number that's usually, in his words, *incompatible with life*. It's a symptom he's never seen in another virus. No, he tells them, you can't leave quite yet.

In other circumstances I would welcome some time at home. I was traveling for most of February. I had a book come out and went to thirteen cities on tour, which means I went on at least 26 flights, though there were some connections in there. The last place I stopped was Seattle, which was the country's hot spot at the time—there had been two deaths in a nursing home in Washington in February, following the hospitalization of a man who had come directly from Wuhan. Aside from more masks in airports, even then life didn't seem much different than usual. I did the event there with my friend Mary Ann and then she and her husband and I had dinner at a pub. The turnout was good, too, we agreed.

It was the longest book tour I've ever done. The first three days were fine, but after that it started to take on a horrible eerie quality, and for a week in the middle it turned into a single long dream in which I did nothing but listen to Radiohead and walk through a single infinite airport, like the looping train at the end of *The Unconsoled*. It's only been a few weeks, but I'm not sure I could say which store was in which city from that time. I missed Emily and our dog Lucy and having time to write and being at home, but it was more than that. In retrospect the dysphoria may have come partly from the instinctive sense around me (I was in denial, as my question to Nathan showed) that everything was on the verge of getting bad.

There were always four good hours a day, which was the exact amount of time it took me to arrive at a new hotel from the airport, go for a long walk, shower, change, get to the signing (and I loved those without reservation, the readers and the bookstores alike, particularly the booksellers, the heroes of my world) and then go back to my hotel, eat whatever was free on the table in my room, and watch an episode of *The Haunting of Hill House* on Netflix. (Pretty good show.) Then I would sleep for six hours and get into another car going to another airport and try to listen to something besides Radiohead before giving up and listening to Radiohead—the music of not knowing how to feel on this earth.

Of course, I was lucky to be on tour. Every so often someone tells me how many writers make a living in America, and the number constantly gets smaller. At first it was a few thousand. Then it was a thousand, then four hundred, then, not long ago, in a Weimar-like bit of deflation, seventy-one, according to a poet I know from Chicago.

People love to ask what it's like to be a writer. I'm still not sure myself. In the midst of writing, when I forget what I'm doing, I love it. But those are infrequent times. As for praise, I never believe a word of it, not deep down. The only good compliment I ever got was at a reception after a lecture I gave at a small college in Missouri. The provost's wife, who was handing out prizes to the students who had written the best essays about my book, was sitting next to me, and after we had talked about her life, she said, in reference to absolutely nothing, "You know, I didn't like the book."

"No?" I said.

"No." She thought for a moment. "But you could tell all the words were in the right place." Then she nodded firmly once, as if that sealed the subject of my attributes forever, which no doubt for her it did. But I treasure the memory of her impartiality, which held a rare vindication—because she was right, I put every word in the right place. It took for fucking ever, and I hated it, but I put every word in the right place, and it was fine with me if she didn't like the novel itself. I was just so grateful that she noticed.

At any rate, I have nothing to write for a few weeks. I can just worry about politics, dying, and tweeting. Huge relief.

One of my favorite announcements comes from Missouri's governor, Mike Parson, a Republican, via Twitter:

Missouri specific:
- ZERO confirmed cases
- Nearly 17 people have been tested
- Testing CAN be done in Missouri
- Prisons, nursing homes & mental health facilities are a concern

Nearly 17! God love them. Is that 16? 15? 16 and a dog? Also it's good to know that there's not an invisible border coinciding precisely with Missouri's state lines that prevents testing from being done there. Testing CAN be done in Missouri. Will it? Don't hold your breath? CAN it? We haven't yet found a supernatural reason why not!

According to a news article, the NBA team the New Orleans Pelicans announced last week that they would have to release their staff for the remainder of the season. The owner of the Pelicans is a woman named Gayle Benson, 73, whose two signal achievements in her life thus far have been first the selection and then the demise of her husband. According to reports, she has $3.1 billion. Anyway, a little while later, the team's best player, an extravagantly gifted nineteen-year-old named Zion Williamson, who plays on a rookie scale contract that pays him a small fraction of the tasteful .1 that Gayle has managed to append to her three billion other dollars, commits to covering the salaries of the Pelicans' employees.

A dad on my street is teaching himself to skateboard. Calamitous news. All that can happen is that he gets hit by a car or, worse, improves. He carefully puts a beer on the curb of the street in front of his house at about 6:00, a gentle time of day in this mildest part of the Los Angeles year, and then over and over does that thing new skateboarders do—I've never been on a skateboard—where you ride about five feet and then sprint forward off the front of the skateboard for twelve feet all mad, as if you just missed doing a really good move, while the board chases your heels. (I witness the birth of this hobby over the course of several walks, I'm not

Harriet the Spy.) Social media, too, is alive with new endeavors: sourdough bread, couch to 5K, scallions growing in jars on city windowsills, everyone doing something different to take advantage of being home and also to try not to feel permanently afraid. Well. Godspeed street dad. I wish you'd wear a helmet.

It seizes me up in the insides, that oxygen thing. Just suddenly—incompatible with life.

March 16

Today, for the first time, Trump says that the virus is "not under control." I can't tell why he's backed off his courageous stance that it was. He had previously said the virus *was* literally "under control" (either "totally" or "very much," depending on his mood) on January 30th, February 22nd, February 23rd, February 24th, and February 25th. Those last four days must be when the warnings in even his famously abbreviated morning briefing got so fearful that it was impossible to ignore them—that is, when a real president would have started to act, and he instead began this verbal triage with himself and us.

Yet it's a small victory for rationality that even the world's most incredible pretender of things not being a big deal can no longer pretend this is not a big deal. Though he still won't come close to admitting the full danger of the virus. "He's just going to look so foolish for so long," Nathan (rarely especially political) says.

It was on February 25th, the last of the dates Trump said the virus was "under control," that a doctor named Nancy Messonnier, head of the CDC's National Center for Immunization and Respiratory Diseases, said, accidentally contradicting him with facts, "This is going to be bad" and the time had come "for hospitals, schools, and everyday people to begin preparing." After her comments, Trump threatened to fire her, and she was left out of all subsequent public briefings. The same day, Trump's economic adviser Larry Kudlow, a former TV host who looks like a wooden dummy that came to life and developed a legally actionable addiction to sun beds, called the containment of covid here "pretty close to airtight."

The widely understood reason for all this subterfuge on the right and in the financial sector is that there's a desperation to keep things "open" so that corporations don't lose business because of the virus. Those are the battle lines we've drawn: science versus the economy. In other countries, there are already plans under way to pay people to stay home, which the United States could afford more easily than any of the countries that will actually do it. The stakes of this game are the final number of dead from this virus being 8,000 or 35,000 when it's over—or more specifically, the stakes are us, whether some of us go on living or stop.

Last week the market fell seven percent in one morning, and it triggered an "automatic stoppage in trading." That was breathtaking to me for some reason, though maybe it shouldn't have been. All these good loyal muddle-headed Ayn Rand fans, smart with numbers and bad at sharing, with their childlike faith in the invisible hand of the market when it's at work on *other* people, when other people are losing their houses or living in the streets—if they lose too much of their own money, they just *stop*. Instantly. It's over, they take their ball and go home. What about the invisible hand, guys! The free market!

Of course we've known this story since 2008—those things are only for the poor. Grocery store clerks across the country had to show up for work today and take their chances or risk losing their $9-an-hour jobs. Meanwhile, the airline industry, which just spent

$45 billion on "stock buybacks," a tool for enriching the rich, wants an immediate $50 billion bailout. The casinos are coming with hat in hand, too, and the cruise lines. Let them fail I think. Enough. Nationalize the airlines, or they can wade through it and try to survive, as companies are supposed to do. If we go a few years without casinos, if the cruise lines have to sell off their four-story waterslides, so be it. "Jobs," they cry with big eyes; but as soon as they get the money, if there aren't strings attached, the first thing they'll do is cut jobs and start self-dealing again.

The shellac-haired weirdo who is our current Vice President, Mike Pence—he once wrote a lengthy essay about how the movie *Mulan* was a covert attempt to normalize the idea of women serving in the military—is the head of our "Coronavirus Task Force." His chief qualification for this is that if he fucks up, Trump can fire and blame him.

When he was appointed as head, Pence promised that by today, March 16, 1.5 million tests would be available to Americans. Still not enough, but a start. Apparently he went home after that and just watched *Mulan,* though, because the date has come and fewer than 14,000 tests have been done in the entire country. As for ventilators, Alex Azar II, the HHS Secretary, won't say how many the country has on hand because of "national security," per *The Washington Post.* Presumably like eleven, then, all made by a subsidiary of Halliburton or Taco Bell during the George W. Bush era. I don't know how exactly that information will play into the hands of our enemies, nor, I strongly suspect, does Alex Azar II. The only fact we know with clarity is that it's our obligation to stay home (or "shelter in place," as the parlance has become) to protect one another. We're our own best chance of getting the virus under control.

Yet according to Nathan, Dr. Anthony Fauci, who's become visible this week, is a good and legitimate public health official. (Some of the doctors appearing in public, for instance Jerome Adams, the surgeon general, are write-offs, Trump loyalists.) Perhaps his integrity means that Fauci will appear at a few press conferences and be quickly sidelined, like Nancy Messonnier. Or maybe he's the one who will organize us, the wartime general we need, a real person, directing governors and mayors and the people, and we'll be able to meet in bars in two weeks for late spring drinks. People are already a little stir crazy.

A columnist named Daniel Hannan writes an article in the British newspaper the *Telegraph* titled *If Coronavirus Has a Silver Lining, It Should Be the Return of the Bow and the Curtsy*. Well, Daniel Hannan, you're a dreamer. I don't personally think it's going to happen, but if we are all bowing and curtsying by Christmas I promise to formally apologize. I'll have to figure out some kind of physical gesture to pair with the apology, but we can sort it out then.

March 19

Schools in New York and Texas close, nearly three million children in New York's system, more than five million in Texas's, incredible numbers. I think at moments throughout the day about the ones for whom school is a break in life's problems. We have to hope we can figure out a way to get them back into school, but there are not many optimists on that subject. Early May at soonest.

The rain has finally stopped, and my long walk falls during that hour of a warm evening that can make anything look beautiful, a lawn, a stop sign, the Grand Canyon. When Nabokov moved to America from Russia (under gunfire, on a ship called *Hope!*), he was amazed by the beauty of mundane objects here, the diners, the cars, the "humble fluting" on the garbage cans in Ithaca. To a native New Yorker, the sunset in L.A. seems the same. You're just allowed to look at it, every night, free.

At five o'clock the domestic workers leave Los Feliz, and the leafy streets empty of a certain kind of car, older Camrys and Corollas, newer Hyundais, and the swishing of the trees in the breeze grows more audible. Meanwhile, those cars wend their way toward smaller homes and second dinners to cook. And of course their own dread about covid. Yet their drivers victimize people, too; they have clothes and electronics made by tiny hands, as, inescapably, nearly every American does. The complicity winds all the way down to whichever humans are last, over whom we will all be born, live, and die in tyranny. At least that's the current system. I'm not sure who let it get so bad.

I wonder, walking every day and seeing the streets and highways empty, if maybe we're going to give the earth a break. I look around environmentalist Twitter and have my enthusiasm dampened slightly though. It turns out climate change is "not an easy fix."

More and more people are video chatting, and I spend a long time talking with my friend Rachel in her apartment on Riverside Drive. She's also in the group chat on Slack, with Ben and Nathan. I knew the crisis was peaking in New York, but I'm still startled by her tone. They're in the hurricane the rest of us are awaiting. I ask about the lockdown there, which started last week, and she says it was non-negotiable, there was no real hesitation; the numbers were staggering. I ask if it feels like New York versus the world, and she thinks and says, no, it feels like New York versus Trump.

She's addicted to New York governor Andrew Cuomo's briefings at noon every day, because it's new information, and even better, information she knows she can trust. I ask if it's true that he has nipple rings. To her credit she doesn't know. Some of our experiences are the same, we both wipe down our groceries with neurotic care, and in every ad and show all we notice now is people touching their faces. But we have more not in common at the moment, really. She says the streets are completely empty there. A handful of the more fortunate or cautious people we know have already left New York. (One couple, the husband Danish, went upstate in the first week of February and have no plans to return until there's a vaccine, which could mean 2022.) Rachel can talk to Nathan about medicine more knowledgeably than I can—she was a biology major—and says it's hard to see an off-ramp. She thinks we'll be inside for two months. And it will be all of us.

I haven't even considered that it could be that long. "Two *months*?"

"Some people think it will have to be until we have a vaccine."

"People won't do that."

"No, I know. Especially parents."

While we're chatting, she gets a snap from a friend and laughs, holding it up to show me. It's a picture of a toddler with her hands and face covered in dirt, standing next to a terrorized-looking fern.

Hour 1 of distance learning, it says underneath.

Nathan has started going into work a few hours early, at around three or four o'clock in the morning. He usually arrives not long before morning rounds, which start at 8:10 a.m. at his hospital, and reads the 6:00 a.m. update. But the covid patients are too volatile; information that's two hours old about them is already obsolete. He sends us a picture of himself on the train into work, standing near the car's doors in his shirt and tie, and behind him a sea of those blue-and-maroon vinyl seats familiar to anyone who's lived in the tri-state area for longer than a month. He hasn't seen a person but the conductor on the train in days.

He passes on one piece of good news. There's been "a flurry" of studies on surgical masks released in the last few days, in his words, and though he wants to wait a few days before saying anything firm, he thinks that it can't hurt to wear a mask, and will probably help. It's a real medical win, he adds, the first concrete good news.

I immediately spot the flaw in this new plan, which is that we, America, don't have any masks, a fact that's been in the news as people have been speculating that masks might be a solution. Anyway, according to Rachel, if you wore a mask in New York right now, someone would shout at you from across the street—the feeling there is so strong that we have to get all possible "personal protective equipment," or PPE, to frontline workers. At the moment many of them don't have it; nurses and orderlies all over America are improvising with garbage bags and masks made out of old t-shirts (there are clever tips online about how to do it).

We ask Nathan how corona *presents,* shallowly conversant with the subject he's dedicated his life to, and he says "Yeah just flu" and his terseness makes it clear what a wide gap there is between practical and theoretical encounters with the virus. Later, on his way home on Metro North, he tells us he's worked the past nine days straight. He says he's fine. We ask him what it's like. "I get a call every twenty minutes from a long lost friend who wants to know if they can fly to Cleveland on Thursday," he answers.

Of course, he doesn't know how this will turn out either. He knows so much more than the rest of us, yet he's ultimately in the same position. And indeed, two nights ago a college friend texted Nathan and me together with an update on his life, some pictures of his kids, then casually asked if his parents should still take a trip to France next week. "I wouldn't geaux," Nathan replied. He's this phlegmatic with all his patients and long lost friends, I'm sure. But somewhere inside him there must be a voice that wants to know when he can go to Cleveland too.

"How is your health, by the way?" Rach asks me before we get off the phone.

"Oh, fine, I think," I say quickly, too quickly I'm sure, so she knows to change the subject. She says she looked up the nipple ring thing and it might have been tape.

New York! My city. I feel like a traitor. I know those wintry New York days of March, with mica-glints at random of spring, a line of little white flowers on a median, an hour of strong sun. Not long after I first moved to Los Angeles I met a famous actress at a party, the friend of a friend. She was great, full of smart tips about beaches and restaurants. Before she left, she stopped to say goodbye to a group of us, and in the flow of the parting conversation she welcomed me to the city again and added that she thought I'd like it. She had been a new arrival once herself and expected to hate it, but couldn't imagine leaving now. "There's nowhere quite as . . ."

She thought for a second.

"Congested?" said someone, a little joke floated into her presence as offertory.

She ignored it, and we waited, full of patience, until she was ready. "*Warm!*" she said at last, and then she beamed, beautifully, so pleased to have found the word, already turning away from us with one last little wave goodbye.

March 21

A group of backpackers went on a 25-day rafting trip without any connection to the outside world and returned to find out about the existence of covid. Charlie Warzel of the *Times* interviewed them about the trip. He got a text from one just after they'd spoken, he reports, which said: "Forgot to mention this, but my river name is One Chain. If it's at all appropriate to mention that, that would be tight."

Other than One Chain, however, people seem depleted right now. For me today is the hardest so far. We'll probably have to be inside for at least a month, quite possibly longer, and the bleakness of a month stretching ahead of us without friends, bars, restaurants, concerts, little league games, travel, family . . . every day is already a hundred years, and an awful tiredness is beginning to displace those initial nervy amygdala reactions, a prickly numbing you can't fully feel and process but can't rid yourself of either. Nobody thinks schools can reopen before late May, suddenly—if then. An idiot is in charge of everything. And we as a nation are out of pasta. That may be calculably the least important problem of the pandemic, but it's close to my own heart. Last night I smoked pot (the second day in a row, something I try not to do) and in an agreeable haze ordered whatever I could find with an actual shipping date, ten boxes of De Cecco spinach fettucine, ten boxes of Barilla elbows, and five boxes of generic spaghetti. The first of them will arrive on April 19th, a date so far in the future I don't believe anything I ordered will actually come. But if it does, I will be glad to have ten boxes of spinach fettucine. An enlightened interlocutor might point out that this is a good chance to make a positive choice for my health, pasta is bad for you, for one thing it has gluten, for another it's carbs, and for a third I overeat it, whereas most foods I can take or leave. To which I would reply, with just a subtle haughtiness, intended to really sting, fuck off.

A sure sign that things are darker is that I'm listening to Norah Jones for the first time in twenty years. In the bleak minute by minute anxiety of last week, I watched the rain and played Led Zeppelin unendingly, especially "Physical Graffiti," an album I've never liked that much but whose sheer heaviness clicked into the place in my mind where art goes when you really need it.

But now that would be too much, ten ginger days into this quarantine.

I think of Norah Jones as the best music available in the worst category of music: unrepentantly affirming, lived-in and comfortable even when its mood is "sad." There's no great art without at least traces of either doubt or fury in it, which on my shallow acquaintance with her music disqualifies Norah Jones from the start. Yet it's also what makes her so seductive. Listening to her songs is like entering the dream of what you hoped adult life might be like as a teenager, legible, vaguely sexy, full of coffee and sun slanting across rumpled bedsheets. A few minor beautifying regrets, tempered by a basic, foundational contentment, like birds in a blue sky. Is this thing—this nirvana—what boomers feel all the time? If so, no wonder they're reluctant to give it up.

I'm not alone. My friend Matteo, who lives a few miles away, "can't stop" listening to Phil Collins, even though it "sucks," because, he says regretfully, it's also "amazing." My theory is that all of us are so tender that nobody can handle songs with real emotional content. Listening to *Come Away with Me,* I realize that if I heard anything that was actually meaningful to my life, from Earl Sweatshirt to *Diane Young,* I would dissolve into Lucretian particles of sorrow, grief, self-doubt, love, death. Even the soft world of Fleetwood Mac seems like too much suddenly. Can I handle the seasons of my life? Unclear!

By contrast, Nathan, who's now briefing members of Congress when he can get ten minutes away from his patients, cheerfully reports that he's added "two new jams" to his rotation, *I Got 5 on It* by Luniz and *Pony* by Ginuwine. So it's possible I may be in my own head a little.

"I've learned a lot. I've learned a lot. It's incredible," Trump says of modern forehead thermometers, per Maggie Haberman of the *Times.*

March 22

The period of anticipation is over, and the news of death and severe illnesses is here. It's centered in New York but with brushfires in towns and cities everywhere in America. I read the accounts as closely as I can, my useless duty.

Trump's primary interest remains in the optics of the virus, obviously. What a helpless feeling to see him flounder in front of the mics; what comically exact proof of concept for the idea of an Elizabeth Warren or Bernie Sanders presidency, for capable bureaucratic progressivism, I think. But the race is over, and indeed the whole primary season, which was so recently the most important thing ever, seems to belong to a different era. Who would win "Iowa," we were obsessed. It was a fun game until we boarded the Death Star. Now the question is whether we can stagger into Joe Biden's arms and cobble the country back together from its pieces.

But Trump could so easily win. That's the troubling truth that takes up most of every day like a big ox wherever you turn. He's so dumb and hateful, and he's behind in the polls, his unpopularity both rock solid and historically high. But it's hard not to think he does have some goddamn voodoo. Look who he bothered to get impeached over, after all: Joe Biden. I find that chilling. When Biden finished fourth in Iowa and fifth in New Hampshire, people roasted Trump for cheating to beat someone who'd had no hope anyway. But he knew who his competition was better than we did, evidently—the other old white guy. On Twitter, I'm all grins and let's go, you can't comfort the enemy, but christ. As Matteo puts it, the boomers just won't get off the goddamn stage. I liked both Sanders and Warren, which was relatively rare I think, but even Sanders had the demerit of meaning a lot to his fans. It will be when we no longer need our president to *mean* anything that we'll have triumphed over this youth of ours, America. Or we won't, and we'll become just another story—like Avatar, or Prussia.

Rand Paul, Kentucky's tiniest senator, has covid. Now this cosseted princeling of the libertarian right, who was handed a Senate seat thanks to his father's political clout, then used it to try to deny basic rights to people in the service of a completely incoherent ideology, will receive the best health care in the history of humankind. There's no chance it will be Rand Paul that dies. It's going to be someone's grandfather they loved who was born in the Dominican Republic seventy years ago and was planning to take everyone back to where he grew up next year to meet his cousins and go fishing.

Reading a general history of the Greeks for research. "The usual Attic dinner consisted of two courses," it says, "the first a kind of porridge, and the second, a kind of porridge." I glance forlornly at the lentils. Wish we had spaghetti but it's gone.

March 24

Since I know I won't be listening to Norah Jones forever, I have to concede to myself that in actuality the most significant development in my personal sense of aesthetics over the last ten days is that I've become a "candle guy." A humiliating turn of events. I've never understood the appeal of candles before—profligate, minimally rewarding—but after we shut in I found a three-wick candle and decided to give it a spin. Now I'm addicted. That particular candle had a light lavender scent. A long search leads me to an almost identical three-wicker on Etsy, which I quickly buy and put out next to the chair where I read during mornings and evenings. The candle's called "Calm the F— Down," unfortunately, but you go to war with the army you have.

The good news is that the benefits of wearing masks have been proven incontrovertibly, according to Nathan, numerous independent studies confirming that in tandem, masks and keeping a six-foot distance from other people help stop the spread of covid. They're not sure about surfaces. Two pieces of decent news though.

What's really worrying him at the moment is that some people aren't coming off ventilators. Six of his twenty patients on any given day are on ventilators right now. (Normally that number is zero.) The next day when he returns, two will usually have improved enough to go home, two will be on the mend, and two will be dramatically worse. Or dead. They have no tools to help those people, he says. It will take time to test drugs ("therapeutics") that could help. Herd immunity is effectively impossible in anything but the very long term—the deaths it would take to reach it would be unimaginable, conceivably in the hundreds of thousands here in America.

Every day he has to decide whether to sedate someone otherwise perfectly healthy and put a huge tube down their neck, which I guess is how you ventilate a person.

There was a medical staff debriefing at Nathan's hospital, and everyone in the room talked about how their mental health had been affected, even nurses and doctors with a reputation for being "tough as nails." What surprised Nathan was to hear that one of the most harmful things was the White House, that people actually do care about what Trump says: to work a sixteen-hour shift, watch five people die by drowning in their own lungs, more or less, and then look at Facebook on the bus ride home and scroll through their relatives parroting the Trump universe talking points, nothing's wrong, it's just like the flu, the only reason it's on the news at all is that Democrats want Trump to lose.

The contrast between the gravity of that and Trump's tone ("some of the doctors say it will wash through, flow through") is so stark. He's selling his version of the virus like it's Trump Steaks on the downslope of its two-month existence in 2007, flailing for answers, promoting a drug named hydroxychloroquine, which he hailed as a miracle even though no one knows if it helps yet. Nathan said every patient started asking for it immediately, liberal and conservative alike. In the rush to get it, a few days ago a woman's husband died—she's in the ICU—after ingesting an aquarium cleaner called chloroquine, unrelated to the medicine despite the similarity of their names.

Stocks are way up, I see, better halt trading. The market has taken on a new interest for me since I've been asked to murder people based on how it's doing. Elon Musk tweets, "Based on current trends, probably close to zero new cases in US too by end of April." Elon would you care to bet a billion dollars.

March 27

At dinner I chaw through a dish of whole wheat penne. It tastes like someone with a personal grudge against me made it. On *Love Is Blind,* the signature binge watch of the pandemic's first week, a woman named Jessica declares that she arrived on the dating show looking for "that can't eat, can't sleep, over the fence, World Series kind of love." Fair enough, you think, but then a TikTok user remembers something astonishing: that this is a *verbatim* quote from the Mary-Kate and Ashley Olsen movie *It Takes Two.* Why does this seem so vitally important? Because it's quarantine. It's Chinatown, Jake.

The show is terrible but Emily and I watch it. There's a new communitarian yearning in the online chatter about favorite shows and podcasts and books, same as the Zoom cocktail hours being organized and the old friends who want to talk again for the first time in years. There's such rawness in everyone—the mix is so different than usual, the same amount of anger, but more fear, less certainty, and I think more love. It reminds me of the story of the first pictures sent back of the earth from space, when for eight or nine days there was a sudden belief that since we had seen that we all lived on the same small blue planet, a new era of peace might begin. Needless to say everyone started fighting again, but what a lovely week; and how much truth contained in the thought, if we could only get out of our own way. Right now we're thinking about work less, ourselves and each other more.

The foreboding after two weeks of covid is less acute but deeper. At the start it felt the way HIV did when I was young, predatory, fatal, and unpredictable. It seemed like going outside might mean dying, the way that when I was 16 I thought having sex without a condom meant you would probably die. Now at least we have some information, and there's new, hopeful vocabulary, *flattening the curve, six feet apart, mask up, social distancing.* We know the dry cough is the dangerous one, and if anyone coughs around me I loop the sound back in my head to see if it was dry. At the same time, as Rachel said, you can do everything right and if your number's up, that's it. A law blogger she reads, David Lat, who's 44 and runs marathons, was eating dinner out in New York last week and realized he couldn't taste the food. (Loss of taste is one covid symptom.) He ended up nearly dying. As Rach said, none of us run marathons.

———

The one cost that we are not even trying to pretend to deal with is mental health. In the middle of writing normal work e-mails I write and then delete long paragraphs saying, but jesus, listen, here I am, talking as if I have rational feelings, but that's fraudulent, because adjusting to this new situation doesn't even fractionally change the terrible internal disquiet I am feeling, I'm rational at the moment only by tremendous exertion, and the vigilance is exhausting. As a result my usual capacities have slackened terribly, e.g., responding to an e-mail seems like summiting a small but difficult peak in the Andes, like even having to *get* to the fucking Andes (open your e-mail) is part of the feat, but then to be coherent, friendly, to address the times without being personal or if you have a personal relationship to leave the door open for confidences without prying, to adjust by what cities your correspondents are in, and then to pretend that the business you're conducting is of *any fucking importance to either of you* in the middle of this pandemic . . . but there are more choppers overhead every night and more ambulances in the streets and I'm listening to Zeppelin again and staring up at them and reading nothing much. I'm yearning to scramble to the comfort of someone like P. G. Wodehouse. But I can't, the ability to be comforted by books has gone out of me, and even after two weeks there's still not a single roll of toilet paper on the shelves.

There are moments when it's clear people are finding a rhythm in quarantine, embarking on long novels together, walking their dogs, excavating their rollerblades from the garage. But even these signposts of adaptation are not so much hopeful as neutral, factual, for the simple reason that, even leaving aside the relentless acceleration of heartbreaking news, we still don't yet know the most important fact: where the road they're marking goes.

I text with Wulf, a friend who loves candles, lit mostly while listening to vinyl in his dim, comfortable, smoke-hazy apartment across town, and confess that I've become a candle guy.

He shoots back *I've started doing day candles* and I feel better.

A neighbor's acquaintance claims to have seen hand sanitizer on the shelves in large quantities at the Gelson's in West Hollywood, which I'd like to believe but doubt. My approach, if I were in charge of the hand sanitizer industry, would be simply to make much MORE hand sanitizer and then SELL it for a profit. But this kind of radical outside the box thinking is why I could never make it in business and must settle for being a writer.

Then, this evening at seven o'clock, after I've spent a long day worrying bootlessly about shit like this, my Emily comes in the door, cheeks cold, long hair windswept, but smiling. She's carrying grocery bags. "Look what I found," she said. She holds a box up. "Spaghetti."

Ben was right, it's not my favorite brand, in fact I've never heard of it, but it's plain old spaghetti, and my gratitude is overwhelming. I give Em a squeeze that crinkles the light blue North Face windbreaker she's had on for the last ten years, still just chill to the touch, and thank her a hundred times. The writer M. F. K. Fisher once said, "It seems to me that our three basic needs, for food and security and love, are so mixed and mingled and entwined that we cannot straightly think of one without the others." I salt the water and put in half the amount of pasta I usually would and take each bite the way they tell you to in mindfulness classes when they give you a raisin and ask you to experience the smallest details of consuming it.

———

I've never written about my family, and as I sit outside tonight, listening to music, I realize I don't think I could. I'm among the most fortunate people in my circumstances for this situation. I have a house and food, for a start. Besides that, though, I know people who live alone and are already craving human touch—with less than half of this prospective quarantine over—and people with health risks and a single mother of two young children, whom Emily and I discuss with some worry. I'm at home with people I love of various sizes and generations (all with newly robust opinions about dinner, since it's become the main event of the day), and though our house is not that big we have the yard, and I can find time and space alone, which is the thing I need to work.

I met a writer once who made his living by writing biographies that non-famous men (always men) commissioned. Most were businessmen in their retirement years—guys who had been third-in-command during the heyday of Chrysler or whatever, old, stuffed full of memories and money in Scarsdale, Winnetka, Falls Church, Ladue. His job was to make their stories heroic, while also being accurate about things like their childhood schools and the birthdays of their parents, and (in tone) quite stiff, "like a real book," as the daughter of one of his clients once said.

"Did it make you hate them?" I asked, and he said that in fact no, it didn't. To do the job well he had to go through their papers, carefully handle the relics of their youth, tactfully discuss children dead from overdoses and suicide, fathers numbed by war, mothers killed by cancer. "What it really made me think is that everyone deserves a biography like that," he said. I thought that was profound. There are people who can write about their families casually, a lot of whom I admire and even love, Gerald Durrell just for a start. But to me, these people I'm in the pandemic with are so much more interesting than I could possibly demonstrate, every detail of who they are is so private and significant and alive with meaning, it would take so many decades of thought to do any of them justice, such mad care, that only silence seems like an option. I barely know myself.

March 28

A survey of notable economists by the University of Chicago strongly indicates that coming out of economic lockdown prematurely would do more harm than good for the economy. "Abandoning severe lockdowns at a time when the likelihood of a resurgence in infections remains high will lead to greater total economic damage than sustaining the lockdowns to eliminate the resurgence risk," they say, a dry but remarkable sentence.

In other words, though the terms of our political debate about covid are irrevocably set, the economy versus public health, the two problems have an identical solution: lockdowns. Chicago is conservative, too, the echt freshwater school, and even their survey indicates that both the economy *and* public health would benefit from lockdowns. Because we live in a two-party system, though, and one of the parties took peyote around 2016 and never looked back, it has become another subject of desperate, scientifically moot debate, like climate change. "Reopening" the economy, as if you could just do that anyway, like a bottle of Pepsi. But it's in the ultra short-term interests of the banks and hedge funds, so it will happen, some kind of brokered reopening, if we actually even manage to shelter in place until after we flatten the curve, hopefully after June 1st. Even the most well-meaning reporters seem to accept the poles of the debate, ignoring the fact that the solutions for the economy and the virus are not opposed but identical.

March 30

The first Monday in a while to feel anything like a Monday. Yesterday there was a Zoom with the people I went to school with in England, incredibly dear to my heart and whom I rarely get to see or catch up with, scattered around the world in London, Sydney, Vancouver, Hong Kong. Of the innumerable video calls we've had, it might have been the happiest. Everyone seemed like themselves—a scared version of themselves, but there, drinking wine and making jokes about the pandemic. It was like seeing an old part of myself to be together with them and Emily. I wrote a whole novel about going to school there, and a lot of the sentiments in it embarrass me now. Yet as Hawthorne said, "the young are apt to write more wisely than they really know." And the remainder of life, he went on, in his beautiful style, "may not be idly spent in realizing and convincing themselves of the wisdom which they uttered long ago."

After the Zoom, I go outside and walk with a surreptitious joint. Sometimes I get obsessed with a song for a day or two, and currently it's *This Is the Day* by The The (tough band to google) with its chorus ("This is the day / your life will surely change") too apposite to even be interesting. I've been managing to read some fiction again. Other people seem to have committed to long novels, on Twitter there's an *Anna Karenina* group read, but I've devoted most of my career to reading long novels, long and short books, I've read that one specifically untold times, and suddenly the idea is totally unappealing. What I've found myself reading here and there is a history of science in the romantic age, partly of the story of William Herschel. He was an outsider to the London scientific establishment who designed his own telescopes while living in Bath and began to observe things in the sky that nobody had ever seen before, including ultimately the first new planet to be discovered in a thousand years—since Ptolemy, which says something about the interval. Herschel's sister, Caroline, sat with him for almost every hour of his decades of nightly observations. She made numerous discoveries of comets and stars with her own telescope and was highly esteemed by other scientists, but the fame has always been her brother's. When it was especially cold at night as they sat there taking readings until dawn, Herschel warmed himself by cutting onions and rubbing them on his face and hands.

It does somehow feel as if history is in motion again. Between this bizarre unnatural child-monster improbability of a president and this unprecedented virus, ground is getting rucked up that hasn't been disturbed in a long time. There are moments, if you allow yourself to look at the polls, to consider Trump's loony handling of the virus from essentially the first moment, when it seems just distantly possible that the outcome of that might be good. There are whole regions of language my foreign friends, some of whom were on that Zoom, never understood while I lived in England. What exactly is a "deductible," they'd say. Is it true you sometimes have to pay $10,000 because your child didn't have the luck to grow straight teeth? Because braces are free in France and Greece and Spain—why, even in Mexico, and Colombia, somebody else would chime in, from a table away. Did you know that? Yes, you did. No, you don't know how it got that way in America either. You have some guesses.

I see a tweet from the critic Michael Schaub that says, "In these certain-ass times," and I startle myself by laughing in real life, because dozens of pitches from book publicists for the past two weeks have started with the phrase "In these uncertain times." No company is not deeply concerned about my mental welfare. "In these uncertain times, your friends at Mountain Dew urge you to be extreme safely" "Here at Philip Morris, where we have actually studied lung health for some years"—and so on.

As I'm sitting outside this late evening, listening to the quiet sly warmth of Kacey Musgraves, an acquaintance I've been trading a few friendly catch-up texts with asks about my health, someone I barely know. I stare at the text and get hot in the face, take off my big headphones, jam my phone into my pocket, furious and worried and wondering how they even knew about or remembered that.

March 31

On a spring night when I was nine, my stepfather told me to take the trash out before dinner. It was one of my normal chores. We were living in Virginia at the time, my mother, my stepfather, my beautiful baby sister, and I. The outside trash cans were in a fenced enclosure off the back porch. I didn't mind taking the trash out—the recycling was nothing—and sometimes when it was dark I would illicitly run my fingertips along the smooth side of the car on my way back inside.

That night the trash smelled, for whatever reason, and when I was lifting the lid of the big trash can outside, something smelled bad in there, too, and all at once I threw up. I hadn't been feeling sick. The throw up was on the outside of the big can and on the ground. I sort of looked at it for a minute and felt a panic and wondered if I could get away with not saying anything about it. I decided no.

The kitchen was the nicest room in that house because my mom was there. It had a big Mexican-style table with wide wooden slats in the middle, where an "island" would go these days, and where she graded papers. I quietly told her I'd thrown up.

She touched my forehead. "Oh, sweetie. Are you feeling okay?"

"Is there a mess?" asked my stepfather.

I nodded, and he shook his head grimly and went outside. My mom gave me a hug and said I didn't feel hot. We heard the hose turn on and I went up to my room to read—at that time I was reading the *Babysitters Club* books over and over and over—before dinner.

A week later, or maybe the next fucking day, who can tell with memory, it's so tiring and endless, the same thing happened again. I was brushing my teeth and threw up randomly. The day after that, I threw up right when I got home from school. It was then that my mother took me to the doctor.

He said it was a stomach bug, and indeed for the next few weeks I was fine, until the same pattern of illness started over. The doctor said it was probably just a different stomach bug, and he said the same thing the third time, which was around Christmas, and it was then that I started to hate the words "stomach bug" (stomach bug stomach bug stomach bug) so much that I still panic when I hear them. My heart is beating fast this minute. That was when we changed my diet, and I also started to eat, I can see in retrospect, much more salt. I only wanted hot soup or pasta, both very salty. After school I would eat a full sleeve of saltines, and for dinner I would have a bowl of vegetable soup, as hot as possible. That fixed me. I still threw up once in a while, at night. But we had gone to five or six doctors by that point, and the tests hadn't turned up anything. We made it through the winter, and in the spring and summer I stayed in the same strange but tolerable holding pattern.

Then in the fall—I had started fifth grade—things took a turn for the worse. I started to throw up again, but more frequently now. At first it was two or three times a week, then at some point it became daily, then suddenly in a monthlong period I find hard to remember two or three times a day, then six or seven, and then (this is when I stopped going to school, in late October) it was kind of continuous, something like twelve or fifteen or twenty. We went to every doctor again. They gave me every kind of test again. But nothing worked, they were baffled. I had started the school year weighing that fall 110 pounds, skinny but normal, and by the middle of November I weighed 79.

Things reached their worst on Thanksgiving. For a day or two beforehand, my feet and lower legs had started to experience a kind of pain I don't like to think about but can come close to reproducing even now if I close my eyes, the memory is so intense. It felt like razors were nicking my skin at random places up and down my lower legs, sort of. It hurt so much I was shocked into a weird clarity, and I could talk and read, things I'd been too sick to do for a while. It didn't really stop except for a few minutes after I ate soup, but then I'd throw up the soup. I threw up 30 times on the Tuesday before Thanksgiving. My mom told the doctor the number on the phone. I was sleeping in the bathroom. (There is no euphoria in the world purer than having just thrown up and feeling the cold tile of the floor on your finally relaxed body, endorphins shooting through it long enough that you could have fifteen or twenty or sometimes even forty minutes of really no pain at all, before nausea returning and the wait to throw up beginning again.) My mother was on the phone with one doctor after another at this point, asking if I should be admitted to the hospital. I suppose they said not yet.

On the day before Thanksgiving, I was better. I went downstairs and ate. Even in those last few weeks, when I had the prestige of a bell in my room and there was no thought even given to my schoolwork, I remained uneasy about bothering my mother and stepfather at night, which was their time together. They sat downstairs and watched TV, tired and with full days ahead of them, full of my problems, I remorsefully understood. They liked *Thirtysomething,* which at the time struck me as a really inscrutable concept for a show, that "something" as if fucking *birthdays* could stop mattering. They also watched the Ken Burns Civil War miniseries, when you had to do that at an appointed weekly hour. Anyway I didn't like to bother them.

But that night I woke up at around ten o'clock and I had to, even though I knew they were doing something more important than TV, which was getting ready for the next day, Thanksgiving, by cooking and cleaning. But I had to. I was in my own bed again that night instead of the bathroom, which was a sign of how good I'd been feeling. It was an hour after my bedtime. I remember it in fragments, but with clarity. For one thing, it felt as if there was suddenly lukewarm water trembling right beneath my skin, all over my body. That sounds mild I guess, but it was the most frightening thing I had experienced up to then and it probably still is. At the same time, my stomach was convulsing in a new and unexpected way that was almost nice (genuinely) as a distracting sensation—but I don't know, the details of an experience like this are never more than a lie about the totality of it, what mattered was how desperately I needed the whole feeling to end, the way you need the feeling to end when you pick up something hot from the stove by accident, and your brain doesn't say, "Oh, shoot, yes, this is too hot," your brain says "Whatever is happening has to stop immediately." Except I couldn't drop the pan. Or however you want to put it. Has a bear attacked you? Everything that tries to explain being sick is wrong-sounding, at least to me, because the experience is the opposite of words, of speaking, in some pivotal way. I threw up and shouted out hoarsely (my throat had been fried from stomach acid for a month) for my mom, but she couldn't hear.

That initial truly unbearable pain, which I experienced sitting on the side of my bed, lasted for about a minute I think, and then I threw up down the front of myself, trying and failing to lean forward, and all the pain and nausea subsided. I tried to walk to the door but had to lie back down on the floor, sweaty, with my shirt weighed down at the hem by throw up, which I hated. I steadied myself. I spent about a minute on the floor, knowing I would be stable enough to walk after exactly one minute more.

I opened my eyes and looked at my bedroom. I felt very far away from it, thousands of miles. My body was trembling. I looked at my cherished baseball stuff (my glove, cards of Yankees first baseman Don Mattingly, my hero, a small old statue of Stan Musial from my Uncle Will) and even that didn't matter, and I looked out at the dark lavender sky that usually worried me for being infinite, and realized, without knowing the word, or at least having it close to hand, that I was indifferent. It didn't matter either.

I started to feel sick again. Before it had returned all the way, I dragged myself into the hallway and called for my mom, who heard me, because after a moment she came to the foot of the stairs and said "Oh my god!" and finally we went to the hospital.

I had only two bad days left to go after that. It was a neurologist who figured it out in the end, even though his specialty had nothing to do with my diagnosis. All of the doctors were coming in one by one to take their shot, apparently, and the neurologist, I remember his build and his dark hair distinctly, though not his face, suggested a kind of IV. They consulted, a nurse said, "It won't help but it can't hurt," as if I didn't have ears, and they changed my IV, and whatever was in it worked after a lag time of no more than twenty or thirty seconds. It didn't even take a minute. I remember the warm liquid pumping into my arm, that strange feeling, I didn't know anything, I was ten, but I knew I was suddenly better, within the hour infinitely better. I ate something and fell asleep. I slept for 24 hours. I woke up starving. I ate whatever was on the tray, an apple and some graham crackers. All the days of needles and tests were over, my mother said as I ate—she had slept in the chair next to me—and I remember looking at her and seeing the area around her eyes had loosened, though I hadn't known it was tight, and I ravenously ate some pizza she'd brought and fell back to sleep again.

I saw the neurologist one more time. He knocked on the door and asked how I was doing. My mom thanked him, and my grandmother, too, her mother, who had arrived, and who was in many practical and all emotional senses my second parent. The doctor smiled, winningly, and said, "I came back to pat myself on the back." We all laughed, giddy. He talked to us for a few minutes, then wished me luck and left.

I still have the endocrine disease that the neurologist had found in the recesses of his med school exam memory. It still is not the best, but my problems now are mostly chronic rather than acute, a good trade, besides which lots of people have much worse diseases, terminal ones just to start with. It takes every tenth or fifteenth day from me, and often an hour or two, sometimes at inconvenient moments. But on the spectrum of human illness that's almost nothing. Occasionally I get sick again and have to stay in the hospital, but it passes, and it's no longer a mystery, which is half of the badness. I'm lucky enough that only once have I felt close to as bad as I did the first time. And that I live near good hospitals and well-stocked pharmacies. And that I have health insurance. On and on it goes, my luck, a permanent debt.

Salt is the "poor man's" version of the medicine I take, it turns out, that was one of the last mysteries we solved. The first doctor I had at NIH, where I started going that year for specialist care, was the one to ultimately teach me, which is why eating the saltines had worked, the soup too, and why I still eat those things—along with pasta. Except my sense memories, the idiots, who eat so much spaghetti so ferociously, but evidently draw the line at whole wheat, which is what we're almost back down to.

My doctor says it's still unknown how this disease would interact with Covid-19, but advises me it's "best not to find out." I'm immunocompromised, both because of the nature of my disease and the medicines it requires, and I have to admit I have been wondering if I will be one of the people who gets covid and just goes, twelve hours in the hospital and then a mortuary. It should be on my mind more, I think, but in a way I don't care. I'm not acting more cautious than the averagely cautious person. I've been struggling to think why. What I think is, there's a voice in my mind that sometimes speaks up on behalf of my childhood self, and to him, this is not a surprise, and with his eyes I've been looking around the world and thinking, finally, the world matches how worried I have always felt we should all be. So when my regular self, passing a Starbucks with boarded windows, thinks, "Strange times," that other part of me, pissed off, four days without the relief of smoking a joint, thinks—when is it not strange. When is it not times.

The one thing those who have been sick really know, which thousands of people are learning from covid every day now, is that ultimately you have no control over your body. I will try not to get covid, but I might get it. If I get it, I will try not to die, but I might die. That's what having a body is. Only when you get sick, or maybe have a child, do you realize what a half-familiar mammal you've wound up living inside—that you can no more tell it to stop feeling horrible than you can order your stomach to be flatter or your eyes to be bluer.

I hate talking about being sick. I've never written about that either. Or talked about it. For years people close to me have teased me for my eccentricities (I take a lot of naps and a lot of hot baths, I eat enormous bowls of pasta at random hours of the day) in the same way I tease them, and it's fine, I really don't mind. They say silence about trauma—if getting sick counts—is invidious, but even the minimal amount I have to tell people in order to function in society, to have relationships, causes me more pain than the silence. Silence has been a relief, if anything. Partly it's because some people are sick as a way to get attention, which I understand, but for myself I hate it, I reject it, I want no trade in that marketplace. Everyone can be sicker than I have ever been. Fine. The 3,815 people who have died of covid in America as of this evening know more than any of us, I guess. "How is it with all your health stuff?" another old and not particularly close acquaintance texts me today. "Fine," I write back curtly, and as far as I'm concerned that puts a lid on the getting in touch with old friends part of this pandemic.

APRIL

April 1

Members of Congress were "floored" to learn that South Korea is testing ten thousand people a day. America has tested about that many in the past three months combined.

One of the minor coincidences of the virus is how it has synced up in these two countries, America and South Korea. Both had their first cases of covid and their first official covid deaths on the same two days, weeks apart. But as of this morning 4,000 people have died here, a terrible rubicon, while in South Korea that number is in its way just as stark: 4. And our President, who opposed increased testing from the start to keep his numbers down, of course, has apparently asked the South Korean government for "as many tests as possible." So we go hat in hand to an economy dozens of times smaller than ours, but with basic functionality in matters of centralized government.

America by contrast, has billionaires underfoot in every direction—David Geffen has fallen silent on social media after getting incinerated for posting a picture of his quarantine site, a

$590 million "superyacht"—but the cost is a government from which the last ounce of excess has been cut away to please the rich.

The trouble is that excess is a skill in government. Usually it's not even excess. A trial in Stalinist Russia was a bullet in the head, which is much more efficient and market-friendly than the arduous process of gathering jurors, hiring court stenographers, etc., but which has the crucial benefit of saving people from getting shot in the head. Now countries like South Korea have masks, tests, thermometers, ventilators, and plans, and we have low enough taxes on the rich that our Secretary of Education, Betsy DeVos, owns ten yachts, has two helicopters for them, and employs a "yacht scheduler."

The exception to this demented governmental cost-cutting is of course the military, which every day seems more like one of the great surrealist art projects. It's the most expensive enterprise in human history; the loser of several consecutive wars; and a direct thief (in General Dwight D. Eisenhower's words!) from art, education, science, the poor, the environment, and so on, in favor of allocating that money to businesses that produce new ideas for killing human beings.

Which would all be bad enough even if the military could MAKE ME A FUCKING MASK. But they can't! You would think they might be able to divert just a couple million dollars from building new supersonic jets that don't work to produce some ten cent masks, some tests. But instead we're asking South Korea for that stuff. This, even though our military's budget is way north of $700 billion a year—not far short of South Korea's entire GDP.

If you step back even a foot or two it all seems like a piece of the real, high insanity, rare stuff, no different than Caligula making his horse a senator except perhaps that it's more dangerous, because if you support the military, you get a badge as a "realist," a hardheaded maker of tough choices. As if only the people who spent a lot of time negotiating with the horse had anything really smart or relevant to say.

By contrast, we spend $70 billion a year on education. Sometimes I think about what America would be like if those numbers were flipped: $70 billion and $700 billion. I would put my money on the kids who came out of that education system being able to make masks. I really would. For a while after the war, before its own asshole tax conservatives mutinied, Britain invested special care and funding into its education system, even paying for young people to go to art college and technical schools for the first time. (English, my own major in college, began as a subject for miners and factory workers in night school in England, because classics was considered too sophisticated for the lower classes.) Out of that brief experiment came, besides a generation of visual artists— well, most of the music that people who want their taxes cut listened to for the last fifty years: John Lennon, David Bowie, Pete Townshend, Mick Jagger, Roger Waters and Syd Barrett . . .

What if it didn't have to be war? That's the real point. At the end of *Monsters, Inc.,* the monsters figure out that they don't have to scare children into screaming to fuel their city, which is the movie's premise. Laughter is a superior power source. We don't have to terrify and murder twenty-year-olds because they grew up without money. That's not written anywhere. It doesn't make you serious to think we should. With the same exact money we could give the same exact boys and girls (because anyone honest knows that's what they still are, the prefrontal cortex of the brain doesn't even fully develop until you're 25) time to think quietly and make weird paintings. But that privilege is primarily reserved for George W. Bush.

I don't know, it's all too much, the seized-up numbness of March, the fear and fury, the predictable but nevertheless incredible mishandling of this virus by the Trump administration at every step. The bad faith, the waste of lives. Worrying about whether you've sanitized your car keys and how much disinfectant you even have *left* and if there's going to be toilet paper again soon and how a person really actually *gets* covid and just the whole fucking thing.

"Unfortunately, the enemy is death," says the President. "A lot of people are dying. So it's very unpleasant." Not a big fan of his work generally, but I have to agree, unpleasant! He's still refusing to wear a mask. Many of his supporters follow suit.

April 2

Late at night, we get a message from Nathan that he woke up soaked in sweat, feeling delirious. He doesn't have a fever, though it sounds as if it had just broken to me. (Everyone's a doctor.) He says he drank a gatorade and went back to bed. If he doesn't have a fever in the morning, he'll go to work, since they definitely can't spare him at the hospital. He has no idea if it's covid. He says he'll check his oxygen when he gets in but he's sure he's fine.

It reminds me of the time he came directly from Botswana to a fifth-floor walk-up I lived in on 55th Street, above a dry cleaner whose only exterior signage read "Tailor Genius." He had been in Botswana to study the Ebola virus, sitting in a tree house in the jungle.

"Do you *have* the Ebola virus?" I called out cautiously while he was in the shower, where he had gone right away after he arrived.

"Don't think so!" he said. There was a brief pause. "My nipples are bleeding."

"Jesus!" I said.

There was no reply.

"Is that a symptom of Ebola?" I asked.

"No, I ran too far before my flight."

That was something he did, like Forrest Gump. He would go out for a quick run and return four hours later, having somehow seen Yonkers. I don't have that gear, and my theory is it's the same way he can put up with being a doctor. He'll also eat anything under the sun. A sandwich artist at Subway once refused to fill his order because it was in her words "too gross."

After his shower, Nathan came out of the bathroom in mesh shorts with two of my band-aids on his nipples, said he felt like a million bucks, ate a chicken parm, drank a gatorade, and then instantly fell asleep on the couch in the living room. The other four of us celebrated his return quietly in the bedroom, drinking vodka and listening to the Darkness while he rested.

Nathan tells us his Brooklyn hospital is affluent enough that a "friend of the board" was able to send a private jet to Ontario to buy supplies, so if he does have covid and goes in, he's not worried about infecting people, he'll have appropriate PPE. Many nurses and doctors still don't. And they still can't get tested, not even Nathan, which is the very first step every other country took toward managing the virus. But he doesn't think he has it. He adds that Cuomo just announced New York has enough ventilators (the chief tool of life extension in severe cases of covid right now) to last for six days before they have to start choosing who receives them—"rationing" them, he puts it.

April 5

Trump again urges people with the virus to take hydroxychloroquine. It's a relatively harmless drug, according to Nathan; he uses it to treat people with lupus. The problem is that after some initial excitement in February because it killed covid in a test tube, scientists found out that hydroxychloroquine does absolutely nothing against the virus in people. But Trump won't let it go, and Nathan says he still has families screaming at him because he hasn't given their relatives hydroxychloroquine. Because *Trump* said to? we still ask, and he says they tell him the President is the leader of the free world.

Nathan's better this afternoon. His oxygen never fell. Probably a bug, he thinks, or if covid, a mild case. Lots of people who get it never experience any symptoms at all. There's a chance I got it on my book tour I suppose. But no way of finding out. That would take an antibody test, which is months if not years away.

The ventilator problem was resolved equally quickly: New York gets a thousand from the government of China, after the intervention of "Chinese billionaires Jack Ma and Joseph Tsai." At an absolute minimum I was sure we had our own billionaires. It would be nice to hear from the Silicon Valley set. They've been congratulating themselves on disruptive innovation for three solid decades, and now, when we could actually use it, utter silence. Not a fucking peep.

New York is still the epicenter in America. Last week, the USNS *Comfort* docked on the Hudson to take overflow patients from the city's hospitals, and though I didn't make much of it when I heard the news, Rachel says it's really unnerving to walk outside and see the ship, and when I come across a picture of it, I see why; it's a blinding white vessel with alarm-red crosses fifteen feet tall on its hull, like a ship blockading a port until the plague passes.

"Javits is crazy too," Rachel replies when I mention the ship, and texts me a picture of the convention center: curtained off "rooms" with narrow cots, masks sitting on their pillows, and in each one a bedside table with a small succulent on it. The plants are from a local flower show that was canceled.

Groceries are still tough there. Here it's improving. In New York, though, there's ferocious competition for delivery slots at midnight, when you have to be waiting to click with a full cart and hope for the best. (Rachel's dream is a weekly slot from Fresh Direct.) Even if your order goes in, you might get half or so of the items you asked for, and a lot of odd substitutions you overpay for. When Ben misses out, he puts on a mask and nitrile gloves and goes to the supermarket. There's still no toilet paper, and meat and milk are rationed, when they're available: two packages of meat, two half-gallons of milk. Yet he says the thing he finds most ominous is that the mail has stopped—it comes once or twice a week, he conjectures because the sorting centers have been overrun with covid, though who knows under Trump. The hamburglar is probably postmaster general.

"Does it feel different?" I ask Rachel when we check in.

"Yes!" she says, in a tone of disbelief that I could even ask.

"How?"

"You walk out and just see . . . no one."

Ben and she both say Manhattan and New York more generally are empty. In a rich friend's building, two of the nineteen units are occupied. Everyone else has gone to a second house or a rental. "East Hampton is not built for this!" an escapee we know says in a post, apparently in earnest.

The exception to the emptiness of New York is the Orthodox Jewish parts of Williamsburg, apparently, which are carrying on as if nothing posterior to the composition of the Talmud bears any practical relevance to daily life. That is morally wrong, bad and selfish. Spiritually, who the hell knows. Maybe they're the only ones going to heaven. Nobody knows a single thing. Deconstruction has never seemed more correct to me than at this moment—all of the things we believe to be real, from presidents down to words, just things someone made up and then forgot someone made up. We're not tethered to anything permanent. At least that's how it feels on April 5, 2020, in the United States of America, almost a month into quarantine. In an aerial picture circulating today, hundreds and hundreds and hundreds of cars wait in a Texas parking lot, neat as legos, for a food bank to open. Football fields of minivans and pickups, motionless and scared as rabbits in a spotlight at night.

Rachel and her husband, Dan, also a good friend, have tried to shield their daughters, Beth and Jane—Jane, really, who's older—from the whole thing, and so Rachel says it breaks her heart when she overhears Jane's voice saying "coronavirus" on the phone today. Yesterday they took the girls out to do bubbles in one of those little sections of Riverside Park along Riverside Drive. They were having so much fun, Rach said, and lots of single adults stopped to just watch them—you could feel how starved they were for connection or joy, or anything, she said. She sent us a picture and it was true, five or six very different people staring at the two children with naked avidity for their effortless joy.

April 9

Somewhere in the last week time went flat and fast. It's like summer camp, when the first few days are infinite, and then, as soon as you've found out where the lake is and everything, the remaining weeks go by in an instant. None of these days seem quite distinct, as people lie unendingly on their couches, all meaning and moment dissolved. For a bit in there everyone was talking about *Tiger King,* a show about the people who own semi-legal wild animals, and occasionally get eaten by them, but those jokes then just sort of stopped. That's how fast new things get digested when everyone's paying attention. I spent the whole day listlessly practicing the solo to *Rikki Don't Lose That Number* by Steely Dan, occasionally staring at social media. I still haven't found the right book. Two friends who are novelists tell me independently that they can't read fiction. One is reading about serial killers on Wikipedia, and the other isn't reading anything, for the first time since she was five. She tells me so after she recounts a theory belonging to the critic Marie-Laure Ryan called "the principle of minimal departure" in fiction, which says that unless you're overruled by the text, the world you're in as a reader is presumed to be identical to ours. My friend adds that she thinks we can consider ourselves overruled by the text.

I'd been thinking of a less clever analogy. In the Civil War, the soldiers called marching to the front "going to visit the elephant." To me it's as if we're all visiting the elephant.

"Don't be a cutie pie," Trump tells the reporter Jonathan Karl after he asks whether everyone who needs a ventilator will get one.

A friend's father-in-law has covid. I don't know anything about him except that he wakes up at 2:30 every morning to do the *New York Times* Spelling Bee game. I play it too, though at normal times, like for instance when I should urgently be working. I can bring him to mind, a typologically perfect old white fellow in a blue button-down and khakis, a ballcap (to protect his skin!), with a ready smile, a delight in being a grandfather. He's achy, has a low fever. He should probably be in the hospital, but because they're overcrowded, hospitals aren't admitting covid patients without fevers. And so the dice get rolled.

But Wuhan reopened yesterday. It's the biggest moment of hope since we found out masks work, a time span I couldn't even begin to measure of my life, longer than whole summers of the early 2000s—three weeks ago. If we're a month behind Wuhan in the timeline of this virus, that means we could all be out again in May, conceivably. Of course it's China, so the possibility lurks that it could be a potemkin reopening. But equally plausible is the idea that they have better public health planning than we do. We could lag their reopening for that reason. Anyways it's nice to hope. Otherwise this is all too desperate and eerie. There are no sports on—even in *Children of Men* there was soccer playing in the pub—and day after day ESPN has to fill up the air with nothing, with stories from the past or the future, because there is no present. It's not that stores are closed it's that everything's *so* closed, everything we love has been closed for a *month,* and we miss going to the library and not feeling jumpy and tense at the grocery store and seeing our moms and walking down streets that aren't boarded up and windswept. We miss seeing people's faces. Wherever you are, everything's just so radically closed, so for somewhere that went through this to *open* is like a gleam of sunshine under the door after a snowbound winter.

Little flourishes of pandemic invention are popping up all the time. Rachel went to a Zoom funeral. ("How was it?" I ask. "It happened," she said, an accurate description of every funeral.) A friend in Chicago, where Em and I lived for several years, is getting carryout cocktails most nights. They're left up for you on a ledge in front of the bars and restaurants, with all the ingredients sealed in separate baggies, payment "contactless." The laws against drinking in public have been suspended in many places, in part to help restaurants. It sounds great, walking the sunny Chicago streets with a drink in these later and later sunsets. But also like a zombie movie. Have resourceful ideas during wartime always felt tinged with insanity? I think it must have been so—the recipes for making a cake for 12 with half an egg, the ingenious ways to wrap a parcel with no string. Burnt cork for mascara.

I drive to pick up medicine at the Walgreens on Sunset. There were rumors on the message boards that it was hard to find the 20mg size of the most important pill I take, which spooked me enough to refill my prescriptions early. When I get back to the car, I look down—a bag of Twizzlers I bought at the register is in one hand, my keys in the other—and realize I'm trembling. I can't tell if it's simply being out of the house, and I'm Boo Radley henceforth, or the relief of having the medicine. I think that one. I would have died very quickly if I'd gotten the same disease any time before around 1950. If I didn't have these pills for a day now, I would get sick, and a day after that I would probably go into a coma, and then I would die. Don't be a cutie pie.

Even Marx admitted that the great benefit of the capitalist phase of society—which he thought came after the feudal phase and before the socialist one—was its capacity to invent new technologies, to supply a marketplace continually demanding new goods. In that sense I'm a hypocrite, because medicine is a participant in that feverish race, and I'm glad to have the pills. So, thanks, I guess, Walgreens? Anyway, socialism, who knows; I would like more of it at least, please. As with so much of life, the problem is that we only know how things are, rather than, with any precision, how they could be.

It's the boredom and the terror in combination that make these days so sleepy and wrong, i.e., the terror is very much not gone. A month of everyone's lives. When the British were rationing there was a cause, there were young people at a front to pray for. Now we're all always dully at the front, people dying daily, some proportion of them daily specifically for the cause of Donald Trump not feeling embarrassed to wear a mask and admit he underestimated this disease. It's almost impossible to remember what the vitality and righteousness of the women's march three years ago felt like. The lifeblood of the funny signs, the evidence that other people *care*. Maybe history is on the move. Then again, maybe not, since I have been on my couch for fifteen hours, not quite reading, as lentils simmer on the stove.

I fell asleep today from one till five, time I should have been working. There's a legend that the father of the philosopher Epimenides sent him to look after some sheep, but he accidentally fell asleep in a cave for 57 years instead. If someone ever asks me what the start of April 2020 was like that's what I'll say. We're frightened and alone in our houses, and sleep, non-being, is the most rational conceivable response I can see to the situation. It's what I'm doing.

When I was very little and we went to the beach in New Jersey, my grandfather used to go outside to sleep whenever it rained. He was a businessman. As soon as it started to rain, he would go find his blue windbreaker, and put on a fishing hat and a pair of loose fishing pants, then walk barefoot out to a dune between our house and the ocean, where he would nestle himself in a spot among the reeds, hood cinched up tight, beach towels beneath and around him, and watch the ocean until he fell to sleep. I loved that. It seemed so snug and alone, alone with a world that makes rain and seagulls. He was alive from 1920 to 1997, my grandfather. He had two children and was on Nixon's enemies list and served on the board of Planned Parenthood all the way back in the 1950s. That's a pretty great life, just that. I don't know how well I ever really knew him. His name was the same as my own.

April 11

Very suddenly the U.S. death toll from coronavirus passes 20,000. It was five minutes ago that Nathan was telling us there had been 15 deaths, then 70, and so on. The number was still under 1,000 a few weeks ago. Now it seems clear that we're more likely to lose 75,000 people than to stop at 50,000, or even 100,000. Though my sturdily logical friend Jared and I agree that that last number sounds a bit melodramatic.

In March there was at least a novelty to the situation. (As Churchill said, nothing more exhilarating than being shot at without result.) In these April days, people are both more enraged and more bored. It's not heroic any more.

In South Korea, too, a surge: 214 people dead from covid there now.

One of those 20,000 people who has died of covid is the country musician John Prine. It feels like a huge loss. His fans are bereft. I loved him, for that matter. He was what we hold out to ourselves as the part of us that is uniquely and decently American, plainspoken, wry, humane, unpretentious but confident, almost like the doctor in a frontier town who's messed up here and there, sure, but come down the road in one piece all the same, with a few tales to tell. Sitting outside and looking at the lonely palm trees against the white sky, I listen to *Clay Pigeons* and *In Spite of Ourselves,* and think of what John Berryman said when Robert Frost died: for a while there we had an unusual man.

At the corner of Western and Santa Monica, the woman who usually sells makeup to people waiting for the bus has masks for $5. One of them says, "Social Distance This!" The fact that this makes no sense is comforting. Last week I saw Dodgers and Lakers masks, this week we're up to nonsense. Hand sanitizer has to be back soon.

My review of actually wearing a mask is that it sucks and I hate it.

April 12

I may be regressing. The evidence is subtle, but if you look closely, it's there, for instance, I'm wearing a fleece with my high school's name on it that I got as a present the day I *got* there; I'm listening exclusively to the Dave Matthews Band; and I am decidedly moody. I didn't even like high school! But today Nathan (*Ants Marching*) and Rachel (*Jimi Thing*) both confessed that they too have been listening nonstop to "Dave," and we fantasize about a time, this summer even, though Nathan is an Eeyore about that suggestion, when we could go see this terrible band we love so much in concert together.

Things I've bought because people recommended them on Tik-Tok this week: an Aztec clay mask, a small but very powerful wet vacuum for carpets, "Everything But the Bagel" cream cheese from Trader Joe's.

It's Easter, the date Trump said the country would reopen a month or so ago. Not close. Still, there's hopeful news from New York, where hospitalizations and deaths are falling for the first time. It shows that it can be done. There and in Maryland there are mask mandates, and recommendations in a host of other places including California. Good measures, but on the right there's an equal clamor to use the data from New York to show not that masks work but that we can reopen. We can be as virtuous as we want, but as Nathan said, there are no red states in South Korea.

"Satan and a virus will not stop us!" a Louisiana church expecting 2,000 people today declares. They're right about that, it will just be the virus.

April 17

With statesmanlike calm, Trump reacts to stay-at-home orders by instructing his Twitter followers to "LIBERATE MICHIGAN!" and to repeat same for "MINNESOTA!" and "VIRGINIA!" He's escalating to the language of armed insurrection in defense of this ongoing lie about the virus. But the grind of this presidency is twofold: first, that it's always impossible to pin him to the meaning of his words, because he's always pouring out new words, he's tweeted with the same passion about Robert Pattinson and Kristen Stewart's relationship; and second, related, that there are too many insane things happening all the time to process moments like these, where we should really reset to the regular metabolism of a new cycle and try to assess together how dangerous this could get. It only takes a few hundred people to "liberate" a state if that means assassinating politicians and causing terror, and sixty million people voted for Donald Trump.

This is where the media has failed. Every article in the papers still implicitly bows to this notion of the "President," as if we were in Sam Rayburn's secret club in the House or an episode of *The West Wing*. "President Trump has nothing on his schedule today," they'll loyally report, when a more accurate headline would be "Insane Person Remains Still in Charge of Country."

You can sense the election hoving into view, like an enemy ship that's a long way off but getting closer, not farther. The one that scares me (the TV critic Emily Nussbaum was the first person I saw point it out) is Ivanka. Ivanka has youth, looks, and plausibility, plus a husband who can pass himself off as calmly knowledgeable if you've never actually met or seen someone calmly knowledgeable. She could fuse the huge dumb power of the white suburbs with her father's radical base; the same chaotic lies and distractions could cross into the public without ever passing from her lips. If somehow they can steal this election and begin a transition from this idiot to his daughter, I don't think it's unreasonable to imagine we will be entering a new phase of history. 1776–2016.

Or he could lose in a landslide. It's not likely that either *will* happen, it's that the window for either to happen is open. After the election, my friends thought I was being alarmist. And they were probably right—the overwhelming likelihood is that America will not end, or even change substantially, because of Donald John Trump. But there's a chance. If you played out Hillary Clinton's presidency a thousand times on a computer, none of the simulations would end up with American death camps for asylum seekers. Under Trump, that number goes up, and even if it's just to sixteen times out of the thousand, or sixty, the difference is unmistakable in our atmosphere. (A small way: Every day of my life is filled with anger now.) As Rachel, an optimist, says, maybe within those thousand Trump simulations are a hundred that result in Democrats taking the reins of power next January and rebalancing economic inequality in our country dramatically, perhaps for the rest of our lives, and Ruth Bader Ginsburg and Stephen Breyer retiring and the Court getting more liberal and younger. In fact maybe there's more of a chance of that leftward movement to come from Trump than could ever have come from Clinton. It was Bill Clinton who abolished cash aid to poor families. But in a way the worst outcomes are the ones that matter; in five years Malia Obama will not be supervising the logistics of death camps, but Jared Kushner might be. Stupider people have done worse things to better people than us.

"The Age of Coddling Is Over," David Brooks, probably the most coddled living human being, announces in the editorial page of the *Times*. Yeah, that's the problem, we're all being coddled too much. This is too easy.

April 18

I saw the name Pauli Murray unexpectedly today. It was the first time I'd thought of her much since 2016, when Yale, where I went, announced with great fanfare the names of its two new residential colleges. The residential colleges are a big deal at Yale. Mine—and Ben and Rachel's—was named after the empiricist philosopher George Berkeley, who never saw Yale but donated some books to it from England. He's the one who said you can't prove a table's still in the room after you leave.

They named one of the two new colleges for Benjamin Franklin, and the other for Pauli Murray. I hadn't heard of her before the announcement, so I read a lot about her at the time. She was a lawyer and a priest, and more famously, a lifelong activist, and what's more the rarest person in any movement, one who is at once an inspiring on-the-streets organizer and a brilliant mind. In 1940, she and a friend were arrested for sitting in the "Whites Only" section of a Virginia bus, fifteen years before Rosa Parks's identical gesture changed the country—luck that it fell out that way, really, or the slow long grueling battleship turn of a society's morality.

Today I saw Murray's name in the historian Leon Litwack's crushing, magisterial book *Trouble in Mind: Black Southerners in the Age of Jim Crow.* For the past several years, I've been working on a novel about a boy at sleepaway camp, which is on its fourth or fifth draft, and some time during my book tour in February I realized also its final one, at least in this incarnation. I broke it from caring too much, like a fucking donkey with a pet chick. Now I have to put it in a drawer and see if in a while I can return to the original idea and find a book in all the dense agonized fog that it's become. "A perpetual succession of calculations, a monstrous four years' up and down," Kafka once said of writing a novel. Harrowingly accurate.

A month ago giving up on that book would have destroyed me, but a month into covid I don't care. That's partially because I've turned my attention to an idea for a new novel (the new novel is always going to be so good, that's one of the traps) that's been percolating in my mind for a little more than a year, about a graduate student from Chicago who tours Georgia in the 1930s, on a grant to collect and record regional music.

The idea really began when I read a book called *Remembering*

Slavery, a selection of the interviews that the Federal Writers' Project conducted with living survivors of slavery in the 1930s. I read it in 2015, and I can picture the room I was sitting in, the experience stands out so vividly to me—it was in my study in our house in Chicago, a room with windows running along the top of the wall, where as I read the book I could see the snow flurrying down with unrushed calm, sure in the knowledge it would be falling through the white air for the next eight hours and then through the black night—it was in that light, on that day, that I read about the pregnant woman an overseer forced to dig a hole and place her belly in it so that he could whip her without harming his "property," in the account of a witness seventy years later—that and a hundred other stories like it, in one sitting as I recall it, though I suppose it must have been two or three.

For years afterward I thought about that book every day, until at last I started to read more books about it, I needed to know more, sometimes I reach that point. So I read, which has always been my reaction to life. Litwack's book is astonishing, one I wish I'd found earlier in retrospect because it's so comprehensive. It's a painstaking history of what went wrong between the end of the Civil War and Rosa Parks, with a simple thesis: "What the white south lost on the battlefields of the Civil War . . . it would largely retake in the late nineteenth and early twentieth centuries." With an avalanche of data, stories, and testimonials, often so intense that it's hard to read more than a few pages of the book at a time, he puts the argument beyond dispute.

It was when I thought Litwack had carried me past surprise that I saw Pauli Murray's name. It was in one of many similar stories that he assembles, which establish the patterns of deliberately unpredictable, supremely effective violence that white southerners used during Jim Crow, a ghost structure in our nation's history as significant and far reaching as slavery itself, I think Litwack ultimately shows.

"Pauli Murray," he writes (and I experienced a quick confusion, until I placed the name as a Yale one) was a child when she saw a sight she would "never forget." It was the body of a man named John Henry Corniggin, "lying out in the field, where he had been shot to death," for walking across a white man's watermelon patch earlier in the day.

For a long time I was proud I went to Yale. I would never have admitted it, but I was, I worked myself up to the edge of misery and often past it in high school to get into the best colleges, and I did. My motivations were suspicious in retrospect—I think it was the armor of a word like *Yale* or *Stanford* that partly drove me— but even so, I'd done something difficult. That was undeniable: it was difficult to get in there!

But as time has passed, and as I've maybe needed that armor less, and also seen the damage caused by credentialism in our society, and above all as I have realized how thin the band of people is who were in the correct context even to *try* to get into Yale, my pride has melted away until now I think it's mostly gone. What's left is the true and shocking happiness I experienced there (you get high school or college, an intelligent friend once observed to me) and an affection for its streets and places and stupid Berkeley courtyard that will last until I die. I think it's just how we're made.

Pauli Murray was six years old when she saw John Henry Corniggin lying dead in that field. Litwack provides no other details; there are too many other stories for him to include, most worse.

I look it up, and that would have made it 1916, twenty-four years until she was arrested on the bus, and exactly a hundred years before Yale named its new college for her.

Six is just so small. Nothing bad that happens to you then goes away, not for real. Tiny Pauline Murray must have been so bright and alive at six too, such a dazzling light to her family, given all that she went on to do. But for all her intelligence she knew nothing. No six-year-old does, or should. Everyone remembers the little boy at Sandy Hook who told his teacher he would go fight the shooter, he was taking karate lessons. But Murray had to stand in the field and absorb the fact of a murder based on skin color, her own skin color.

And then beyond the shadow of Pauli Murray is this person John Henry Corniggin, whose memory would likely have dissolved into time forever if a little girl who became a writer hadn't remembered it. Why do I find this all so much, so intolerably moving? Is the pandemic getting to me?

The circumstances of John Henry Corniggin's murder in retaliation for crossing that watermelon patch reminded me of a different book I was recently reading, from which I learned the reason for the long-lived slurs about black people and watermelons: after the Civil War, watermelons were the cheapest, most efficient crop black people could grow, and some of the few black families that attained financial stability in that time were watermelon growers. So the origin of this myth of Black—what, gluttony? laziness? as if anyone could not like watermelon!—has its ancestry not even in an innocuous fondness for a fruit but in jeering mockery directed at freed slaves trying not to be destitute.

Two of the most common expressions in the south during the era when Jim Crow was forming were *work like a nigger* and *lazy as a nigger.* You were caught coming and going. Aside from the violence, this is the heartbreak of Litwack's book, the absolute power of what Frederick Douglass presciently predicted would become the defeated south's "sacred animosity" for freed slaves and their descendants. Well-meaning leaders from both races alike at the time drove home the lesson that only rectitude, thrift, and hard work could lift black people out of poverty. Black people responded by behaving with rectitude, thrift, and hard work. It didn't matter. "We thought we was goin' to be richer than the white folks," recounted a man named Felix Haywood of the decades after emancipation, "'cause we was stronger and knowed how to work, and the whites didn't and they didn't have us to work for them anymore." In fact what happened is that in every part of the south after Reconstruction, any black person who achieved any kind of success was likely to meet with violence and the destruction or at minimum the theft of his (almost always his) property, if he was fortunate enough to live. As a man named Pierce Harper recalled, "If you got so you made good money an' had a good farm, de Klu Klux'd come an' murder you."

They did it to his neighbor. "Dey taken him an' destroyed his stuff," Harper said. "Hung him on a tree in his front yard."

There was a second person it surprised me to find besides Pauli Murray's in Litwack's book. He was from rural Georgia, born in 1899, and as a boy witnessed a group of drunk white men beat a black man to death. The men attested that it was because he had been "sassy," though in fact his specific defiance was one of the most common that provoked violence from whites against blacks, per Litwack, which was that he refused to hand over his paycheck to them on payday.

For years after he saw the murder, the boy later wrote, he gave in to the satisfaction of "despising" white people. He said, anticipating the language of PTSD with eerie precision, as so many of these accounts do, "It helped me to deal with the memories, the terrible dreams." Eventually he became a Baptist pastor, and lived a long life—dying in Atlanta in 1984, having outlived, by sixteen years, his second child, first son, and namesake, and one of the other rare souls like Pauli Murray who possessed genius both as an activist and thinker: Martin Luther King Jr.

In late February, a young black man in Georgia named Ahmaud Arbery was shot and killed while he was jogging. The right ran the usual attacks up the flagpole—he had a history of petty crimes, he might have been trespassing on a construction site. (Michael Brown was "no angel," in the infamous words of the *Times*.) In this respect only the terms have changed. Slightly at that. Being "sassy" was the catchall offense for which slaves were punished before the Civil War and which for many decades into the twentieth century remained a strong enough accusation to give full retroactive license for a white person to kill a black one extralegally, on the rare occasion that there was even an investigation. "Impudence" was another common word that Litwack records, and of course any accusation, however far-fetched, of sexual interest in a white woman. "Uppity," too; I suppose it was regional, I don't think Litwack says. Anyway now the passwords are "trespassing" or "loitering" or "acting suspicious." It's far from clear that Ahmaud Arbery was trespassing—it seems more likely he was simply jogging. But of course, say he was trespassing—so goddamn what? He deserved to be *shot* to death?

"Fucking nigger," said Travis McMichael, the shooter, while Arbery lay dying, according to a witness. That word has not changed.

April 23

50,000 deaths in the U.S.

April 25

"Outcry after Trump suggests injecting disinfectant as treatment," *The Washington Post* reports. It's true, there's been a bit of an outcry about that specific suggestion.

Trump says he was being "sarcastic," but I'm not quite so sure, primarily because I watched it, and he was not. "A question that probably some of you are thinking, if you're totally into that world," he started (I would doubt it), "so, supposing we hit the body with a tremendous, whether it's ultraviolet or just very powerful light" (nice of him to leave this up to the docs) "and I think you said" (here he gestures to Dr. Deborah Birx, who looks like someone just pointed a gun at her) "that hasn't been checked, but you're going to test it. And then I said supposing you brought the light inside the body, which you can do either through the skin or in some other way."

Again it is very generous of him to leave all these avenues open for scientists other than himself, though he did trail off there, saying to the journalist who asked what I can only presume was a totally unrelated question, perhaps vaguely aware that he had lost his bearings, "Sounds interesting, right?"

But he wasn't through!

And then I see the disinfectant, where it knocks it out in one minute and is there a way we can do something like that, by injection inside or almost a cleaning, because you see it gets in the lungs and it does a tremendous number on the lungs.

His brain always goes back into the comforting vagueness of New York steak house dialect ("a tremendous number") when he swerves too close to the actual terrifying truth of what's going on with the virus.

> so it'd be interesting to check that, so that you're going to have to use medical doctors with, but it sounds interesting to me. So, we'll see, but the whole concept of the light, the way it kills it in one minute. That's pretty powerful.

Yes, super powerful. Thank you, Mr. President. At this point the reporter, to his credit, asked if Trump was actually talking about INJECTING DISINFECTANT INTO COVID-19 PATIENTS, to which Marie Curie over here replied

> It wouldn't be through injections, almost a cleaning and sterilization of an area. Maybe it works, maybe it doesn't work, but it certainly has a big effect if it's on a stationary object.

You don't want to bleach a moving human. I've always said that.

The makers of Lysol release a statement that "under no circumstance" should its products be used in the human body. Looks like they're not fans of textbook sarcasm!

Rachel and Wulf find a trove of old pictures of us from college. I write back on Slack "Thanks, literally hurts to look at them." I am not a crier, but as I study them, for too long, my face does get warm, I feel so assailed, not by Rachel and Wulf obviously but by this situation, by the past; how much more innocent the present is of knowledge, really, how sure the people in those pictures seem.

They would mean nothing to anyone, snapshots, but they matter to me. And one day I'll be dead. Me! The unfairness of it. Who will keep track of the fact that for a solid decade Wulf wore the same "day shirt" every weekend day and the same "night shirt" every weekend night and you could revive me from a coma and show me either garment and I would say, "Hey, the day shirt," before I went into cardiac arrest and died? This sadness is quarantine.

Finally, two nights ago, after a few weeks away to clear my head, I smoked pot, and was again amazed and a little angry that I had forgone the overwhelming relief of it so long. It's an unsettling feeling to have about a drug. I don't drink often—I stopped a few years ago except on special occasions, because after I turned 36 or so (I'm 39 now) it left me actually unable to function the day afterward. I had only smoked pot a couple dozen times in my life when I moved to California two years ago, and the first time I went to the dispensary it was with a furtive feeling that still hasn't completely vanished. If you want, you can go to one that looks like a Gap, though most are still nicely poised, aesthetically at least, between legit and shady, and they have the "budtenders" who tell you what the marijuana's like.

Etiquette forbids talking about what pot makes you feel like, except perhaps within the sanctuary of a group of people who are smoking it. Iffy even there. But it's a little like dreams, which are in fact not boring but incredibly fascinating. The problem is that people are terrible storytellers, and a dream is the hardest kind of story to tell well. Kazuo Ishiguro won the Nobel Prize for it.

Anyway, for me, it's a feeling primarily of relief, tremendous relief. When the budtender who was helping me this week (like liquor stores, the dispensaries were correctly deemed essential busi-

nesses in March) asked how I was doing, I surprised myself by saying, not what I would describe as fantastically well. She laughed
and said "Who is!" and then guided me in her mask toward the
indica, which is the "relaxed" kind of pot, while "sativa" (all of this
terminology is cursed as far as I'm concerned) is more conversa-
tional and active. "In da couch" is how you're supposed to remember that indica is more relaxing, if you're 13, or in my case that
times three. A friend who's a "marijuanaentrepreneur" says that
most of the strains are in fact hopelessly mixed up at this point, and
since the dispensaries sell pre-rolled joints that describe a feeling
instead of a strain—"Calm," "Sleepy," "Create," etc.—I usually
choose those. This week, though, I come away with two glass jars
of what people in this weird part of the country call flower.

Aside from pleasure in the world, which is short enough rationed
itself, what the drug does for me that's new is to give me a well-
ordered sense of freedom: the sense, passing through no interme-
diate states from anxiety to calmness, that of *course* I can put down
the eleven things (private, political, existential) that I have, like
a dunce, been shouldering along through my day; and suddenly
the trees look so true to themselves, and the world so accurate and
clear and beautiful and sad, and music sounds especially good, and
I understand myself—forgive myself. No medicine has done that
for me, yet I am unsure where I fall between using the drug medi-
cally and for mere enjoyment, and for another person that might
not be worrying, but for me, I feel such shame, an emotion whose
origin is obscure and radiantly powerful in me, to smoke two days
in a row, or even *three,* as I've done now, that I vow (lighting up,
tonight) that I will take another break, even as I chide myself for
the last one.

I've been listening to country music while I end each day looking at the clouds and smoking. Like the pot, it's a newer development; for a long time I was an "everything but country" person (everything but the bagel! ha, ha, I'm losing my mind) but at some point I started to dislike that part of myself. The south is infuriating, but it's there, and the people there are of my country, and I decided it was wrong to ignore their music because of something as thin and suspect as culture. So I went into country music looking for why the people who listen to it are stupid, and immediately stumbled over, in an appropriate reproof, a bunch of geniuses. Because we're in a real actual golden age of my favorite kind of country, which is female singers who play guitar: Taylor Swift, Brittany Howard, Kacey Musgraves, Maren Morris. I listen to these four so often with the intense concentration of the high that even the subtle tambourine shakes and background voices in their songs sink down into my consciousness. There are so few better feelings.

Country music has the unbelievable advantage over other genres of being about stuff. It's like being allowed to play inside the Canadian doubles lines. So many indie songs are called like *St. Lucia* and have incomprehensible lyrics. (Every the National song is lyrically identical, they did a study.) Then you listen to Maren Morris, and she has a whole song about how she really needs to hear a love song, she used to be able to cure the blues by drinking, but maybe she's getting a little too old (at the time of recording she was 26), before realizing, in this beautiful, soaring, I guess what could be called "cheesy" chorus, that what she needs is just the right love song to stand her up straight, and then she can keep moving. I can't stop listening to it.

The magical thing about Kacey Musgraves and Taylor Swift, who have moved on to write both more poppy and abstract songs, is that both are still too deeply rooted in their country instincts for saying something tangible to leave it behind completely, and so they both have a kind of ethereal realism. It's that Winslow Homer feeling, or Hopper, a longstanding American strain. Taylor wrote her first hit when she was 16. It's called *Tim McGraw*, and it's about how she hopes the boy she's addressing, who held her by a lake that summer, thinks of her when he hears Tim McGraw songs. It's four guitar chords that anyone could learn in an hour, but with the real geniuses it's always four chords at the start. Even at 16, Taylor Swift already understood how she could sing a melody to inflect the actual music playing behind her the way no one else but her could with those four chords, how to lag or go ahead of the changes to introduce unexpected nuances of emotion into the song.

Of course, there's a problem when a song's about something, which is why it's so easy and fun to avoid if you're a coastal pop star: you have no deniability if it sucks. The worst country songs I've found are EXTREMELY about stuff, specifically *Guys Named Captain* by Kenny Chesney, about the traits of people who are named "Captain," and *Ten Rounds with Jose Cuervo* by Tracy Byrd, about the perils of drinking ten shots of Jose Cuervo brand tequila. The problem is those songs came to my attention because they're the *popular* bad songs, and thus the ones that make playlists for novices, and so they're incredibly catchy. A playlist of them would be like a cosmic slippage from our earth into hell. (Hell should be fun in parts, or there would be too much dignity. If you ask my opinion. Which has not thus far been done. It's like Larkin's great and weird opening hypothetical in his poem *Water*: "If I were called in / to construct a religion / I should make use of water.")

I would hate to think that I listen to so much country music because Donald Trump was elected, like I'm fucking David Brooks, but I'm sure that's part of it. It's not political once I get lost in the music, especially with my favorites. But listening to some random singer (your Kelsea Ballerinis, your Thomas Rhetts) I'm conscious of searching for clues about their culture. It's as if the election drew out a deeper feeling, it was so surprising and appalling, something like being in childhood, a little—the dim and scary sense of being surrounded by strange animals and not knowing if you can trust them. What are they. What do they feel. How do I survive.

Instead of understanding more about Trump voters, though, which I don't, my taste has been enlarged. This is tied together at least in mind—and in habit—with the pot, which I tell my credulous self is good for me. I was always too well behaved for pot; I cared so much for so long, worked so hard in high school to get into college, in college so that something good would happen after that. The shame of going to a place like Yale is rightly yours if you are a white guy, I guess. I often think about the great poet Kay Ryan, who after she got famous turned down jobs from all the best colleges and went on teaching composition at a community college somewhere in rural California. ("Those kids at Harvard don't need me," she said, as I recall it. "They'll be okay.") On the other hand the part of me that needed to go somewhere like Yale then is the same part of me that needs the ability to stop paying attention to my mind for ten minutes, which pot gives me. I had internalized it all so deeply, that to go to Yale meant having done something permanently right. Then it turned out starting in March, or maybe when Trump was elected, or before that if you're someone else smarter than I am, that the world is sand, I should have just been getting high.

My favorite country song title (and a good tune) is *She's Actin' Single (I'm Drinkin' Doubles)* by Gary Stewart.

April 28

ALL my pasta is here. Look on my works ye mighty and despair. Is it back on the shelves? Sometimes, sure! Do I feel stupid? Yes, when I look at the thirty boxes of pasta sitting in their little battalions, I feel a bit stupid! Would I rather have them or not? Shut up!

It's Wulf's birthday, the fifth friend in our daily Slack and the only one besides me who lives in L.A., one of the people I see the most here besides Emily. He's the one who's on day candles now. He had been planning a party, but instead drives up the Pacific Coast Highway and listens to *Aja* and *Gaucho* back to back. I told him it's sad but that's a great drive. He did not seem especially consoled.

April 29

"It's gonna go away, this is going to go away," Trump remarks. Nice to hear the hits. Mike Pence (whose asshole wife Karen Pence gets in a car every day and drives from D.C. all the way to Virginia specifically so she can teach in a school that doesn't allow gay or trans kids, as I am reminded by my own angry, overtaxed brain when I see him) says, "By Memorial Day weekend we will largely have this coronavirus epidemic behind us." How largely, Mike.

I asked Nathan why the diseases always seem to come from bats. He says there's interesting new research about that. Scientists think the reason is that bats are the only mammals that can fly (something I didn't know) and apparently flying is impossibly stressful on a mammalian system, as a consequence of which bats have evolved in such a way that their immune systems are nearly indestructible. When bats get something like Ebola, their body "just chills" (Nathan's words) whereas the human body gets overheated, starts hemorrhaging blood, and then dies. So bats can effortlessly carry diseases that destroy us.

It's going to become more and more of a problem because of climate change, he says, scientists are tracking it very exactly. Deforestation means that bats and other animals everywhere are searching in cities for new habitats, which is how people get viruses from bats. However this strain of the coronavirus turns out, we can expect more "zoonotic" infections (I had to infer what that word meant, or possibly still don't know) leading to new and different viruses with unknown traits. For a time there was a government program called PREDICT, which was used specifically to catch bats and see what the next viruses to jump to humans might be, like this one. But Trump canceled it in the fall of 2019.

April 30

Reopening.

It's been coming: Though we are still "strongly advised" to stay inside when possible, there's a huge wave of openings across the nation, including "small retailers, restaurants, and other businesses." Most schools are still closed, arguably the thing we should have been fighting hardest to reopen. But not profitable. In Georgia, Trump ally Brian Kemp lifts restrictions even more broadly, on gyms, hair salons, elective surgery centers, short-term vacation homes, and dine-in restaurants. But the distinction is only political in minor ways—here in L.A., too, you can walk into a Starbucks and order a drink. There are clever, expensive-looking plastic dots and arrows to show you how far apart six feet is. Capital is here to take care of you. I haven't chanced it yet.

So it's only sort of the moment we all hoped for. People in my neighborhood are out on lawns, shiningly happy to be in each other's company again, listening softly to music and chatting, six-feet-apart-but-it-can't-travel-outside-anyways, sipping wine by candlelight. And elsewhere, of course, obviously a lot of people are cavalierly doing jackshit to stop the coronavirus, and elsewhere from that, even, are lots of people committed to isolation for as long as it takes. For them, this is all a mirage, a terrible, indeed tragic moment of false happiness for a country about to be laid wreck to by an invading army without any notion of mercy. Nothing has happened to the *virus*.

I'm at a terrible kind of simmer. Thinking about either the virus or Donald Trump I could do, but to think about these two threats has shattered my brain a little. The weirdo genius polymath Sir Francis Bacon once said that war is like the heat of exercise, but civil war is like the heat of fever. This is like the heat of fever. I have violent thoughts.

Should I throw a rock through the window of this Bank of America. How can I get them *back* for caring so little. It feels like the years of lead in Italy, Lila in the factory. The left has nothing left but our anger. We simply gaze on as Larry Kudlow and Steve Mnuchin (or whoever controls the economy) decide that we will strike the bargain that prisoners, old people, and the homeless die so that "the economy" will keep whirring.

Those three groups are not a mistake. The prison population in America is made of people from deep poverty, and half of all homeless people in America have sustained a traumatic head injury. In other words, these are the people we should be taking *best* care of, like the people who come here seeking asylum. Instead we've agreed to let them die for the sake of Apple's quarterly earnings call.

Oh and old people. Well! Old people! There's a saying in Africa about that, which is that every time an old person dies, a library burns to the ground.

A long, long walk this evening, full of melancholy feelings and doubt. It's gray. People say Los Angeles has no seasons, when in fact April alone has hundreds of little ones. For a while in spring something new is blooming almost every day. A lot of it is ugly, some of it is weird, some of it is impossibly beautiful. Right now it's purple petals. I walk longer than I intend, into an unfamiliar part of Koreatown, every shop in it intoxicating looking to someone starved for the normal world. I'm back on Norah goddamn Jones. For a while I was only listening to Stevie Wonder, and then I retreated into the comforting high school sound of the Wailers, now here we are at *Don't Know Why* again. Not great.

When I'm almost home, it gusts up with a little storm. I can already see the white edge of the cloud where it will be over, that's how slight the storms are here. I could probably walk to it. But I would never, because it's beautiful here, everything shining newly with the raindrops, the streets darkened and slick for once, and above all, the purple petals that just came out a day or two ago falling in deliriously happy swirls, thousands of them, until the familiar street I thought I knew so well looks unfamiliar and beautiful and lunatic. They get stuck under windshield wipers, even, where they flutter, pinned, as if a drunken meter reader from another, more beautiful planet had mistakenly strewn his tickets everywhere.

MAY

May 3

"Time has stopped," says Jon Lovett of *Pod Save America*. People are comatose; people are down; people are tired; people are sleeping. It's a shit show, it's a clown car, it's a dumpster fire. It's Groundhog Day. It's bad vibes; it's a coup; it's matcha season; it's the end of the world; it's just pandemic; it's the end of time; it's spring; it's 2020. On TikTok, teenagers confined to their houses post videos of elaborate Rube Goldberg machines that send a golf ball (for instance) through dozens of crazy obstacles before it ends up in a basement or a pool, where in the most popular videos there's usually a crowd that belts out a huge cathartic cheer when the ball teeters on the edge of a tiny plastic cup and then drops in. The contraptions are the opposite of life right now, complicated. Life is simple: Don't go anywhere and be afraid.

Last night I did go somewhere. It was the first time since the start of quarantine, not counting the grocery store and the drugstore. The place was Wulf's, where a small group of us gathered outside for a few hours at six feet's distance to celebrate his birthday. You see it every night in this mellowest Los Angeles month of the year, people out in yards and on stoops, laughing and drinking until late enough that the sun has set and the cold stars are out. Last night they were us.

We met on the neat green lawn in front of his apartment building, which is in a six-unit hacienda of a type scattered throughout L.A., little run-down portals to old Laurel Canyon, with inner courtyards covered in haphazard pink vines, and actresses who influence ("on the side") drinking on juliet balconies. Someone is usually playing an acoustic guitar, unfortunately, or, just sometimes, in a passable enough way that it suffuses the whole night with a feeling of intimacy.

It was dizzying to be together. We sat on separate blankets, listening to "Europe '72" by the Grateful Dead (Wulf's birthday choice) and talked. We were all carefully attentive to each other at first, as if it was a board meeting, but slowly, after we'd each had a drink or a gummy, the conversation became more natural. Then I forgot to notice what it was like, until all at once I was laughing in a way that made my whole body feel as if I'd been doing plank pose since March 10th. It was disconcerting, but marvelous, like the spark of life coming back into me. We stayed for three hours, a good longish time, but at 10:00 on the dot we got up and dispersed as smoothly as ball bearings on a skillet; as if none of us could have taken a minute more. As Matteo said afterward, it was emotional even to be around people. Wulf met a flight attendant on Hinge.

May 5

"Look, we're going to lose . . . anywhere from 75,000, 80,000 to 100,000 people," says the President. *Look* is one of those words shitty people figured out they could start a sentence with and seem automatically serious, as if everyone but them is afraid to face up to tough facts. ("Look, there will be some civilian casualties in Iraq.") But you can't say "look" about 100,000 people dying that *you specifically* could have saved. It's not a meteor that fell on Indianapolis. Wear a mask and listen to the public health agencies.

Stories of death everywhere now: perfectly fit 26-year-olds, a heavy tranche of men in their sixties with preexisting heart and lung conditions, random mothers who had recently celebrated their 40th birthdays at small gatherings. Did they get it there? Anyone can find a story of a person almost exactly like themselves that's died. There are pictures on the news of little children saying good-bye to their grandparents on iPads, hugging the iPads, presumably whispering last words of that ferocious toddler love, if they have a notion of what's going on. It seems like a special cruelty that these old people die alone, with heavy metal rectangles in their hands if they're lucky; born before the television, dying via one. In my mind is the ghost of a memory of a line in the English poet and soldier Siegfried Sassoon's memoir, which I care enough to seek out and find on my bookshelves. "Elderly people used to look like that during the war," it read, "when they had said good-bye to someone and the train had left them alone on the station platform." The situation is the same as now, but with the ages reversed.

On the right, the most pressing story at the moment is still the need to "save" the economy. The panic on the financial networks is total. The chyrons (*U.S. Economy Collapse Imminent?*) are like lamentations from the Book of Ruth, the gnashing of teeth in coldest outer space. If you only watch this hysteria for ten minutes, it seems to have so vanishingly little to do with reality. But no doubt if those channels are your world and you watch the ticker all the time, it quickly does come to seem like reality. In that instant of tilt-shift so much seems clear, how so many probably basically moral human beings, with kids and Audis are suddenly telling us, in panicked suburban second mortgage–anxiety tones, that lockdowns will ruin our economy, and we must reopen, even if it means accepting a "9/11 every day" starting on June 1. That's the phrase that keeps coming up as people try to contextualize the statistics of a disease that started out with such a small handful of cases, so few deaths, so recently. Of course, the difference that guarantees we will lose and companies like Amazon will come out of this stronger than ever before is that it will be an invisible 9/11 every day, taking place in thousands of hospital and nursing home rooms across a huge country. In this sense the problem is like climate change, just hard enough to feel threatened by that we're going to meekly allow it to slaughter us.

And obviously there are enough psychopaths in banking to carefully curate an atmosphere in which any moral qualms are minimized to the people violating their own principles; who in their green suburbs would never take out a gun and shoot a stranger in the face. But look, 75,000, 80,000 people—a single death is a murder, a million is a statistic. An American died of covid every 45 seconds in April, I read. So it goes.

And of course the appeal of reopening is profound. Look at us the other night. It did feel like "freedom." That's the word so many people on the right use about guns and now masks, and it's such a maddeningly dumb abuse of that word. But the notion of freedom isn't dumb. It has real meaning in this country particularly, that's why its roots are so stubborn. Imagine coming from a family of peasants that had farmed the same tired soil for fifty generations, then arriving in America, where all that mattered were two things besides being white: work ethic and luck. It must have seemed like magic. If your family had the good fortune to find prosperity across more than one generation here, of course it might revere the idea of "freedom," in whatever attenuated, mutating forms it assumed over the generations. And indeed, revere America with the same lack of precision.

The radical danger is that, as the artist Joseph Beuys said, capitalism always has the word freedom on the tip of its tongue. "Freedom" is the sleight of hand the profit-makers pull, because they have encouraged enough people to think that *freedom* doesn't mean freedom from want, or fear, but being able to own an AR-15 and say racist stuff. "Freedom" is how they dump poison in a river. As long as most Americans don't have access to those truer, less tangible, and deeply unprofitable freedoms—choice, education, destiny—then not wearing a mask will be what freedom feels like for some of them.

A boat parade in a lagoon in Florida for Trump makes me think we're fucked. There's just so many of them, and they're so proud and delighted! By Donald Trump! When he ran, it was hard for me to imagine a single person who could look at him and think he should be President. I am very alive to my mistakenness.

"Thank you very much to our beautiful 'boaters'!" the President tweets, clearly moved to his core by their shared respect for his feelings. "I will never let you down!"

May 6

Nathan says school closures may have made things *worse* because they increased "intrafamily contact." An incredible loss if true. But so much remains unknown. In a year all of that information will be available, and hopefully also obviated by the new vaccine we have, or some over the counter drug that stops covid in its tracks. The chances of either are pretty slim, though a vaccine will eventually come, one way or other. He also reports that he's debuted a new joke on rounds: "Me, my kids are studying at SUNY-Downstairs!" followed by a wink. Joke met with universal opprobrium by those close to him.

Twitter's most disarming picture of the day is of a school reopening in China, tiny giggling humans in gray jackets and pin-neat ties at their desks, and on each of their heads an air-light foam hat six feet across, like a motionless propeller, so that they stay safely apart.

Grimes and Elon Musk had a baby boy named X AE A-XII. "Still a better name than Elon or Grimes," Wulf points out on Slack.

May 9

Georgia senator Kelly Loeffler is in the news for having invested in a company that makes body bags shortly after getting a briefing on Covid-19 in January. She then continued to "downplay the virus in public," presumably so those body bag checks would get fatter. Loeffler was already the richest member of the Senate, not a slight feat. Her husband is the head of the New York Stock Exchange. It amazes me that this woman is one of just a hundred senators for the 350 million of us, is already rich beyond imagination, and her first thought upon hearing about the risk of a pandemic that could kill millions of people was to invest in body bags. Truly a freakish moral outlier.

My favorite last word of a book is from *Tristes Tropiques* by Claude Lévi-Strauss, a memoir of the time he spent studying Brazilian tribes, combined with quite a lot of, arguably too much, info about those tribes. It's also a lament (*triste* means sad) about how by the middle of the 20th century, imperialism, consumerism, and tourism had conspired, in Lévi-Strauss's view, to mostly eliminate cultures like those of the Brazilian tribes, in favor of what he called "the monoculture."

The last word of the book comes after Lévi-Strauss has spent his final paragraphs pondering whether peace of mind is possible for humans. By this time it's come to seem like the question that drove him to write the book; Lévi-Strauss was helplessly in love with anthropology (an affliction he claims can befall anyone, at any time, which is kind of exciting) but was more interested still in searching for peace of mind for himself. It's exceedingly rare in modern society, he thinks, coming only in the flashes of experience "in which our species can bring itself to interrupt its hive-like activity."

He offers examples of the moments of attention he means, increasingly strange, until the list culminates in his great ending. Such a moment of peace can come, says Lévi-Strauss

In the contemplation of a mineral more beautiful than all our creations; in the scent at the heart of a lily and filled with more knowledge than all our books; or in the brief glance, heavy with patience, serenity and mutual forgiveness, that, through some involuntary understanding, one can sometimes exchange with a cat.

I remember the disorienting thrill of reading five hundred pages about indigenous South American tools and then landing on the word "cat." What a Lévi-Strauss-like moment in itself! The cat's familiarity is crucial to his point, which is that there lurks within us the capacity not to be distracted by television or even our selves, to really look hard at what's around us—in short, to see more than we see. All of us have that power, he believes, and may need it as the world shrinks and grows more intricate. And the result of his long and moving trip to Brazil is that these mysteries are not always necessarily far, you don't have to travel to Brazil to see them. They are in your own house; and the part of ourselves that seeks them out only dormant, never dead.

That is the peace of mind I am trying to cultivate because I'm going fucking crazy. So is everyone I think. Sixty days inside, when at the start two weeks seemed like a long stretch. At Wulf's, the subject that elicited the most naked yearning in people was travel—leaving. People's choices were weirdly sensual ("Italy, but take it slow"). This is my level of affluence, of course. Personally, I would like to go everywhere right now, anywhere, shifty and alone, transporting by blink between cities and towns all over the world, sitting in cafés in unfamiliar squares and having coffee at one, retsina at the next, writing in a journal, looking at people. The possibility of it seems so, so far away.

I haven't traveled far. I wish I could go to Japan, that's my first choice. Actually I think I'd most like to visit Africa, but I can't be far from a good hospital, or rather I can, but I might die, which is not presently a risk that seems worth incurring. (Give it two more weeks.) Instead, I've hugged the shore, Paris, the Netherlands, lots of time in England, a bit in Greece and Germany, anywhere someone went to die in a Henry James novel. I love them all. But I've never even been to . . . I don't know, Copenhagen, for example, and Copenhagen's probably so beautiful and odd, full of cobblestone streets and ancient nordic eccentricities and rum-looking bars, that it deserves a lifetime of attention just itself. On Wulf's lawn, a friend said if she were daydreaming then she'd like to go to Baja and rent a car and drive to the famous Mexican beaches. She imagined taking slow roads, drinking lots of beer. A carful of people without a mask in sight, listening to music. And the deserted beaches she says they have on the west coast down there—she has friends (she's Californian—their travel dreams are always surprising me) who have been, and for a brief moment as she described it she went somewhere closed to all of us, before her eyes came back and she smiled. "As soon as the pandemic is over."

I rarely use Instagram, I remember telling them, but sometimes I drift around it for an hour or two, looking for things as different from my own life as possible. I like to see what tattoos people are getting in Tbilisi or what the counter food is in the hipster district of Suzhou. I do it by following random hashtags in languages I don't understand. Wulf, who's from the Adirondacks, pointed out that a lot of people talk about no Americans having passports, but they're off, Americans travel all the time. They just stay in America. He's right. Hundreds of thousands of people ride their motorcycles to South Dakota every year to gather. They go to Destin and Lake of the Ozarks and Bethany Beach and New Smyrna (shark capital of the lower 48!) and Las Vegas and Bridge-hampton and hundreds of other places with incredible emotional meaning to those who love them . . .

I was once in the concessions line at a Cubs game and met someone who had driven his family twenty hours instead of flying, so they could afford the tickets. I have never rooted that hard for a team to win. The ache to travel crosses all lines of class, obviously. It's been years since I read *Tristes Tropiques,* but a day or two after the party I went back to look through my notes from it to see what I had underlined and halfheartedly started transcribing some of them, a chore I often put off. I fell into reading it again instead. There are 365 churches in Bahia, says Lévi-Strauss, one for every day of the year.

May 10

Here in California, more businesses, including bookstores and clothes shops, are opening. The curve is flatter. In New York, Nathan only has two patients on vents. Cruise ships are once again taking bookings for trips departing from "Miami, Port Canaveral, and Galveston" on August 1. (Thank you to our beautiful boaters!) And in what almost seems like an end point to some definite period of our lives, there's hand sanitizer on the shelves at drugstores.

Altogether, then, the collective focus has shifted from the next ten minutes to the next ten months. It's not that anything has been solved. As Ben observed, the choice has come down to whether we go out and risk it, guaranteeing a rise in deaths, while trying to manage as sensibly as possible, or wait a year and a half for a vaccine, doing this—the remote work, the remote learning, the inability to see loved ones. Two bad options.

So while the pure early terror is dissipating, we walk forward into a fog of calculations about what's safe, who's safe, and all of it now up to no one but us. If we were doing our best it would be one thing, but a haphazard mosaic of companies, states, mayors, and CNN isn't the same thing as a federal government, and we've gone from 7,000 deaths to 70,000 with the velocity of a fall. After reading them my whole life, I feel as if I understand the numbers of war. Hearing 40,000 and hearing 70,000 felt indistinguishable. It will go where it goes next. We've come to terms with it each in our own ways. It was all going so slowly, and then it started doubling, and doubling, and everywhere, even where we flattened the curve, people had to take chances to go to work or take care of family members, or else just did it out of selfishness, and now the receipts are coming in.

May 11

Unsurprisingly, the election is sharply back in focus. It never left the conversation, of course, but Joe Biden became the presumptive nominee almost exactly as the virus emerged, and the polling between him and Trump has been basically static since the matchup was confirmed: Biden ahead by a wide margin in the national vote, by smaller margins in the states where the election will be decided because of the Electoral College.

There are days I think Biden could win forty states. It's easy to forget given the daily mental pressure of living in his America how improbably lucky Trump got in 2016. No one thought he could win, which depressed turnout; he ran against a historically unpopular candidate; the Russians and Jim Comey and who the fuck knows who else helped him; and since his improbable victory, even the Democrats (not notable for their political savvy, a shortcoming in a political party, it turns out) destroyed him in the 2018 midterms, while underlining it all is the fact that last time he lost by almost three million votes. Biden is popular, safe, and unchaotic, and every sane American I know would camp out on a cold sidewalk to vote against Trump, whether it was for Joe Biden or a lump of dirt.

Sadly this is the same part of me that watched Trump march through supposedly insurmountable obstacles to get here, convinced that each one would stop him, wrong every time. And now we live with a real chance that he will seize power illegally. People are waking up to that at least. When you read about Nazi Germany, this is how it happens, like Hemingway's description of how you go bankrupt—gradually and then all at once.

The President met with some of the country's oldest veterans maskless. "They're so pure, it will never happen, alright?" he says. "They've lived a great life." Well, I hope so, because if Trump has coronavirus a bunch of them will be dead this time next week. It's the kind of thing the whole nation should pause on for *weeks*. Not only is it not a scandal, though, it's not news. Nor is it news that the Secretary of State, Mike Pompeo (whom I think we have to take as nature's last word on how closely a human being can resemble a toad) keeps calling covid "the Wuhan virus." Other Trumpers call it the China flu or, among the more overt racists, "Kung Flu." Meanwhile incidents of violence against Asian-Americans are spiking, including bullying among children.

If the Trump era ends I think what will be hardest to convey is how things happened every day, sometimes every hour, that you would throw your body in front of a car to stop. But there was nothing to do to stop them. Those children getting bullied. The money for billionaires, the last protections stripped from waterways and forests, the children suddenly skipping meals again because the Republicans are back. Day after day after day. The knowledge that Ben Carson is somewhere wandering the halls of HUD right this minute, doing damage we can't even see, and Betsy DeVos is over with her Dolores Umbridge self-certainty at Education, *permanently* harming children every day. Whole lives. But we barely have time to focus on even the President's offenses.

There are so many times it should all have ended. Everyone knows them without thinking, the things that would not only have ended other presidencies but banished whole parties into the political wilderness: Mexicans being "rapists," the tiki torches in Charlottesville; the 25+ more credible allegations of sexual assault by different women from every walk of life, with no relationship to each other; the picture of the little girl in the fluorescent pink top, sobbing at knee height to a border agent, watching her mom being taken elsewhere, that became the stark viral representation of our child separation policy (what a disgusting phrase). It should have been over ten times this month already. It should have been over when he accused frontline workers of not having the PPE he failed to get for them because it was "going out the back door." But it will all be forgotten because we forget everything. As Marshall McLuhan said, the price of eternal vigilance is indifference.

I can see the pointlessness of all of us who spend time repeating these points on Twitter. There's a part of the progressive left, a lot of them Bernie supporters, who laugh at #resistance Twitter, which I guess is what I do in the sense that I am unable to stop shouting about how pissed off I am about whatever Trump is doing that day. They're the same people who mocked Warren's plans because only Bernie would do. Bet you'd like some plans right now fuckers.

What those criticisms don't acknowledge is that not only do we know it might be fruitless to rail against Trump on Twitter, that fact is FOUNDATIONAL to the exhausting rage of the situation, the probability that all our furious, detailed condemnations of child separation—of that girl in the picture ending up in a position to be in that picture—achieve nothing. That our donations to food banks and RAICES achieve nothing. Of course we know that. But it's also too wrong to just be aloof from it, or make nihilistic jokes. You can't. What's happening has to be said, and noticed, and deplored, it can't transition into being part of the grim lols of online monoculture without a layover in our consciences. Someone has to pause on it all, and even if I'm not traveling to the border to help, even if I'm achieving nothing, I don't care. The whole point of "Never forget" is to not in fact ever forget—to head things off before some Stephen Miller grabs the reins after Trump wins in November and nine months from now we look up and people are being killed for us by our army. I want to have said something before that happens. He really could win again. It really could happen. And does that mean we'll have concentration camps? No one knows. It doesn't have to end like Nazism to be like Nazism.

"Anger is better," says the narrator of Toni Morrison's *Bluest Eye*. "There is a sense of being in anger." I don't think you're supposed to identify with that line, but I felt a chill of recognition when I read it. Anger is better. There is a sense of being in anger. I don't follow Trump's offenses so closely because I'm a great guy, or something. (I am a great guy, it's just for other reasons.) I'm angry.

If Nick Carraway was right, and everyone suspects themselves of one of the cardinal virtues, mine is that I hate unfairness. I'm all sorts of awful things, selfish, deceitful, small; but I hate unfairness, I just fucking hate it, involuntarily. "Kung Flu," I don't understand how these people live with themselves. Trump hasn't left my mind since the moment he was elected. You have to watch bad people when they're in charge of you. That's a lesson some childhoods yield.

Anyway, I would have to respectfully disagree with Jared Kushner's take on the year so far and his father-in-law's handling of covid, that "This is a great success story" and "that's really what needs to be told."

That's the tragedy of Bernie: Bernie would have been a fuck you too. If the electorate wanted to throw a bomb at the system, an understandable feeling, it could have been Bernie. He was a great candidate, and he won a lot of people over, including a lot of Republicans. Play the whole 2016 election out a thousand times, first to last, and I bet there are fifty scenarios where Trump wins and fifty where Bernie wins. A few dozen each to the various mutants who made up the Republican primary field, and then 700 or so for Hillary Clinton. We could have landed on any of those bingo squares and we pulled Trump.

May 12

"*Guarding Jordan* with Jeff and Abby Hornacek" is airing on some new atrocity called "Fox Nation." Even at this absolute peak of Michael Jordan nostalgia I have to question how much Abby Hornacek knows about guarding him.

The President's mind is on former Republican congressman Joe Scarborough, a morning TV host sometimes critical of him. In retaliation, Trump is implying that Scarborough murdered someone twenty years ago. Which is quite an escalation.

"Concast" should open up a long overdue Florida Cold Case against Psycho Joe Scarborough. I know him and Crazy Mika well, used them beautifully in the last Election, dumped them nicely, and will state on the record that he is "nuts." Besides, bad ratings! #OPENJOECOLDCASE

A detail-rich tweet, between the shot at Comcast, the recapitulation of his close relationship with the person he's accusing of murder, and the inevitable swipe at their ratings. This might be the hardest he's worked since he took office. Could his time have been better spent? Hard to say. According to Buzzfeed, three Russian doctors treating the coronavirus have fallen out of windows in just over a week.

May 14

Thinking it over, I pick Amsterdam. A canal there, having breakfast with Emily and some friends, feeling the warmth of the peaceful daytime break over the delicate trees by the canal, drinking coffee. I love every part of the day in Amsterdam. At noon it's tranquil but busy, and late mornings and later afternoons it's full of the most beautiful light, echoing reflections of water and glass. (To protect the canals, houses in Amsterdam can't weigh over a certain amount, so they have a lot of windows.) I like the city at night, excitable, druggy, fringed with sort of insane possibilities, and I like the museum afternoons, and lunch in a brown café with fogged up windows on rainy days, and the chocolate shops where they melt a bar in a brass pot in front of you to make it (though I very virtuously only get a coffee and a modest 5,000 calorie pastry). I love passing local teenagers playing intense games of soccer on the public tennis courts under the gaslights at night, a few dozen older men with bagged beers ranged around. I love the weed shops that look like midwestern basements, and the weird Dutch breakfast buffets and antiseptic old CNN International, and I love *The Night Watch* and Bas Jan Ader. It's a perfect city to be tired in, nothing is far, and there are sleepy parks and restaurants and museums for that dusty half hour of afternoon when the whole world wants to fall asleep. I like the Amsterdam airport. I like the leaves that fall on the roofs of the houseboats in the fall. How peaceful it would be to drag my tired body back to an unfamiliar hotel in an unfamiliar place, that's what I feel now. Home is partly being able to leave.

"Holy fucking SHIT my children need a lot of attention today," texts a friend who had her second baby a month before the pandemic started.

I go for my usual walk. I try to walk 10,000 steps, because it's a number I can't reach lazily, which I know of myself that I would if I could. At some point you really have to be out there marching around to get 10,000 steps. If I die this year it will either be from coronavirus or stumbling on tree roots in the dark while trying to give other walkers space.

I'm a few inches over six feet, which means that 10,000 steps is about four miles. That's not as far as it sounds, and I see the same places over and over, a few calm streets in the upward slope of the hills. As I walk today, I call the friend whose kids needed all the attention. She's trying to balance work and distance learning. The most infuriating part she says is the amount of printing she has to do for her daughter's kindergarten class. Anecdotally, it certainly seems like the moms who are dealing with these problems.

May 18

Trump is still taking hydroxychloroquine. The point of this is probably something about the stock market, but the other point of it is irreality. It's like drawing the little sharpie balloon to include Alabama in the official map he was showing of Hurricane Dorian, because he'd said incorrectly earlier that Alabama would be within the affected area. The right seized on that as a symptom of "Trump derangement syndrome," and while I don't deny that I'm deranged because of Donald Trump, they've got that part wrong. That map was in fact one of the most distinctive and important moments of his administration because it was so sheerly stupid, because he was asking his people to embrace the most naked, pointless lie. And they did. They did. So.

May 21

"His continued refusal to wear a mask in public and a bizarre reference to Henry Ford's bloodline notwithstanding, the president was on his best behavior" is a hell of a sentence to read and completely understand.

May 24

In a day or two we'll reach 100,000 deaths.

The approach of the milestone catches me by surprise. I thought I was inured to the rising numbers, but then maybe everyone's brain is wired to have awe for round numbers.

There's anger rippling across the country. The cover of this morning's *Times* (whose record of courage during this presidency has been mixed) is a wall of unadorned text, under the banner headline **U.S. Deaths Near 100,000, An Incalculable Loss.** The text itself is made up of obituaries for people who have died of covid. Too many of them are my age, thinks everyone at once. It's a grave, memorable front page. 100,000 people, a war's worth, and no end in sight. None of the jokes are funny any more. There's nothing interesting about the pandemic any more. There's nothing interesting about the supply chain, or the new lingo, or the daily reports. Nothing except my friends, my family, and one or two bare little shreds of music, usually Kacey Musgraves, is keeping me tied to life. 100,000! How did this come to pass? How could I have ever believed in a place where this could happen?

Nathan reports that he's goofed in his domestic duties. He likes doing the grocery shopping and the dishes and his wife, Heather, loves cooking, so they divvy up the chores that way. According to Nathan, when he goes shopping he pops an onion in the cart automatically, assuming it goes in most recipes. But today he was putting the groceries away and found a drawer in the fridge with *twelve* onions in it. He asked her what they were doing there and she said she had no idea why he kept buying them. Why did she keep letting him! That's his question.

Fond recall among friends of the time Heather asked Nathan to "bring home some fish for dinner" and, unsure of what that meant, he bought five pounds of flounder. He ate flounder alone several times a week for a month after that. He also relays that he got another promotion at work. Doctors are extremely odd. My personal theory is that medical school drives them insane.

"Our human capital stock is ready to go back to work." So says White House adviser "Kevin Hassett" in a TV hit. #Human CapitalStock starts trending on Twitter. Where did this person, this Kevin Hassett, slouch in from? Yet he is not wrong. The human capital stock is ready to go back to work. It has no money, which it needs to buy shelter and food. Otherwise it will be dead, of use to not a single corporation (and incidentally in direct contravention of the human capital stock's own wishes). Can't have that. In Canada everyone gets a couple thousand dollars in a month, in Germany even more. Here we get work. A one-time wealth tax on the fifty richest people in the country could see us all safely at home, hundreds of millions of us, for as long as this lasts. But those fifty people would never allow it. In *Eichmann in Jerusalem,* a regular German woman says, fairly early in the war, "The Russians will never get us. The Führer will never permit it. Much sooner he will gas us." In March there was a moment of wondering if perhaps history was on the move again, somehow. Now it seems clearer than before the pandemic, bitterly clear, that nothing will ever change in this country.

May 25

A video appears on the internet of a black man in Minneapolis being killed by a white police officer. It's agonizing. The officer kneels on the man's neck for several minutes as he begs, in increasingly muffled and desperate tones, to be let up. Then he dies.

I watch the video once and close my computer, even though I have a book review I should be working on. The rest of the day is terrible, and only late at night do I realize it's because I watched someone die. So did millions and millions of other people. His name was George Floyd.

Every night for the last few weeks I've been waking up around 4:00 in the morning, which happens to me intermittently. The doctor I once asked about it said, "You have terminal insomnia." "Terminal!" I asked. He glanced up at the distress in my voice. "It doesn't mean fatal. It means that you fall asleep well, but wake up in the terminal sleep period, the third period of sleep." I told him they should change the name but as far as I can tell he never got on it.

Tonight though I can't even get as far as that, can't get to sleep. I go for a long walk in the dark. Usually it helps but when I get home I realize I didn't see a single thing, I was thinking about the video of Floyd. On my side, looking at my phone, trying to get back to sleep for a few hours before the day starts, I see that a lot of people on Twitter are having the same trouble sleeping.

May 26

Protests overnight in Minneapolis; what started as another story of police brutality is becoming a national one. In clips, the protesters are organized, peaceful, and have a look of utter determination on their faces. They haven't been anywhere since March 10th and they all watched that video.

May 27

The original protest in Minneapolis is growing, and protesters are amassing in Memphis, New York, and here. George Floyd. His name is the name of the moment; the question is whether it will join the others: Ahmaud Arbery, Philando Castile, Rekia Boyd, Jamar Clark. Freddie Gray, the perfectly healthy 25-year-old who died of "spinal cord injuries" sustained in a Baltimore police van; the officers acquitted. When did it become police protocol to kneel on people's necks? How could you kneel on a person's neck for more than eight minutes as they begged you not to? Something essential is shut off inside a person who can do that.

Millions of children today are seeing what Pauli Murray once did in that field: a black life forfeit to a white whim.

May 29

In response to the protests, the rhetoric on the right is getting more violent. Both the right and its news organs, particularly Fox, are on war footing. Tomorrow a thousand protesters could be lying dead on the streets of one of our cities. I really believe that.

"When the looting starts, the shooting starts," Trump tweets. Twitter restricts Trump's tweet for violating the company's policy on promoting violence. Over at Facebook, the slightly less morally keen version of Twitter (ha!) Mark Zuckerberg has decided against removing the quote, letting it stand, the naked threat of a sitting President, top commander of the largest military in human history: "When the looting starts, the shooting starts." Facebook employees protest en masse. My heavyhearted prediction is that it won't achieve much. Incitements to violence must be incredible for the algorithm. Remarkable how much power our system has reposed in a single man for having the idea to rate whether or not girls at Harvard were hot.

The phrase "when the looting starts, the shooting starts" comes from Bull Connor, who shocked even the conservative parts of the country in the 1960s by turning dogs and fire hoses on civil rights protesters in Birmingham, Alabama.

May 30

At some moment between yesterday and today, the protests went supernova.

There's electricity in the air—the thrill of something good happening, something righteous, and tens and tens of thousands of people in virtually every American city have flooded into the streets. Here in L.A. we're under a curfew, as most cities nationwide are. But the protesters don't care. They're screaming in the police's faces, furious, united, unyielding. I've never seen them so reckless in my lifetime, not in 1992, not in 2003, not in 2017.

It's a Saturday, and we had been planning to get together on Wulf's lawn again to have drinks, as we had for his birthday, but everyone else cancels.

"I don't know," he texts me. "Do you still want to come over?"

I do. It's one of those days when being inside for the pandemic scratches at you like a wool sweater. As soon as I start driving over toward West Hollywood I wonder if I've made a mistake. The sky in L.A. is always full of choppers, but tonight is different, they're just hovering, unsafely close together it looks like to me, dozens of them.

I turn west onto Santa Monica to cross the city to Wulf's and immediately see a blockade. My heart skips and I turn onto Normandie instead and take back streets the rest of the way. On the big arteries on either side of me I can hear sirens, glimpse militarized cops in matte black cars and tactical gear. "LAPD is stopping everything at 3rd and La Cienega," a friend texts me and Wulf. La Cienega means Beverly Hills. So we know who's going to stay safe throughout this at least. She says there are about a thousand protesters around the Grove.

I almost turn around, but when I get to Wulf's—parking quietly on Formosa and 2nd for a minute first, a side street, just to be absolutely sure of something that I don't know what it is— I'm happy I came. He's out on the lawn with some drinks and a speaker, listening to MF Doom. We shake our heads at each other and I sit down.

Over here, close to the Grove, the noise of the choppers and sirens is constant. "Look," he says. In the air directly in front of his house, six helicopters wait in an uneven static scatter, effortfully stationary. The last daylight is still in the sky, giving everything a terrible lavender glow, underlit by the protests—an image from Saigon, the peculiar indifference of the palm trees standing up into the sky whether they're wanted or not, the lush quiet street from which we watch.

Wulf grew up in a town in the Adirondacks, and is now a screenwriter. He's one of the funniest people I've ever known. His father is obsessed with their Austrian lineage, which apparently includes some nobility, and that's how Wulf got his name. There's a door his Dad calls "Salzburg Gate" leading from their backyard onto their back porch ("normal door" Wulf muttered when I was first getting the tour). At the start of quarantine Wulf bought dozens of boxes of Spam and Hershey Bars, though, as Ben points out, only two rolls of toilet paper. I love him—I love all four of these friends, a familial love, and for some it seems that has been the lesson of the pandemic thus far, the importance of friendship.

We open cans of Guinness and settle in to watch the world end.

Almost immediately four firetrucks pass down Wulf's small street with their sirens on the loudest setting, or if there's a louder setting then you could hear it in fucking outer space. "They're just circling the block," Wulf says. For a while we talk about other stuff, but then two more fire engines come ("Circling the block") and then six new ones ("They're circling the block") and then a last one ("Maybe joining the others"). People in different text chains keep sending videos from Twitter and Insta. In one, from Minneapolis, National Guard and city police are in full hysterical *Call of Duty* cosplayer mode, indistinguishable from terrorists, going up and down a quiet suburban street, screaming, "Light 'em up!" and shooting paint canisters. (Why paint canisters?) A woman named Tanya Kerssen gets a video of being shot at with one of the paint canisters while standing on her own front porch. The east coast weighs in on the video, the shock of it; Wulf and I are sitting there watching it again and again, wondering if we're closer to bloodshed and even urban war than we thought. Around the Grove, not three blocks away, one or two protesters are throwing bottles at cops, while thousands of others, more by the minute according to the news, are marching with signs. John's crazy neighbor, a striking woman of about 50 with a Havanese, comes home with a milkshake.

"The 7-Eleven got looted," she reports.

"On 3rd?" I ask.

"Yep." That's where I had stopped and picked up beer before coming to Wulf's an hour before. I don't say anything. She takes a sip of her milkshake. "I had takeout waiting in Newport! I told them."

"Told who?"

The woman has curly dark hair. She must have been insanely attractive once. She was in a few movies in the '80s, but never made it, as the saying goes. "Told the police! They were literally trying to stop me going to Newport! I said, I have takeout in Newport."

Not sure what Newport is and afraid to ask, I reply, "Wow."

"So I picked up the takeout in Newport."

Suddenly my vibes are getting dark, and I concentrate on the skyline while Wulf talks to her until thankfully she wanders off. I light a fresh joint. The light goes at last and the sky is ablaze in unfamiliar ways, high stars, low-flung city effluence, and the helicopters with their beams searching the streets, the ad hoc police checkpoints flaring light out too brightly. Two cops pass on horses. "Just circling the block," I say. We both die laughing (I have smoked a whole fucking gram-sized joint already and am unstrung and happy and looped out of my mind) and put on "Eat a Peach" and wait to get lost in *Mountain Jam*. After that it becomes a normal and oddly welcome lawn hang. Neither of us has any desire to leave. I don't want to go home until as late as possible, when I'm sober, when things have died down. Hours pass. For most of them we listen to Sly Stone, who's on Wulf's Mt. Rushmore of musicians, along with the Dead, Doom, and Zeppelin. He's also been to more than thirty Phish shows. The Lord survives the rainbow of his will.

At midnight we put on the Doors song *The End* in order to make jokes, but it turns out it's twelve minutes long and halfway through the joke has vanished, and the moment takes on an evil submerged aqueous feeling. This is the end. When the song is done, we fly into the sweet home of "Abbey Road," whose musical choice takes on a miraculous soul-inevitability when you're high enough. Wulfgang feels that way more about Sly. He might be the world's biggest believer in Sly Stone, that Sly is an indisputable, god tier genius. (By his own description, he spent our whole junior year at Yale running, playing *Mario Kart,* and listening to *There's a Riot Goin' On.*) We hear the Starbucks on Melrose might have been vandalized. The protesters there are lying down to honor George Floyd. Two more LAPD choppers and a news chopper come by. Kobe Bryant died this very year in a helicopter. There are murals all over the city of it. That man kneeled on George Floyd's neck for eight fucking minutes and forty-six seconds. You have to be a person without a conscience to do that, we say to each other. You just must. Otherwise there's no way. But at the back of my heart I know conscience leaks out in odd moments. All the police wear the same uniforms and drive the same cars and believe a lot of the same racist sexist bullshit. They have stickers of the Punisher on their cars together. Once you're part of a team maybe the team is kneeling on that neck with you. Maybe you think you're the Punisher. I don't know. Chauvin's partner is a man named Tou Thao, who's Hmong-American. Numerous complaints have been lodged against him, we're beginning to hear. In 2017, the Minneapolis Police Department settled a lawsuit for $25,000 with a man who claimed Thao handcuffed him for no reason, beat and kicked him, and broke his teeth.

Meanwhile, Chauvin's wife is a Hmong refugee who competed in the Mrs. Minnesota pageant not long ago. She has already filed for divorce. Good for her. I wonder if this is why Chauvin and Thao were partners, though, this connection, or if that was chance. Thao was standing there, watching, as George Floyd died. It's confusing. Is this a story about the police or about race? Both, always both. But there is even a Hmong story lurking within the details of this terrible white and black one. In this sense, the last few days have been truly, neutrally, terribly American. If we're nothing else, we are an experiment. With the choppers in the sky and Donald Trump in the White House and people dying of coronavirus everywhere, unnecessarily, it's hard to know what kind. We talk this over and smoke more weed, noise from the 7-Eleven and the Grove still audible, until after several hours everything just lessens, slightly; one or two choppers depart; the firetrucks come back across town, silent now; we listen to album after album of Zeppelin, as if it were the start of quarantine all over again. Wulf says that the first day after quarantine ends, he's going to listen to *The Rain Song*. Then he pauses (we're both far gone) and starts talking about a car bombing when he was visiting his girlfriend in Beirut in 2008. At 2:00, when things are quiet and both of us are finally jittery but sober enough and tired, we say an emotional goodbye (it's hard not to give each other a bro hug, what can you say) and I put on my mask to walk back to my car, and drive home. I hate myself for not being all the way sober, but I'm not, I realize after a block or so. I drive with unbelievable, no doubt noticeable care, the last thing you want, but the streets are empty, screaming with emptiness. Even Santa Monica and Melrose. Just before I get home, I see a huge orange pyramid in the street ahead of me and flinch, wondering what it is. I slow down as I approach it, only to realize that it's hundreds and hundreds of Nike shoeboxes. Someone must have gotten into their store. Well, fuck Nike. As the famous story here in L.A. goes (who knows if it's true) they wanted to do an ad with Zach Galifianakis and he played nice until they were all on a big corporate call together. Then he said "So are you guys still using sweatshops?" Silence. I don't think anyone wants looting, but I asseverate to myself with stoned conviction that we can't get distracted by it, let the looting become the story and not the protests.

George Floyd's "crime," ha, was using a possibly fake $20. I would bet good money Donald Trump paid less than that in taxes last year, but of course he won't release them, here in year five of his routine audit. Yet the second people walk down the street, asking that black people not be killed by the police constantly, the government can roll out billions of dollars' worth of absolutely state of the art killing machinery and blame the results on "looting."

Everything is trembling at the edges; everything is permeable; everything is fearful; the protests (by late at night, when I'm home, checking Twitter for news) have spread further, there are plans for them in Europe even. I fall into sleep only by accident. In the morning, Wulf says on Slack, "I was hearing phantom helicopters and sirens all night. Chas, makes me think it was scarier than we were thinking." Well, not me. He says he took a walk this morning to assess the fallout. "The few places in this neighborhood that made life normal (the Coffee Bean, the Thai place) are boarded up."

There are new skirmishes between cops and protesters coming out on video continuously. Even Walmart is closing hundreds of stores and boarding up their windows, apparently. It's an unpleasant turn of events. If that huge invincible idiot giant is scared, should all of us be? We should. On the other hand, would anyone I know put a stop to the protests? No. People are thrilled and energized and alive. Too much has been unfair for too long to too many. The protests are like waking up from a nightmarish collective enchantment. Breonna Taylor, Trayvon Martin, Ahmaud Arbery, George Floyd. It has to stop. It has to. No options are left but for all of us to stand shoulder to shoulder and say that it cannot go on. Even if everyone's in a new danger and Trump is Franco and we have to fight for the next 50 years, fine, thank fucking god. The old safe danger was intolerable. And in the marches and on social media and in conversations, there's a sharp new consciousness, all of us commandeered by it at once, that nearly everyone in this country's first task is to look at themselves.

JUNE

June 1

More than two hundred cities have imposed curfews and states are rapidly activating the National Guard. (I had no idea they could do that. What happens if Delaware and Texas decide to fight each other? I'm not a military lawyer!) Wulf, who's been at the marches the last three days, says a lot of the white protesters go right up to the police line and snap pics. He hasn't seen anyone black do it yet. But it seems like a net positive that white people across the country care so much—that it's stirred up the brunch crowd, as he says. Moods are dangerously on edge among protesters and police; a nation of Fergusons. If there'd been one shot fired at the protest, Wulf said, he knew the people around him, people exactly like him or anyone, were ready to explode. Boards have gone up on store windows overnight, faster than Christmas decorations after Halloween. Only the 7-Eleven on the stretch of Vermont near me is open.

Between Trump, covid, and the murder of George Floyd, forces are alive in this country that were asleep before. We have no real idea yet what they are. The protests have seen none of the rioting the right predicted from the start, particularly Fox News. There have been minor incidents of looting, proportionally nonexistent. Anyway the suspicion that every protester is a possible looter is an effect of exactly the systematic racism being protested.

The large rallies in L.A. are in West Hollywood, while on my side of town, in Los Feliz and Silver Lake, there are a vast assortment of small protests. A few dozen people are generally gathered on the median as you go into Griffith Park, wearing masks and holding up signs that say **Black Lives Matter** and **Justice for Breonna Taylor.** A mom and three kids with masks and a homemade **Remember George Floyd** banner stand for hours in front of a five million dollar house in the Hills, chatting at social distance with passersby, a pretty table of lemonade and water standing near the curb to refresh the protesters. *BLM* is written in dust on cars, on loose-leaf paper taped to random windows, in spray paint on the street. At 5:00 every night, people gather at Normandie and Franklin and march up Hillhurst, to Ralphs, the grocery store, though if you'd transported me from six months ago and given me a glimpse of them, I'd have said they were the crowd at a St. Vincent concert.

The stubborn idea that rioting and looting are inevitable when people protest is why it's crushing (and why the internet rushes to the barricades) when the *Times* runs an enormous A1 headline that says *As Chaos Spreads, Trump Vows to 'End It Now.'* So much so wrong there; the conflation of protests and out of control cops as "chaos," the bizarre credibility they're willing to give Trump with the word "vows," as if he were a person whose vows have ever meant a thing (more than 20,000 lies so far, according to the *Washington Post* tracker, not to mention the three wives to whom he made—well, vows), and finally the trusting regurgitation of the phrase "end it now," as if he had any such capacity. The paper's white-collar Ivy League faith in the systems of power is so deeply rooted that they're going to normalize us into getting murdered in our beds. As Graham Greene said in *The Quiet American,* innocence is a kind of insanity.

Armed and black-visored and body-armored ranks standing on the steps of the Lincoln Memorial. A chill breeze runs up the back of Twitter, the jokes about it halfhearted; because it's scary. It's strange to experience fear and hope running so strongly through our bloodstream simultaneously, the protests and this aged empire readying itself to strike back at them.

A few hours after the outcry, the *Times* changes the headline to **Trump Threatens to Send Troops Into States.** This feeds into the conviction on the right that relatively neutral news sources (CNN, the networks, the major newspapers) are "fake news." There's a frenzy on MAGA Twitter that Alexandria Ocasio-Cortez made it happen, which shows what a gifted politician she is.

June 2

Trump, who was rushed to a bunker the instant large-scale protests arose, disputes the idea that he went there for his safety. He gives the real scoop only to "Brian Kilmeade," the Furby-like personage who co-hosts *Fox & Friends.* According to his interview with Kilmeade, the Secret Service told Trump it would be a good time to go and "inspect the bunker." All-time coincidence if true.

"I have only two corona patients today," Nathan reports. "Huge change from a few weeks ago." He says he's happy to go in to work for the first time since February—not that he was precisely unhappy before, but I think he saw the disaster unfurling at closer hand than any of us can really imagine, and it was probably not an experience that had anything to do with either happiness or unhappiness.

He's not optimistic that this moment of relative reprieve as far as covid goes—the outdoor meetups, the open bookstores—will last. The fall is the time the doctors dread. Trump "hasn't spoken with Fauci in weeks," it's reported, and fired his testing czar. There are worries about whether the protests will be superspreader events. We have to hope that the people moved to protest are also the ones who believe in masks, which seems relatively likely to me. Lying beyond that is the more serious concern: that so many red states being "open" now will have dire consequences come October and November.

'Let Them Have Eric!' Screams Trump While Pushing Son Through Door of Bunker. One of those *Onion* headlines that is probably closer than any AP report to capturing what's inside the President's heart. The flight to the bunker is so telling; he knows that people despise him and he panicked. Like nearly all dictators, aspiring dictators, dictator-manqués, bad fathers, etc., he is a coward.

Only one piece of nonpolitical news today earns my coveted "click": *Key West High School Holds 'Jet Ski Graduation.'* Extreme and badass. I'm jealous.

June 3

I have a thought: Why am I angry at myself for smoking weed, if it's the first thing in my *life* that has allowed me not to feel anxious? Also to be "present," a word I loathe but can't think of an adequate synonym for? Isn't that an upshot pretty devoutly to be wished?

There's a counterargument, I suddenly have a lot of deadlines looming, but I can't imagine working for ten minutes, much less hours on end. Is that the pandemic or the drug? I feel sure part of it is this moment, when I want to be glued to the internet and the news. Work and ambition and professional envy have never been more alien to me than they are now, into the third month of covid. Only the gentle experience of being smoothed inside myself, listening to music or playing double solitaire with Em, seems urgent. And much of that feeling carries into my sober moments.

The idea of having "sober moments" is itself not wonderful. I read that weed triggers the epiphany part of the brain, and I'm preoccupied by the thought, that by becoming reliant on a drug, I am falling into an abyss that in all but a few subtle details resembles me, my life, myself. A strong piece of evidence in favor of this theory is that I have been listening to the Bob Marley collection *Legend* a lot.

I read on the internet that some people find so much relief from smoking weed mainly because it forces them to take deep breaths. Lord, how fervently I believe that.

It's hard to explain to friends from overseas (though they have a sense) how totally the protests have taken over America. Companies that had zero interest in Colin Kaepernick's protest over this exact same issue a few years ago are rushing to be on the right side of history. "To be silent is to be complicit" tweets Netflix, racing to the lifeboats. "Black lives matter. We have a platform and we have a duty to our Black members, employees, creators and talent to speak up." Sure, Netflix. But then, in twenty years no one will have ever been against Colin Kaepernick. It's the lone bitter part of Martin Luther King Jr.'s deification: a second dehumanization, to erase the first one by all the people who despised him.

There's an unmistakable crackle in the way people are texting and thinking and feeling right now, that's what's hard to explain. Anything feels possible. I thought I had lived through history until I lived through history. It's addictive. The pictures of the protests are addictive to look at. Tens of thousands of people in London, Paris, Berlin, Cleveland. On the side of a lonely country road in patchy-snowed Montana, seven women in single file, holding up **Black Lives Matter** and **Say His Name** placards.

George Floyd's face has become part of the iconography of the movement. He had a face that looked ready to be happy, like he was about to smile—at least, in the picture going around of him. There's a dense but precisely distanced crowd, silent and vast, on the Mag Mile in Chicago, the city where so much of black culture survived, where generations of black writers, musicians, and journalists just about kept the furnace going, waiting out the bitter cold of history—that is a valiant city, as I saw up close at moments when I lived there. Right now I miss it.

Of course there's an entirely different perspective from which a lot of people see the last week. *Send in the Troops* runs the headline to an op-ed by Tom Cotton in the *Times*. The editorial—an actual disgrace for the paper to have published, on which at least there seems to be instantaneous agreement, but christ—calls for using the American military against American protesters. It might be the most appalling thing the paper has published since Judith Miller's reporting helped bolster the fraudulent case to go to war with Iraq. Tom Cotton has the right to think this, as immensely depressing as it is that a sitting United States senator would, but why on earth would the *Times* publish it? David Brooks, responding to the criticism of the decision to publish Cotton's op-ed, says, "I believe in democracy. I believe in a free press. I believe in open debate. I love it when my newspaper prints pieces I disagree with. It causes me to think."

You can see his little brain chugging along. I want to say to him, David, friend: Not every idea you disagree with is intellectually galvanizing. White supremacy is not an interesting idea that can "cause" you "to think." There are beliefs that the marketplace of ideas has correctly dismissed, and the U.S. military attacking Americans is one of them, or used to be one of them. But even if you could sit down with him, David Brooks hasn't actually heard another human speak in decades.

I think it bothers me so much because he's a writer; he's like me. And in that sense he is where I can feel most sensitively, with the skill I've built up through years of practice at my craft—how lax his thinking is, and above all how poisoned his conceptions are by his privilege. He's the obverse of Maya Angelou's great observation: "Black Americans have had to study white Americans. For centuries under slavery, the smile or the grimace on a white man's face or the flow of a hand on a white woman could inform a black person that you're about to be sold or flogged. So we have studied the white American, where the white American has not been obliged to study us." The *Times* editorial page is made up of men (Bennet, Brooks, Friedman, Stephens, Douthat) who have never been obliged to study anyone but themselves, yet believe they are the most expansive-minded of us all.

One of the uglier moments of this week came two days ago, when police in Washington, D.C. used tear gas, riot control methods, and force to clear peaceful demonstrators from Lafayette Square, so that Trump could go do a photo-op with a Bible clutched in his little hands in front of a church near the White House. The outrage continues to grow. The *Times* called it "a burst of violence unlike any seen in the shadow of the White House in generations."

Press secretary Kayleigh McEnany registers her disagreement today, however, comparing Trump's visit to St. John's with Churchill visiting the war bunkers in London and George W. Bush throwing out the first pitch during the World Series after 9/11. Neither of them pepper sprayed peaceful protesters to do theirs, though, so you almost have to give Trump the edge. I'll admit one moment of the whole thing made me laugh out loud, which was when a reporter asked Trump if it was his Bible. He contemplated it briefly. "It's *a* Bible," he replied.

I present my new liberal ideas about smoking pot and not working to Matteo. Frankly he's kind of a wet blanket about it. But he has an amazing new projector in his backyard. We watch the entirety of *Gimme Shelter,* then discuss it as if we were in a college seminar. We listen to *Tumbling Dice.* It's still such a weird joy to see people. Wulf's there. He met a dog influencer on Hinge. "She lives in Orange County, unfortunately," he said. It's his fourth or fifth fling. He doesn't seem to be placing a particular emphasis on distancing, Matteo and I observe. "It seems like pandemic has been fine for you," I tell him. He agrees, great pandemic. We get into a heated two-on-one argument about whether it's acceptable for him to tell people he still holds the women's world record in the mile even though he's not a woman. His best mile time (a 4:13, which is genuinely impressive, unfortunately) was nearly broken by a woman recently, which is how it comes up. As we tell him, it still doesn't make him a women's Olympic gold medalist. "Just a yardstick," he says, holding his hands up. "Just a yardstick."

June 4

Now it's come out that James Bennet, the editor of the *Times* opinion section, admitted in a staff meeting that he hadn't READ Tom Cotton's "essay" before it was published. If it were my job to operate the most influential political opinion section in the country, I might choose to read the articles in it, and maybe especially the ones advising the United States to bomb its own people. I learned on the second day working at my high school newspaper that a sacred rule was never to publish something you hadn't read every single word of. But maybe James Bennet (whose brother is a mere U.S. Senator, poor soul) did not have the benefit of working at a high school newspaper.

June 5

It doesn't fucking stop! From the *Times* town hall: the editorial page pitched the op-ed *to* Tom Cotton. So Tom Cotton was just staring into space wishing he could legally hunt poor people and someone called him to suggest he write this article.

I'm under few illusions about the *Times*. Thomas Friedman has had his column there since 1995, and for precisely seventeen years since he gave Charlie Rose his infamous opinion regarding Iraq: "What they needed to see"—they being the people of Iraq—"was American boys and girls going house to house, from Basra to Baghdad, and basically saying, Which part of this sentence don't you understand? You don't think, you know, we care about our open society, you think this bubble fantasy, we're just gonna let it grow? Well, suck. On. This."

So the *Times* has been giving us the "Suck on this" guy for the past seventeen years. (The part that bothers me most isn't "suck on this," even, it's "American boys and girls." There's that horrible slippage again: bland middle-aged white men, in charge of the universe, fully aware they are sending "boy and girls" to both mete out and risk death.) He's considered one of the paper's more liberal columnists.

The *Times* used to be wreathed in gold to me. In ways it still is, I suppose. When I was 21 and freshly in Manhattan from college, a cool autumn flush with sunlight, I used to pay $2.25 every morning at the deli and get a cup of coffee and a copy of the paper back. Sometimes we would talk about the Detroit Lions, the clerk's favorite football team. I would pet the cat. And I would go back to my walk-up and read the paper in the sunny New York morning light, before beginning a long happy day of writing incredibly incompetent fiction. I can almost be there again if I try. I hope the paper is always there. I hope the clerk made it back to Lahore, which he was saving up for. I hope we get a vaccine. I hope the Lions win the Super Bowl. I hope police have to stop killing black people. I hope Biden wins. It's too much hoping. I see why the protests are expanding. At some point hope gives out and only your legs work. In helicopter shots on the news you can see the vast undulating crowds flowing around buildings and through alleys as they march, with the bright collective sentience of a school of fish.

A week ago I would have said it was impossible for something other than the virus to be the main story of 2020, even the election. Yet in fifty years it may be these protests that eclipse covid or Trump, or it seems that way at this instant; it's everywhere, everything; for the last eight days no other story could conceivably have led the news. Already it seems like an analogue to 1964, 1952, 1865. That the progress made in those years for black Americans was clawed back by racists is part of the reason for the fury of *this* year, these protests. It's as if millions of people were informed at once that you can still shoot a black person in America without consequence.

The organization of the protests (facilitated by social media, part of its wildly unpredictable effect on society) is impeccable. The signs are exhortatory. **Keep your foot on the gas. #BLM**. There's one that says **No Angel** with an arrow pointing down at the black woman holding it. Rideouts in Baltimore and St. Louis. There's **Who do we call when the police are murdering people?** and **That's not a chip on my shoulder, it's your knee on my neck** and **How many weren't filmed?**

And **You Can't Kill Us All.**

Statues and monuments have been stormed and removed. Over publicly erected brass nameplates aged into verdigris, people affix signs that say **This place is dedicated to the slaves who were taken from their homes.** The scenes at courthouses and statehouses are reminiscent of the activist Bree Newsome climbing the flagpole outside the state capitol of South Carolina and removing the confederate flag in 2015. (The image of her clutching the flag was partly so inspiring because she had a helmet; she had a *plan*.) In the present moment it seems unimaginable that the confederate flag flew over the capitol in South Carolina so recently. How did we tolerate it for that long? What were well-meaning white people but part of—perhaps the essence of—the problem?

As noticeable as the clever signs are the ones with slogans of the movement. **No Justice No Peace. Silence Is Violence. End White Supremacy.** Plus, over and over, **Say Their Names,** usually with the pictures and names of George Floyd, Breonna Taylor, and some liturgy of the others: Michael Brown, Trayvon Martin, Laquan McDonald, Akai Gurley, Terence Crutcher. There are dozens from the last decade. **Remember the Central Park 5,** some signs say, referring to the five teenagers wrongly convicted of murder and sent to prison, then later exculpated. In the 1980s, Donald Trump took out a full-page ad in the paper (maybe the single most proactive thing that lazy piece of shit has ever done) calling outright for those boys to be executed. He still hasn't admitted he was wrong, much less apologized.

My whole heart is with the crowds, though I don't go, so I guess not my whole heart. My doctor thinks it's "better to avoid getting covid." I linger near the protests I see while I'm on my walk each evening, standing a block away from whichever I stumble upon, double-masked (the new best practice, according to Nathan) and longing to walk over and join in. "The concept of congregation is an impatient anticipation of eternity," Kierkegaard said. The people in even the small protests seem *like one,* as I heard a news anchor say, and in their unity hint at a truth I think many of us hope for, perhaps even believe, without any proof whatsoever, which is that one day all things, including our selves, will be one again.

———

Military surveillance aircraft deployed against the protests. Cotton's wishes may still come to fruition, which is why the debate about the *Times* is more than academic. "The cops are about to shoot a hundred people somewhere," a more conservative friend texts a group of us from high school. The last time he texted anything was in March, when near the end of those terrible anxious first weeks he sent me a meme of a cow inexplicably standing in the ocean up to its ankles and the caption "Man has retreated. Nature is healing." March is a long time ago.

I worry something bad is coming too. Because I'm on the west coast, I wake up every morning later than the day and sit upright instantly to check my phone and make sure rioting hasn't started in Topeka, or whatever Bull Connor pretext they need to shoot. There have been plenty of rubber bullets flying and batons in stomachs just here in Los Angeles, broken teeth, mass arrests, but no break into total violence yet.

Of the hundreds I've seen by now, the sign that returns to me on my early hours walk is one that a black kid in Silver Lake was holding, standing with his parents. It said, **Am I next?**

"Gushers wouldn't be Gushers without the Black community and your voices," tweets Gushers. "We're working with @FruitByThe Foot on creating space to amplify that. We see you. We stand with you."

June 6

James Bennet—responsible for the Cotton editorial—let go by the *Times*. I take no pleasure in his losing his job, but you have to read the articles. Maybe he can take this time away from his career to find another "t" for his last name.

As the days pass, the protests only grow. The backlash is predictably crazed. "Now that we clearly see Antifa as terrorists, can we hunt them down like we do those in the Middle East?" tweets the ultra-creepy frying pan faced Florida congressman Matt Gaetz.

I occasionally worry that people reading about Trump in the future will think "Antifa" existed. In fact, talking about "Antifa" is an unambiguous sign of how stupid you are. There's no such organization, nor even anyone pretending to lead one like it. It just doesn't exist. Whereas on the right there are the Proud Boys and a million militant variants, local cops blooded into hate-filled fraternities with names and patches and everything. Even Matt Gaetz must know this. So what does he want? In plainer language than he would use, what he wants is permission for our government to hunt down Americans who protest Donald Trump and kill them. That's what Tom Cotton is requesting as well. The strategy for November 3rd—in the event they don't like the outcome of the election—seems to me to be emerging all too clearly. But I'm a pessimist on these things.

The protests have spread abroad, which is encouraging. A worldwide movement is harder to bomb. More than a hundred people in Almaty, Kazakhstan, protest with a banner that says **I Can't Breathe.** Nearly all of them are arrested. In Yerevan, Armenia, a few dozen people stand outside the U.S. embassy, holding up signs that say the names of George Floyd and others. Protesters in Cork, Dublin, Dingle, Kilkenny. A thousand strong in Vilnius, Lithuania. Tens of thousands of people in Paris and London. Thousands in Amsterdam. In the streets of Hamilton, Bermuda, a small crowd kneeling to show solidarity. In Fiji, eighteen people in the capital city of Suva stand silently for eight minutes and forty-six seconds. In Rio, police use tear gas to disperse thousands of protesters— also marching to remember the death of a fourteen-year-old boy named João Pedro Pinto, shot in the back during a police raid. In Ternopil, Ukraine, where any protest can be a death sentence, a tiny handful of students hold one anyway. And in a picture from China, a dozen people stand in an unrelenting downpour to mourn and protest the death in distant Minnesota of George Floyd.

June 9

Don Jr.'s trip to Mongolia to shoot "the world's largest sheep" has cost taxpayers at least $75,000, according to reporting.

As a sum of money, it could change the lives of dozens of people, but whatever, there's more flagrant corruption on every hole of golf his father plays. (Trump makes the Secret Service stay at his own club at, breathtakingly, rack rate.) Yet this seems somehow worse. The undeservingness of the recipient; the fact that none of us can travel anywhere, and Don Jr. got to go to *Mongolia,* which I would be willing to bet a lot of money he couldn't find on a map, only to shoot one of the most harmless creatures ever devised, a sheep—not just harmless, in fact, but literally the creature we have decided on to represent innocence. Everyone has had their breaking points in the past four years, and this is one of mine. I can't let it go. I go looking for the picture I hate most, Jr.'s pudgy little smirk as he holds up a water buffalo's tail next to his simple-looking brother, both of them crouching unathletically by the momentous gray mud-patched carcass of the animal, fifty years of dignity laid waste, a whole inner world we can only start to imagine the first half of a half of a percent of. Just so that this offensive and stupid photo of two grinning fools could exist. What do they imagine themselves to know about their place in life compared to that sheep's, even. It infuriates me. I feel something I don't like and after a moment realize it's hate.

June 14

We're at a rest point in the pandemic. Covid transmission rates are higher in some places but dramatically lower in many others. In New York, Rachel is sending her daughter to camp. It's all outdoors, and there are temperature checks for staff and children, and most activities, particularly meals, are distanced, but both she and all the kids doing similar things on social media look so happy in pictures.

It's on time: There are waves and waves of stories about the impossibility of parenting during covid. A friend of ours in Greenwich is near a breakdown. It's not a term to use unadvisedly, she really is—the combination of trying to manage her two kids' different e-learning (she never liked computers) and of trying to work from home, with little help from her husband, has sent her mind off-kilter. Money didn't save her. The threshold of madness must no doubt be much nearer for people in want, but people who reach it are alike—that's just a binary, crazy or not crazy. To have faced real madness and loss of control is like being sick, something separate from the world, only inside you. None of us can judge it. I think of Gerard Manley Hopkins's unforgettable description of experiencing it himself: "O the mind, mind has mountains; cliffs of fall / Frightful, sheer, no-man-fathomed. Hold them cheap / May who ne'er hung there."

Nathan has been briefing business leaders and politicians on the virus and was at a TV studio with one of them this morning. After he was finished and was putting away his papers, a producer he hadn't spoken to before came over and said to him quietly, "Do you want to meet Anthony Scaramucci? He's right over there."

Nathan: "What?"

Producer: "The Mooch."

Nathan: "Oh. No."

With the shelves mostly full again, Ben makes the devastating confession to Rachel that he (in her terse first-hand reporting) "doesn't even like beans that much."

A day worth noting as I do the dishes for the one thousandth time this pandemic (figure estimated). Three times a day the kitchen looks exactly like you would want for exactly ten minutes each time. If I were given the Ovidian gift of being able to remember this pandemic in proportion to how it occurred in real time, I would have such detailed memories of the dishes, I would become Proust about every coffee cup. Instead I remember stuff like my passwords (sort of).

At his commencement speech at West Point, Trump moves with extreme caution down a ramp, a gentle forty yard incline up to and down from the stage. Between the ramp and his inability to drink a glass of water with a single hand, there's frenzied speculation that he has had a stroke or is concealing some other serious medical problem. There was his emergency visit to Walter Reed last year for an appointment, which he tried to pass off as routine. (Not unlike the bunker.)

"Would be so great if that fat potato fell," a friend observes impassively over text.

Meanwhile there's a true scandal taking place in the country. It turns out the actual postmaster general is a man named Louis DeJoy, whose head looks like reconstituted pig parts were molded into a crude ovoid respiration tank, then installed with the eyes from the dumbest dog species and high-tech, blindingly white porcelain teeth. The scandal is that he's trying to destroy the post office. DeJoy (all-time misleading name) is the first person in his job since the early 90s to have no experience in the postal system. His first priority has been to grind the mail to a halt. There are plans to remove mail sorters, to remove mailboxes, he's banned overtime—and all of it is motivated, as transparently as glass, by the priorities of his former gig, which was to help Republicans "win" elections. It's so dispiriting. A completely unprecedented moment in the history of our country and all these morons can think up to do is dismantle the fucking post office.

June 15

I've got a great deal of work all of a sudden, two fairly complicated articles to write and a book to finish. I've also been reading fiction again for the first time since March, because I'm judging a literary prize and get a dozen or so new novels and short story collections each week. Just with the uptick of obligatory reading, though, I've also found myself reading from a batch of Haruki Murakami novels I haven't looked at in twenty years, first *Norwegian Wood,* then *The Wind-Up Bird Chronicle.* I know Murakami's a kindred spirit because his characters are always making spaghetti, but I'd maybe forgotten how much I liked the early books as the later, less spontaneous ones came along. In a chat with my friend Laura, who lives nearby, it comes up that she's reading *The Wind-Up Bird Chronicle* too. I wonder if more people than usual are. They're worlds you can go into, Murakami's books, worlds not vastly but fractionally different than ours—but different, both because they come from inside an old and complex culture most Americans only know superficially, and because of course they are literally uncanny, the impossible happens there, conduits in time, two moons in the sky. Am I reading them because the impossible started happening here, in real life? The Beatles, too: pasta and the Beatles, two niche interests that Haruki Murakami and I miraculously share, just the two of us.

After two weeks of protests, just as with the pandemic, there is a moment to stop and survey what has happened. One is that part of its force has come from the pandemic. In late March, we all realized simultaneously that everyone in this country needs a minimum of paid leave, benefits, and childcare, and almost no one in the country has them. We don't even have a guarantee of *health care.* The richest country in the history of the world. It's not that the virus is bad—it's that a hundred enormous things are bad, there are a hundred protections people in a country this rich should have, and we let them slip through our fingers. As a culture we had become too numbed to gig economy lives and not having health insurance and continual war. The government is a joke, rigged for the rich, unable even to minimize a virus other countries have subdued. The presidency is an absurdity—all those great men whom our predecessors so trusted (a wrenching part of the Ken Burns Vietnam documentary is the soldiers and their family members who describe how literally impossible it was when they dutifully enlist to imagine a President might be lying) and it turned out someone like this could be President, too. Could go in the Disney Hall of Presidents. Banks, with their friendly branches; rich people, acting as if their manners make them better than everyone else when they are morally at the immediate disadvantage to anyone poor, with a lot of ground to make up; landlords; hedge funds; Apple; fiat currency; the Buffalo Bills; Monsanto. It's all just fucking made up.

One hope is that this disillusionment is what has emboldened the people in the streets. Because if Donald Trump could be President—well, suddenly it seems clear that there's no reason to respect any of this shit. "Citibank" is no more important an entity than a cartoon dog. Fuck Citibank. It's not Citibank suffering during this. "Citibank" is doing fine. And there's a feeling abroad in the land that we should burn it to the ground, every last scrap of paper and debt and interest. Cancel student debt. Cancel mortgage debt. Free childcare from birth. Fuck these companies. It wasn't Citibank that did anything when the pandemic started, except probably ask for handouts. We all saw with our own fucking eyes who actually makes this society work, and it wasn't the partners at "Citibank," it was the people who check out groceries and deliver packages and work in health care. They were the first to sacrifice their safety and they'll be the last after there's a vaccine. Citibank stayed home. Give Citibank the fucking coronavirus and $1200 to live off for three months. Let Citibank move into a tent on the street because the one-bedroom apartment seven of you were liv-ing in has three more immediate family members coming to live there because they can't afford *their* one-bedroom and someone has to make way. Make Citibank watch its grandfather die on an iPad. We'll write the laws and wear nice suits and give to the opera and feel pleased as punch about what good and important people we are, success stories. Why don't we switch that around for a little while, Citibank. You fucking parasites. You should live the rest of your lives in shame that you worked on behalf of such oppression, all for the sake of having nicer things than other people. Repent.

Black Lives Matter has foregrounded economic class again. So much of it is the same fight; above anything else, black peo-ple urgently need money, specifically long overdue reparations, to increase the chances society will stop killing them randomly. Because George Floyd was murdered for buying cigarettes with a $20 bill that "might" have been fake, and the disgrace of that is so deep that it has shaken even our blithe society.

A new line the graffiti artists have been stamping, painting, and stickering all over Silver Lake: *Another world is possible.* Too true. There should be a wealth tax of 90% on anyone with a billion dol-lars (we can means test below that, Republicans love means test-ing, right?) and the minimum wage should be $40 and children of color shouldn't have to strategize about how to try to not get bullied and killed and Donald Trump should be shot into space.

Libraries are a good institution. I loved the library when I was little and I love the library now.

As so many people watch this, it makes me wonder if they're also imagining whether their lives could be different, or if they're too busy working. Probably that one, the merciless grind of life in our society without money. "Dimly he perceived the thing that had happened to him," H. G. Wells writes in *Kipps,* his superb and bizarre novel, "how the great, stupid machine of retail trade had caught his life into its wheels, a vast, irresistible force which he had neither strength of will nor knowledge to escape. This was to be his life until his days should end. No adventures, no glory, no change, no freedom."

I'm lucky enough to be half-disentangled from the machine, yet a part of my mind tugs at me still to quit it all. I've worked harder than I can describe (or than most of my ideas have deserved) to write well. Hard work was what I thought made you successful. But I don't know. Is success in a corrupt society admirable? And even if it is, who said what was success? When did I agree to that? But I did, and here I am, half my life gone . . . when that feeling of hopelessness gets strong, I go into the yard, sometimes at eight at night, sometimes at three in the afternoon if I want, I've stopped caring, and sit back under the same dumb clean beautiful unanswering blue sky as always, watching in stoned peace as the soft clouds float across it, carrying secrets from the bottom of eternity which neither of us will ever understand. Music sounds so pure. For once in this feverish month, the world's grip on me loosens; and I worry about nothing. Today I listen to "Meddle" three times in a row, motionless, thinking and being high. Then I put on *Donuts* and give in to a feeling of not caring and roll a second joint. It's time to let the loose end drag.

June 17

"They've come up with the AIDS vaccine!" Trump announces. No one has any idea where the notion came from, and no one in his camp has subsequently repeated it, not even him. But he said it. In news from actual science, Nathan tells us that it's been confirmed in studies that the virus can only replicate inside a human being for ten days. Therefore, theoretically, if we all put on N95 masks for ten days, we could eliminate the virus. Eliminate it! I get that this is hard to explain to a public already mistrustful of politicians and the media, not to mention masks. But it seems like it's worth someone trying. Ten days! Is Jimmy Carter free to pitch this to America? Dua Lipa? Ken Bone?

Meanwhile, Florida is officially in crisis, the new epicenter of the virus in America. They reported 2,783 new cases yesterday, the most in a single day since the beginning of the pandemic. By now we all know what that means: a massive number of deaths to come in a week or ten days, an inevitable crop. We were overconfident during the declining numbers of May, even those of us whose confidence only increased a small amount. It was late in May that I stopped seeing people's eyes look quite so feral. I started pulling my mask down when I was alone on a street. We thought maybe we'd solved it. Incorrect. So of course, always timing his most outrageous lies to his worst sins, Trump declares that covid is "dying out" and "fading away." It's a desolate feeling to watch him affix the blindfold over people's eyes as they follow him, eagerly, toward the firing squad.

June 19

Kayleigh McEnany: "This President's routinely commemorated Juneteenth."

Reporter: "He said he learned about it this week."

June 20

Brazil has passed 1 million coronavirus cases and is approaching 50,000 deaths, "a new nadir for the world's second worst-hit country." This seems like a sad if unremarkable fact, until you consider that Brazil is run by a man, the far-right revanchist Jair Bolsonaro, who has *twice* been seriously injured while trying to take selfies with ostriches in the last year, according to a friend. That's who we're behind.

Some countries are doing well. Vietnam is a model, as is Germany. South Korea still stands in contrast to us: first case and first death on the same day as the United States, and as of now 280 people in total dead there, 114,674 here.

At a federal prison near L.A. called Lompoc (the kind of place that's name-dropped in reassuring cop shows to add what Henry James called solidity of specification, the sense that the fictional world you are in is larger and more detailed than simply the scenes in front of you, the implication here being: you are safe in the hands of the police) 70% of the inmates test positive for covid. This is murder without any varnish on it. No alibi furnished up. A new nakedness. As for the percentage of the inmates who are black or poor in prisons—well, we all know the inventory. If you're a black man in America who didn't graduate from high school, you have a 60% chance of going to jail in your lifetime.

But everyone measures their own morality where their need

to see each other ends. Indeed, last night I went to sit outside on a terrace in the hills with a few friends.

I didn't know what the hills was until I moved here, incidentally; what it means is that if you have an unobstructed view to the west at night, you see something genuinely extraordinary, a great smooth landmass of black velvet, miles and miles out in front of you, moving seaward, and above it a limitless sky, filled with stars; the little houses to your left and right small incidents in an ancientness—like you.

One of the people there, sitting around a glass table haphazardly peopled with wine bottles, works as a trend forecaster. She says that there's going to be a return of classical silhouettes in 2021. She adds that some people may be wearing togas—"subtle togas." I listen to these predictions, fascinated, even though as long as I've known her she's never gotten one right. Or maybe they occur in such remote fashion microclimates that they don't even filter to a cerulean person like me. Another friend who's with us and teaches high school says the kids are being heroic about learning online. The bitterness in her voice on behalf of her own class when she talks about restaurants and bars opening again before schools would be enough to sway even a congressman's heart, I think, if one of them would listen.

The artist Christo has died. He and his wife, Jeanne-Claude, spent decades making massive public installations in which they draped bright cloth across fjords, around islands, over skyscrapers. The only one I experienced personally I loved, the Gates, an installation of hundreds of sunflower orange cloths hanging from large freestanding orange steel arches at even intervals across the whole of Central Park. I was living in New York for the first time as an adult when they went up, after years of planning. Some people in the city were skeptical at the time, many out of snobbishness. But one step into the park was enough to know the Gates was a perfect piece of public art. It was a cold winter, and I walked east across town, from my apartment above the Tailor Genius, at the beginning of a heavy two-day snow. As I walked into the park, I saw the Gates right away. Children were jumping up to touch their fluttering orange, couples stopping under them and staring upward, and it was one of those moments when the whole magic promise of New York is renewed all at once out of nowhere, just for you. I stood there, cold with my lonely twentysomething thoughts, and watched the snowy scene, like a Breughel, or a Frog and Toad, still at that age when you really believe in the snow, or I did at least, it was still for me—falling evenly from the gray sky across the panorama of the shifting orange canvases, in serried motion along the long arcing pathways of the park, hundreds of people walking across snowy fields, up boulders and down paths, each within their own lives. It seemed immensely meaningful. I sat down and wrote something in my journal. I got a coffee from a cart, then took a long walk across the park to the west side and then up a wooded path to 110th Street. Finally when it was nearly dark I cut diagonally back toward home. When I left the park at last it was night. I turned and looked at the Gates one last time. It had stopped snowing, so I watched the movement of the empty winter trees and the orange cloths. They seemed like a correctly simple and humble decoration of this scrap of nature which even in its cut-down shape so outsizes our imaginations. At a cart near the park entrance on 69th and 5th I bought another coffee and a hot pretzel and walked back east, forgetting myself and my serious silly ambitions. I had big plans that night downtown starting with a pregame (it seems so long ago suddenly, out here in California) at Rachel's on Jane Street, though I forget what the rest was now. Sweet and Vicious, maybe? I feel a pang. 15 years.

What Pandemic? asks a headline. **Carnival Cruise bookings soar 600 percent for August trips.**

June 23

After more than a hundred days almost completely inside, people in New York can dine outdoors again, get takeout, shop, get haircuts, and so on. We ask Ben and Rachel how it's going. She's refreshing Seamless to see if her favorite Indian restaurant is open again yet. No luck so far.

I've settled into a routine despite my lack of will to work: three crabbed hours in the morning, a long walk if it's not too hot, reading and admin after lunch, and then the pure, total relief of smoking. Not sustainable. I've done it before 3:00 the last few days. Time for a break, a week off starting today I've decided.

It was almost possible to forget in the thrill of the first few weeks of this month, but the pandemic is surfacing into sight. Partly that's for the hopeful reason that Dr. Fauci has said a vaccine could be ready by the end of this year: "I believe it will be when and not if." Everyone longs for this to be true. A few doctors on Twitter throw cold water on the idea. Nathan says he hopes Fauci's right, but that some doctors think we might get a "garbage vaccine" around Christmas and then a better one in later 2021. We tell him that sucks. He concurs.

In most places the numbers are better, and in some they're great.

In New York, there were just five deaths today, the fewest since March 15. But in Florida, the numbers are spiraling upward, and leakers claim that the state is manipulating the data to make it look like Florida has fewer covid deaths than it does.

The governor of Florida is a "mini-Trump" named Ron DeSantis who went briefly viral for wearing a mask on upside down at a press briefing on covid. He's a weird, stubby little fellow, a college athlete but in his current incarnation as hippy as Marilyn Monroe, frowning, with sausage fingers and the kind of lobster brown Florida tan that goes forty layers deep.

He's been downplaying the virus since the start of the pandemic and people there are going to die. That's true of many of these governors—none with states as big as Florida—but as it happens I went to college with this one, Ron DeSantis. He was the year ahead of me. I only met him a few times. Sometimes, today for instance, I contemplate the compromises he's making with public health for his own calculated political reasons, and it's too dark to think about once you start really getting into thinking about who's about to *die forever* in Florida, which is a lot of communities without white faces for a start, and a lot of others filled with 91-year-old lifelong smoker die hard #MAGA believers, and reading about more of his stupid bullshit today, it's stressful enough that on the stroke of 5:00, scrolling through stories about "D," as everyone at Yale called him, and then about Trump, I realize, a complete and total reversal, that I can't stop smoking for three days. Oh well. Make me good, but not yet, as Saint Augustine said. And they made him a saint!

In the oceanic peace that comes after the shameful, excellent decision to smoke, I listen to a long playlist of songs from the 90s that my friend Rebecca made because she's writing a book set in 1994. The music fills me with nostalgia; I've avoided listening to these songs for years, because I assumed I was unhappy when I was listening to them first. I was, but it's amazing to hear their familiar shapes again. "Anywhere you go / I'll follow you down," sing the Gin Blossoms. "I'll follow you down / but not that far." If I were the subject of this song, I would answer, "But you just said anywhere."

June 26

Per Fauci, the only reliable witness we have from inside the government, soon the U.S. "could see 100,000 new coronavirus cases a day." Testifying in the Senate, he said of the new surges, "It could get very bad."

Strangely enough, however, Nathan is giddy: They can now say with certainty that a drug called dexamethasone works well on covid symptoms, he tells us. This is good news on any number of levels, but he's this happy because it's a really common drug. ("It costs as much as a slurpee," he replies when we ask how common.) Pharma companies were working on boutique therapeutics that would have cost thousands of dollars a pill, but it turned out this steroid that hospitals have by the barrelful is rock solid.

Though it's not in the press much, for whatever reason, for him (and thus us, his friends) it's as if news of a major victory in a war has come in. Nathan was modestly positive about remdesivir, which doctors think can shave off several days of symptoms, but tells us the steroid reduces the mortality rate of sick patients by a third. An enormous stride forward.

Nathan's not the only person happy on Slack: The restaurant Rachel loves reopened, and she ordered eight chicken tikka masalas for delivery in case they shut down again.

June 30

Another month of covid gone. Today, waiting in the distanced line at Trader Joe's, I read about Derek Chauvin, the police officer who killed George Floyd. Chauvin's facing a felony murder charge that brings a recommended sentence of 12 years. The chances of a conviction are thought to be fairly low. Protesters in Minneapolis— still active, a month later—are saying the sentence would be too short.

Chauvin's wife has confirmed that she is moving forward with a divorce. She and Chauvin's partner on the police were both Hmong-American, I recall, and go into a rabbit hole about it on my phone, waiting in the tense, friendly line at the Trader Joe's on Hyperion. It turns out there's a long-established Hmong population in Minneapolis, with two newspapers of its own, a number of nonprofit and civic organizations, and two members in the statehouse of Minnesota. It's the same reason there's a large Somali population in Minneapolis, apparently, which is that the state volunteered to take in an unusual number of refugees. I hope that's the real Minneapolis. But both sides are real. There's a red and white Trump flag I pass every day driving on Franklin, hanging from a nice-looking balcony with tall happy plants on it: "Trump 2020: Enough Bullshit."

The image I think will come to mind if someone asks me about this time is of a sign at a protest that said **Mr. Floyd's Last Words** which had a full transcription of what he said on the tape. I've read it more times than I can count by now. I think it's partly because he mentions his mother. It makes me think of being little.

Before the Beatles, I had exactly one musical passion, which was the Supremes. I listened to them endlessly on my plastic record player when I was four and five, when my mother and I lived alone together in New York. My favorite song was *You Can't Hurry Love,* because it talked about her mama. I had a mama. We lived in an apartment on Thompson Street together. We had so much fun. After school we would get a piece of pizza and they would slice it down the middle with the fascinating rolling slicer (I thought this was in consideration of our regular custom, but in retrospect my mom just had very little money) and we would split it and walk home and listen to the Supremes, me showing her how MY record player worked as she watched patiently, smiling the same golden smile she has now. I wonder who the mother is that George Floyd remembered and called out to in his last moments. I wonder what she was like, what gentle thing he would have recalled about her when he was five, when he was alive.

The sign captures what was so eerie and gripping about the video, which was that he was *talking* for so much of it, and then he was just gone. From the time he was an infant babbling to the moment we watched him die, he had been saying things into the world. Right up to the end—46 years of speaking, and then, so suddenly, silence, forever. "I have so much trouble with that edge," as the great A. R. Ammons wrote.

Maybe that's part of why people went out on the streets. They realized they had to talk, because it could be too late any time, nobody listened when George Floyd talked. What you could say about that in a speech is something like "George Floyd's voice has never been louder!" And it would be right in a way. He is already a figure in our country's history. But we all know the truth; we watched his life end, and we know that his voice is nothing but pure silence, not louder than ever. We heard the very last words he actually spoke, even. A lady wrote them on a sign. It said:

MR. FLOYD'S LAST WORDS
It's my face man
I didn't do nothing serious man
please
please
please I can't breathe
please man
I can't breathe
I can't breathe
please
(inaudible)
man can't breathe, my face
just get up
I can't breathe
please (inaudible)
I can't breathe shit
I will
I can't move
mama
mama
I can't
my knee
my nuts
I'm claustrophobic
my stomach hurts
my neck hurts
everything hurts

WHAT JUST HAPPENED

some water or something
please
please
I can't breathe officer
don't kill me
they gon' kill me man
come on man
I cannot breathe
I cannot breathe
they gon' kill me
they gon' kill me
I can't breathe
I can't breathe
please sir
please
please
please I can't breathe
I'm through
I'm through

JULY

July 2

"I don't know if you need mandatory," says Trump, "but I'm all for masks. I think masks are good. I would wear—if I were in a group of people, and I was close . . . I mean, I would have no problem. Actually I had a mask on. I sort of liked the way I looked, OK? I thought it was OK. It was a dark black mask, and I thought it looked OK. Looked like the Lone Ranger."

135,000 dead here. Covid numbers are spiking in virtually every red state that pushed reopenings, to the most publicity in Florida. And we're waiting for this child to think he looks enough like the Lone Ranger to wear a mask in public. Then he says the same old line we've heard so many times: "I think that, at some point, that's going to sort of just disappear, I hope." As John Maynard Keynes said, in the long run we're all dead. Still, the embrace of masks and resultant strategic tack away from "murdering their own supporters" could bear fruit politically for Trump candidates down the line.

Some potential good news on the Pfizer vaccine comes out. Everyone's immediate guess, on spec, is that it's bullshit designed to goose the stock. On the other hand, companies are at least trying really hard to make the vaccine, so whether it's Pfizer or someone else, there's a chance we'll have it by next spring. People's automatic suspicion of big pharma means that every couple of pieces of hopeful vaccine news adds up to one, but our bank is starting to make little chinking noises when we drop the new coin in. Spring is nine months away. By then, we could theoretically be free, no masks, seeing the insides of stores and restaurants, meeting up anywhere, new things and places again. It seems shorter than a month did when we started quarantine.

Hugh Downs dies at 99, a television anchor from my childhood. One of those scorpion bites from a distant part of your youth you thought was gone. He had so much authority, with his white hair and stentorian voice, delivering the news on one of the four TV channels—a different world. Also in the news, because he attended Trump's rally in Tulsa last week as a surrogate, pointedly not wearing a mask, is Herman Cain, who has covid. He's in a hospital in Atlanta. Six Trump staff members had tested positive for the virus shortly before the event, so it's an unsurprising outcome. Reports have come out that members of the same staff were getting rid of social distancing stickers inside the venue hours before it started. Cain is a cancer survivor, and probably Trump's most prominent black supporter. I vividly remember his campaign, during which he briefly became the Republican front-runner. His obvious unseriousness and simultaneous popularity was one of the many moments that should have warned everyone, the 16 Republicans who eventually lost to him in the primary first and foremost, that

Trump wasn't the joke we thought he was at first. We had Gold-water, Buchanan, Palin, Cain, Schwarzenegger, the whole motley warm-up act, and still didn't see him coming.

July 4

Black Americans, dating back centuries, traditionally celebrated a holiday July 5th instead of the 4th, in part because July 4th was frequently the date of slave auctions in southern town squares and city dockyards. The greatest speech of Frederick Douglass's career was given on July 5, 1852, because he declined to speak on the 4th. "What is the 4th of July to a slave?" he asked.

According to the *Times,* the Black Lives Matter protests are now the largest in America's history, larger than the march on Washington during the civil rights movement or the protests against Vietnam. Something like 15 million people have marched, perhaps many more. I remember walking up First Avenue in New York to protest going to war with Iraq and not being able to see the end of the crowds in any direction I looked, and thinking, innocently, that nobody could refuse our point. Then the resolution to go to war passed 77–23 in the Senate. Anyway, there were 10,000 people or so at that march. 15 million people is a new kind of event.

The graffiti in L.A.—a city of murals and graffiti—has changed. You can understand more of it. **Black Lives Fucking Matter; No Lives Matter; ACAB; acab; acafb; -all cops are bastards-.**

Rent strike now! and **Black Lives Matter!** and **another world is possible.**

England is reopening, a more ambiguous augury than it was in the case of Wuhan, since that doofus Boris Johnson is involved.

The careful consensus increasingly seems to be that nowhere will actually be "open" until there's a vaccine. I asked Nathan the other day when we can go to concerts maskless. He thought for a second and said, September 2021. Since it will never be 2021, much less September of 2021, the news came as a blow.

My personal feeling is that the protests are fantastic, but I'm ready to go farther. A rent strike, a *general* strike. We're all proud of Gushers, but there's a mood that only civil disobedience will get it done. I have reckless, criminal thoughts. I don't want to hurt anybody, but I would be so happy if I could shake a little sand into the gears of capitalism.

One rallying cry since the death of George Floyd has been to "defund the police"—an unfortunate phrase, because the right has immediately started saying stuff like "Imagine calling 911 . . . and NO ONE IS THERE. That's the future liberals want." In fact the idea of defunding the police is to reallocate some of their budgets, a huge line item for every city and state in America, to (for instance) mental health professionals, so that when a homeless person is erratic, we can help them, not shoot them.

There are more homeless people on the streets here every day. At the foot of a street near us, what is essentially a small apartment complex made of tents, tarps, and various other scrap has gone up along the fence of an empty lot. It's clean and the tents share electricity. Over on Hollywood Boulevard there's another homeless encampment, and two brothers there are supposedly running a body shop from it. Who knows.

People say that future generations will look back on our society and be repulsed that we have the death penalty. Undoubtedly. But I think they'll feel equal indignation about our treatment of the homeless, such a high percentage of whom are mentally ill drug addicts; how can it be that for decade after decade our cities have sent cops out to nudge them along with a foot, like Jo in *Bleak House?* Our taxes, which should be paying for their care—it could be any of our own care one day, anyone who doubts that is a fool—have mostly been given over to the police, the military, and, more recently, returned to the rich in billions and billions of dollars in tax cuts from Donald Trump, one of the most incredible windfalls in the entirety of human history for a few thousand rich people. Which means that the money that should pay for the care of these helpless people is ultimately in the Seychelles, Bermuda, Jeff Bezos's spaceship, etc.

We rail against billionaires, but I still think innumeracy prevents people from grasping how extraordinary their theft is. It's a weird tragedy of the language that the words millionaire and billionaire are so similar, because it makes the progression from one to the next sound natural. The fact that goes around is that to pass a million seconds would take you 12 days from now, while a billion seconds would take you to the year 2050.

July 8

158 deaths in Florida today, the highest number yet in a single day, and more new cases in a single day than South Korea has recorded in total. There are stories about crowded hospitals, and hacking, suffocating deaths at home.

"Florida's Governor Took a Victory Lap on Coronavirus," reads a CNN headline, "But It Was Only Halftime." On May 20th, according to the article, Ron DeSantis "declared victory over the coronavirus." "Everyone in the media was saying Florida was going to be like New York or Italy, and that has not happened," he said on April 28, standing beside Donald Trump. I went back and watched the gloating video, the two of them palling around and bragging in front of reporters like criminals after a surprise acquittal. He was the symbol of successful reopening back then in GOP circles. There were 527 new cases in Florida that day. Today, two months after DeSantis's declaration of victory, there were more than 10,000.

Facing the unavoidable reality of spiking cases, DeSantis at last relents and tweets out a bitchy message about masks, like a sixth grader reluctantly inviting a nerd to a birthday party because their moms are friends. Masks "may" "help reduce transmission," he concedes. It's the closest he's come to admitting his and Trump's error, and it's heartening: facts have won, possibly!

But these people strike like adders when they're backed into the facts. "Holy crap," tweets a local journalist. "Ron DeSantis just held a press conference at a facility with 18 COVID-positive patients, but failed to alert the press." Another, Samantha Gross, adds, "Reporters were not informed that there were already 18 positive people being treated here before we entered this building."

I only have two strong memories about Ronald DeSantis— "D," as he was invariably called—from college. One is, credit it where it's due, that he did an uncanny Jose Canseco impression. The other memory I have is actually of a conversation about him, with a friend who was a music major. Her boyfriend, who played football and whose roommate was on the baseball team, told her that when D took women out, he would tell them he liked Thai food, but he would pronounce it "thigh." If they corrected him, he would make up an excuse and leave the date. He didn't want a girlfriend who corrected him. Also, she said, he always told people he was going to marry a local news anchor: successful, pretty, but not too smart. Apparently he had all these rules like that about women. She also said his only friend on the baseball team was the coach.

I've been trading on these stories all pandemic, obviously. My friend Steph, to whom I told the anecdote a long while ago, forwards me a news story. In it DeSantis is talking about remdesivir and pronounces the name of its manufacturer, Gilead, "Jollied." *It's the thigh food trick,* she says. He's being mocked on social media for it, but she's right, D went from Yale to Harvard Law and got himself into Congress and elected governor. No matter how stupid he looks, he knows how Gilead is pronounced, at least that's my guess. I think he wants people to forget that he went to those schools, and think of him instead as an honest guy trying his best whom the liberals mock for not saying things quite right. It's an adroit two-step. But then, his wife, Casey Black DeSantis, was a well-regarded anchor at the NBC affiliate in Jacksonville before she became First Lady of Florida.

July 15

Ruth Bader Ginsburg admitted at Johns Hopkins for an infection. Her health is often in the news, but god, I hope it isn't the virus. We're not far from the precipice if she goes. A 6–3 court could give the election to Trump on any pretext they chose, and the experiment of democracy here—arguably over already, after *Bush v. Gore,* such a naked power grab that, as Emily points out, the conservative justices specifically demanded that their opinion not be used as precedent—will officially have ended.

There's a long article in the *Financial Times* with the headline **Paris Bubbles Over with Optimism Post-Lockdown.** France has about 500 new cases a day. (We have 62,000.) There will be masks, contact tracing, and temperature checks in public places. Meanwhile, Trump is having a *rally* in a few days, effectively a designed superspreader event. Fury on Twitter. The usual cycle. We have to hope the anger turns into voting on our side and on their side does NOT turn into some militia full of hunting guides seizing the state capitol of Kansas or whatever.

In the midst of many deadlines now, my reading for the novel I want to write has fallen off to nearly zero, an occasional scan of one of the old black-edited newspapers I find so engrossing, the *Amsterdam News* or *Chicago Defender.*

But I've been listening while I write to the *Anthology of American Folk Music,* which is made up of recordings from between 1926 and 1933, compiled from his personal collection by an amateur music fan named Harry Smith. It was influential on the folk scene; it's how Bob Dylan found out about Blind Lemon Jefferson.

I first learned about the anthology from my late and terrific Uncle Will, who bought a used vinyl copy for $215 in 1994, haggled down from a Bleecker Street Records sticker price of $350 as I stared on, beet red, thinking that my uncle was offending the weirdo behind the counter, both of them coincidentally with cups of bodega coffee with Greek columns on the side. Far from being unwelcome, it was of course the highlight of their respective days, as I wish I had realized at the time. Afterward we went to the baseball card shop, where Will studied the cards as intently as I did. He grew up as one of two brothers, my uncle, younger, more diffident, and beautiful. He shuffled through life sweetly and kindly and unobtrusively in a family not oversupplied with those traits, handsome even as he gained weight in later years, and he died after many years of drug and then methadone use. I inherited the anthology from him and sold it along with most of his record collection to a different store, also on Bleecker. It was the height of the CD era. I wish I had kept the anthology at least. I kept his Beatles records, all bought on the day of their release, all battered beyond value by use, knocking out their worth except to exactly one measly person on earth, myself, who doesn't even own a record player.

I've never been into blues or folk, the main types of music on "Harry Smith's collection" (as the real Greenwich Village folk types called it). The reason I want to write this novel, about the musicologist traveling the south, is not the music, it's to write about the survivors of slavery, and I suppose also about white incomprehension of black experience. If any good idea for a novel can be summarized so briskly.

But my uncle knew that music inside out. I remember him with his feet up on his old desk, with a TV on it and books and records stacked everywhere around him, the last person in the roomy Upper East Side apartment in which he had been born and raised with my father. He was a Yankees fan, as I was (passionately), though his second favorite team was the Cardinals, and he followed them just as keenly, which made me wish I could talk to him again one more time when I met Emily, who's from St. Louis. He would have loved her.

After we came back from the card shop, with slices of pizza in boxes, I remember him putting on the *Anthology* and telling me a long and convoluted story about how even though Harry Smith's collection was fantastic, really prime, I shouldn't get fooled into just learning about the blues singers like Robert Johnson and

Charley Patton, the Delta guys (I didn't tell him there was very minimal risk of this, since I was only listening to Pearl Jam), because *he* had been, he had thought for years THAT was the blues, when in fact the REAL stars of that whole era were in point of fact actually the women, if you wanted to know, like Mamie Smith, who had the first hit in the genre that made money, and Bessie Smith, who came just after but was one of the biggest stars in America (and who in 1923 helped shepherd to the recording studio one of *her* heroes, a woman who had spent her life singing in tents with her husband "Pa," Gertrude "Ma" Rainey), but guys like him*self,* guys who hung out at Bleecker Street *Records,* or Rocks in Your *Head* on Prince Street, had built up this mythology about the great men of blues, so that while regrettably he did love the blues as it was commonly categorized in record shops, including Harry Smith's collection, he would recommend to me . . .

Will and I saw each other infrequently, especially toward the end of his short life. He was one of those true New Yorkers, inhabiting a world of shadowy friendships I never really saw, he knew people who lived in Central Park, he spent a while in a clinic with Levon Helm, he would always get free drinks at certain places, for instance the King Cole Bar at the St. Regis, the Cosmopolitan Club and the pizza place Mimi's on 84th and Madison, he knew every doorman on the Upper East Side. But when we did see each other we had endless conversations about these subjects, all of them cycling back ultimately to the home subjects (they felt like home) of the Yankees or the Beatles. I loved him so much. He struggled with substance abuse before we really had the language to talk about that. Now, if I listen to the *Anthology* high, I find myself talking to him, and even going back to some of the books he left behind, which thankfully I did keep, and in which he wrote complex essays and reviews in the margins of the pages.

I even hear what he likes about the tinny old music sometimes, the banjos and jugs. I'd love to know if he ever discovered the Harlem Hamfats. Besides the St. Louis thing, I want to tell him about *The Warmth of Other Suns,* which he would have devoured, and how really what I've learned is that the crucial thing about Bessie Smith was that her music made it up *north,* she paved the way for the blues to be successful in Memphis, St. Louis, and even Chicago, and in this sense of course the musical progress of the blues mirrored the Great Migration. And I would tell him about the Jacob Lawrence show and about how the book—but these are conversations you can have all day, if you let yourself.

July 16

Trump went back to one of his favorite subjects at his rally today, water pressure. "So shower heads," he began. (Huge audience approval.) "You take a shower . . . the water doesn't come out! You want to wash your hands . . . the water doesn't come out . . . dishwashers—you don't have any water!" (Strong audience disapproval. Trump shakes his head sadly.) "In most places of the country, water is not a problem. They don't know what to do with it." Pause. "It's called rain."

One thing the left needs to concede is that Trump is funny. So much of the goodwill toward him that bewilders us is hiding right in that, I think. Supporting him must be fun—he's amusing, surprising, demonstrative, weird. I mean he's not funny to me. You don't laugh at the jokes of the person pointing a gun at you. But if I were in a different room with the gun person I might find them funny.

Obviously he's unintentionally funny more than intentionally, and I wish we could enjoy it. I remember when he took offense

because a reporter said America wasn't a developing country—
"The U.S. is developing a lot!" Trump protested, hurt—and I
think sometimes with fondness about the time CBS reporter John
Dickerson helplessly tried to get him interested in a metaphor.

> DICKERSON: George W. Bush said the reason the Oval Office is
> round is there are no corners you can hide in.
> TRUMP: Well, there's truth to that. There is truth to that. There
> are certainly corners. And look, there's a certain openness. But
> there's nobody out there. You know, there is an openness, but
> I've never seen anybody out there actually.
> DICKERSON: But he—what he meant—it's—
> TRUMP: Sure. Sure.

It would be funnier if Americans weren't in the tragic position
of flushing their toilets "10 times, 15 times, as opposed to once,"
though, as the President has been at vigilant pains to remind us.
"We have a situation where we're looking very strongly at sinks
and showers," fortunately, he says, knowing that in this time of
crisis America wants a leader who will look strongly at sinks and
showers.

A filmed version of the Broadway show *Hamilton* is streaming on
Disney+, which bumped its release up nearly a year for a public
craving new content. The reactions on social media are emotional,
t-shirts and caps dug out for nights at home to watch a full theater
on TV; listen to the songs so many of us love; relive the Obama
years, when, despite hope being advertised to us so often, there
actually managed to be hope somehow. Ben's favorite song is *Wait
for It*. Rachel likes the rap battles ("Guess I'm a bad bitch"). Though

I haven't had time to watch it, I wander around humming *Helpless* to myself all day and listen to the soundtrack while I'm walking. I knew someone who was working at the Public Theater when *Hamilton* came out, and he said that hearing *Helpless* was when he knew the show had no chance of missing.

July 17

John Lewis died today. He was eighty. He was a giant. He was the last living member of the "Big Six," the group of activists whose leader was Martin Luther King Jr. When he was 25, he was in the first row of people walking across the Edmund Pettus Bridge, into the teeth of the waiting Alabama police. They fractured his skull and broke two of his ribs. The nation changed because of that day—Bloody Sunday, as it was dubbed in the press—and Lewis, wearing his backpack on the bridge, became an icon of civil rights courage. Eventually he became a congressman. It's all valentines today, but in my childhood he was one of the most demonized congressmen in the Democratic Party. I remember it vividly.

Where could he have been from but Georgia? Always at the center of this long story, where black people in America were perhaps most brutally abused, and then where they most triumphantly rose as one, arguably, in the person of King. The grief for Lewis on social media is titanic. Pictures of him in his youth, as a leader of SNCC, the Student Nonviolent Coordinating Committee, bring back with astonishing freshness how courageous he and his fellow activists had to be. John Lewis had no idea he would become a congressman or live to old age. There was no proof of concept for what he was doing: sacrificing his body in the hope that people would notice how easily sacrificed it was. For many of the people to his left and right, the sacrifice was their lives. So it could have been for him, rather than a heroic old age. Any of those days could have been his last. The people in the civil rights movement weren't protesting. They were in a war. And they won.

July 19

Chris Wallace, of Fox News: "But can you give a direct answer, you will accept the election?"

Trump: "I have to see. Look, you—I have to see. No, I'm not going to just say yes."

There are days I'm as anxious about winning the election closely as losing it.

July 20

Some encouraging news on the Oxford vaccine ("safe, well-tolerated, and immunogenic"). Nathan advises us not to pin our hopes on it, because the transition from animal to human testing is considered a "guillotine" for vaccines, so many die there. But luck is on our side at this hurdle anyway. Another coin to drop into the bank.

When Trump concedes something, like DeSantis, he has to lash out. So when he has to give way on masks, he makes sure it's racist: "We are United in our effort to defeat the Invisible China Virus, and many people say that it is Patriotic to wear a face mask when you can't socially distance. There is nobody more Patriotic than me, your favorite President!" I've been saying for years that one of these useless billionaires should buy Twitter and keep it the same but ban Trump. But they can't do anything right.

July 23

Tonight I go to Wulf's lawn, a regular refuge this July, and we get to see our friend Mike Still. He and his girlfriend split up in April, a month into quarantine, and he starts telling us about his hobby since she left their place, which is that he bought an "electronic woodwind instrument," called an aerophone. It has six "onboard instruments," according to Still. (We're high, drunk, and listening to Funkadelic.) These "modes" include hyper realistic-sounding flute, clarinet, saxophone, and some others he can't remember. He's really been progressing in all the modes, though, and is thinking about jamming some time with me and Wulf, who plays a good bar piano. He says there are only two drawbacks to his new hobby.

"What?" asks Wulf.

Still pushes back his long red hair with both hands and sighs. "In the first place, you can't really tell people you know how to play the saxophone but then pull the aerophone out."

We ask why not.

"It looks like"—he stares up to the sky, and thinks for a second— "like a recorder."

We both laugh but are quick to say it must look like an aerophone, i.e., visibly have different electronic commands, not be a literal wind instrument, etc., so he finds a picture and shows it to us. It does look exactly like a recorder. As we're laughing, he says, "So, you can't exactly play *Greensleeves* at Christmas for your extended family," and *Greensleeves* takes us about fifteen minutes off track, until we've changed the music and finally Wulf stops laughing long enough to ask what the second drawback of the aerophone is.

Still pushes back his hair again, as if this was just bringing up an even more insuperable difficulty. He's a burly guy, an actor who's been in a lot of car and food ads, you might recognize him. "It *sounds* great, okay," he says (meaning the aerophone). We say okay. "But every half hour or so—this is going to sound grosser than it is." No, what, we say. "Well, every half hour, all the spit that's been gathering in it—I guess you'd say falls out of the bottom of the instrument. Every half hour."

Astonishment, jubilation, consternation in the audience at this, and we say surely there must be a way of predicting when it will happen and discreetly disposing of the expectorant in advance, say during the break in the chorus of *Greensleeves,* a suggestion he rebuts, saying that actually the only way to get the spit out *is* in fact to let it fall, no exertion will do it, he's tried every way possible. We're laughing and laughing with helpless covid-tinged joy, some of it just being together in the pink night, drinking our sundowners, the gently swaying palm trees on Wulf's street so high up and skinny it's like being among the legs of a herd of gentle herbivorous dinosaurs. We tell Still we really would like to hear the aerophone. At home, much later, I think about the careful planning it took us to drink together, and how long it will be until any of us probably congregate again, a week or two at least. You used to see people every day! After we've gone our different ways, Still texts another picture of the aerophone, and it looks even more like a recorder, practically a replica of one, but he details the other settings it has, and I tell them both truthfully that I kind of want one. Maybe we'll start an aerophone trio.

July 24

The average home price in the Hamptons "has hit $2.1 million," according to CNBC. That's up more than 20% from last year. Anecdotally, everyone I know who has a house in the Hamptons except one is currently living in their house in the Hamptons, I think. (She's at her house in Capri.) Because of where I went to school and college it's not a minuscule number of people. I never liked it there, except the time on Ben's bachelor party when a very drunk friend—Wulf, as it happens—was trying to meet us at the bar Stephen Talkhouse and accidentally took a ramble all the way to Montauk, searching with his agreeable minivan taxicab driver for a Mexican food stand called "Stephen's Tacos."

I've felt in my gut since this began that lots of people are going to be pushed by this homebound year to move one valence out, like jumping electrons: city-dwellers to the suburbs, suburbs dwellers to the country, country dwellers into deeper woods, and all the butterfly-fine categories in between. One of my closest friends has spent what I think must be a small fortune to move to the beach on East Hampton for the summer. Her kids' smiles glow in the sun there, as kids do everywhere when they're with mothers who love them, rich kids, destitute ones. Even in this rotten age, so many people are still trying their best. I have to remember that.

According to *The Washington Post,* Ron DeSantis's approval rating among Floridians is "collapsing" "from +20 to -11" as Florida becomes the signature state of coronavirus mismanagement. I don't dare to put much faith in this, the same way I automatically adjust every Democratic candidate downward in my mind four points in every poll for my own mental health. Nathan's rounds are relatively quiet, but he's gotten less optimistic, or at least he's refusing to give in to other people's optimism. "If this is World War II, it's early 1943," he says.

"Another government stimulus package is not in the best interests of the people imo." Not only is Elon Musk not a genius, he may not even be smart enough to speak to. Or if he's a genius, it's a form of genius with absolutely airtight fucking borders, in which politics is constantly trying to make an assault on the fence and getting zapped back every single time. *imo*. The temerity of that; people's lives in the balance, your influence nonsensical but undeniable, and you say you're just giving your "o." There were 5 million unemployed people in America in February, and there are 17 million now. Grow up you fool.

July 29

150,000 deaths in the U.S.

July 31

The country is in a softer frame of mind. The shelves are full in the grocery stores again. Sports are back. Outdoor hangs are normal, frequent even. Zoom is mostly for work. The covid rates vary by state, but everyone who cares knows which precautions to take. And Trump's deficit in the polls is like Planck's constant (which I am possibly misremembering from the great Dr. Perrin's class as being extremely constant). They must have polled every person in Michigan, and Biden has had the same six to seven point lead there for two months, occasionally spiking up into double digits. Say Russia costs us two points a state, Mitch McConnell and the Supreme Court another two each—that's still a narrow win. If we lose with the country so united against Trump and for Biden, we will be through the looking glass, and who knows what might happen. The virus will come back in the fall and winter, Nathan says, possibly really badly, but then, a record number of people are expected to get the flu shot, and the little bank of good vaccine news is rattling—I picture it as the bank from *A Tree Grows in Brooklyn,* that tin can cut into a star, as I fade off into sleep . . .

The real thing of pot: I can feel relief, and even occasionally, fleetingly, joy, pleasure in life. Without anxiety. Is there anything that's not worth that? Yes, probably, but I can deal with a cough. I wish I weren't smoking so often, but then, a lot of people wish a lot of things right now.

I walk a long way every evening these days and sometimes again in the middle of the night, listening to music (a surprise new Taylor Swift album came out a couple days ago, it's incredible) and looking around at the million Los Angeles plants, creatures that have intuitions about earth none of us could begin to have in a thousand lifetimes of communion with nature, fat succulents, runaway orange poppies, cruel ugly cacti. Sometimes I venture all the way up to the Griffith Park Observatory, the serely beautiful white chapel sitting watchfully above Los Angeles. At 7:00, you can rely on hearing people coming to their doors still with bells and tambourines. It's truly neighborly of them, what they do, how they check in on each other. We're still together. I couldn't be a bell ringer myself, so I admire it.

Herman Cain died of covid yesterday. He was only 74. Cain grew up in Atlanta, where his mother was a cleaning woman and his father a barber. He went to Morehouse and then to graduate school at Purdue, specializing in the nascent field of computer science. He went into business and rose quickly to become an executive at Pillsbury, then the CEO of Godfather's Pizza. But he's famous because he was briefly a front-runner in the 2012 presidential race. His political views were inane, self-interested, and superficial, and he never built a large following, but he remained in the spotlight, primarily, I don't think it's cynical to say, because he was a black conservative (and latterly a loyal one to Trump).

At Yorkside Pizza in New Haven, there's a picture of Cain on the cover of *Pizza Magazine,* the industry's journal of record. (Yorkside is mentioned on the cover, which is why it's up; it was up in the early 2000s, before Cain even entered politics. Yorkside is one of the last college places left in New Haven, as anyone who went to Yale before 2015 will discuss with you at morose length, with good pizza, served with sauce and cheese at the temperature of basically lava if it's busy, for instance after Toad's let out on a Saturday night, and the best Greek salad anywhere.) Today I thought of the picture—this graduate of Morehouse, on walls otherwise crammed full of framed pictures of Yale men and women—and thought, it was inevitable that it was Cain who would die of covid. Not Pompeo, that sack of shit, or Rudy Giuliani, with his bizarre drunk cable-ready rictus, or one of the kids who murders leopards, or whatever. It was the black guy. The 9-9-9 guy, the pizza guy, a joke to the left, a token to the right. He should never have even touched politics. It was remarkable that he succeeded as he did in business. He should have retired into wealth and paid someone to write a biography of him.

Trump barely acknowledges Cain's death. Bad politics—his rally caused it. No doubt Cain's name will be buried, an embarrassing reminder of the time the GOP killed their one black friend.

He was in good shape, too, slender, healthy-looking! That gargoyle William Barr, for one—but you can't start, those are dark thoughts. Still, it's remarkable that without even trying, America always, unless perhaps there's a Native American available, assigns its bloodshed and death to black people first.

AUGUST

August 1

All of July passed more quickly than a single day of March. After the nerves of early spring, the tired hopelessness of April and May, and then the volcano of the protests in June, perhaps we're settling in to wait for the only thing that can resolve either problem, the election in November.

The George Floyd protests are smaller in number, but the concrete actions resulting from them are more numerous. Democratic officials are taking action locally where they can. Statues of slave owners continue to come down from public squares, names of schools and bus stations change. In Mitch McConnell and Rand Paul's Kentucky, Governor Andy Beshear, a rare Democrat elected statewide there, has pledged health insurance to the state's black citizens, something close to reparations, which would be my real dream. There's a lively and thoughtful debate about whether the word should be styled "black" or "Black"—the *Times,* among others, recently selecting the latter option—to indicate the specific history of Black America, something that, as a writer, I watch with close interest. The portraits of secessionists in the Capitol come down, and with them one of the last few southern claims to victory in the Civil War: their memorialization as heroic men. The Capitol is better off without them.

It's still quarantine, no day without jitters. I'm listening to Sam Cooke, nothing but the upbeat, good-hearted, sometimes sad immenseness of Sam Cooke. He's the best singer in American popular music to me. You can tell because every cover of one of his songs is worse than his version, even Aretha Franklin's. Ben, who went to two Eagles concerts on consecutive nights just before the pandemic began, hoping the band would play a personal favorite called *Doolin' Dalton,* only to discover instead that the band played the same 33 songs in identical order both nights, reports on Slack that "*Amie* is an incredible yacht rock jam." I ask what he thinks of *Escape (The Piña Colada Song).* He replies that it's "low end, but not as bad as *Coconut.*" I tell him he might be taking it a little TOO easy.

A graphic of new daily coronavirus cases on MSNBC:

> Spain—0
> France—0
> Canada—285
> U.S.—48,489

Get your shit together, Canada!

August 3

It's that time of year when Los Angeles becomes one of the worst cities in the world for two months, hot, airless, squinting, the sky a sullen lightless blue. At the start of August, palm trees (so beautiful in winter) slowly transform into lean, sun-bitten old soldiers, maniacally bent on their emaciated upward growth. The bright red sign for the new Thai place on Hillhurst goes chapped white in a week. The mountains that ring the city are suddenly a stark baked brown, and in this moment their bare rock shape seems more truly Californian than every stripe of beauty that happens to pass, in human or natural form, at their feet. I would leave the city for two months today if I had any choice and return for winter, my favorite time here. But there's a pandemic. In the last place I lived, Chicago, I couldn't take the winters, and so I did go away for two months. And the place I went was Los Angeles.

I love it here. I can never imagine staying or leaving. New York is where my eyes go—as Jonathan Franzen said, the only place where no one asks why you live there. But coming to L.A. has been like getting bewitched. Its cool sunniness, its low-slung tatterdemalion endlessness, give the city a tranquil, dreamlike quality. It's a place of such gentle successes and failures. The weather and the landscape are beautiful enough that every hard fate is softened, every success muted. The city itself spreads out in just such a way that it's impossible to permanently understand it all. And it's janky, no design or order, full of loose ends. It's like the opposite of a Wes Anderson movie. In New York, if your yarn store sucks, it's gone in ten weeks, the market decides for you. But in L.A., crisscrossed with strip malls, you can hang on to the exact same yarn store for thirty years. Still, if you look at any part of it, L.A. starts to pulse with the weird vitality, in part because, as in all great cities, very few people are here innocently. You can get a check cashed on almost any block. Sports bars look like warehouses or speakeasies. Brickwork everywhere is covered with sun-faded paint, advertising things that were once and may still well be in business. On a block you've passed a hundred times, you'll realize the lines aren't for Target but for a taco truck you never saw, just around the corner. The most expensive restaurants are next to dollar donut shops, which are next to noodle shops that are better than the semi-expensive restaurant two doors down, and so on in endless fractal confusion, in the gentle dayless flow of Los Angeles time.

Except now, in August and September. Now it's a place with no geography except the sun, the city as a whole a blank stare. All that lack of order starts seeming hateful when it's this fucking hot.

It's the first place I've ever lived that was not founded on Christianity. The churches here, even the huge expensive ones, have no more purchase than any of us on the identity of the city—none. If Pink's Hot Dogs disappeared, by contrast, there would be pink armbands for sale. In exercise classes in New York and Chicago and Boston, the teachers will say, "Here comes the really hard part, go go GO! Earn that margarita tonight!" In L.A., the teachers say, "Here comes the hard part—even a lot of the teachers sit this out—rest if that will feel better . . ." No puritans were involved in the making of Los Angeles.

It's the only sad city I've ever lived in. The dreams that bring people to it are so dizzying that to fall short of them, which is inevitable mostly, infuses the long residential blocks with a mood of strange sorrow. It's in the faces you see, especially the beautiful ones, a little dazed, twenty years into a search for fame they were sure, on the flight from Dallas, would take twenty minutes. There are little instructional academies dotted everywhere, as if all of us were just one guitar lesson, just one improv class away. When I see them I miss New York.

Trump introduced his Secretary of the Interior this morning. "He loves the Interior," according to the President. Honestly it's an incredible qualification for the job.

August 5

"They are dying. That's true. And it is what it is." For months, even after he wore the Lone Ranger mask, Trump deflected the questions he got about covid deaths. But now, as the numbers surge dizzyingly higher even before the predicted autumn surge, he is at least glancing at reality with a tight nod. "It is what it is"—that's the phrase people are furious about, including even a few meek voices on the right, who want the President to show empathy during a national crisis, or at a bare minimum think it would be wise politically.

You can tell that Trump himself hates to think about death, like all narcissists. I keep turning over in my mind James Baldwin's piercingly correct observation: "Perhaps the whole root of our trouble, the human trouble, is that we will sacrifice all the beauty of our lives, will imprison ourselves in totems, taboos, crosses, blood sacrifices, steeples, mosques, races, armies, flags, nations, in order to deny the fact of death, which is the only fact we have."

It's positive that there's now essentially full public acceptance of the necessity of masks, even if it's reluctant. Too many people are dying—even Trump sees it. The numbers are sickening. In one interview he says, "People question masks, but there's no downside in wearing them." Right, people. The next day he reiterates the point, adding that wearing a mask is "a patriotic thing to do." What a reversal, after the sheer number of easily calculable deaths his refusal until now has resulted in. Even with the lag, no one I know would have dreamed of walking the streets without a mask after, say, mid-May. It's taken until August for the President to do it. I'm sure every one of these Republican ghouls has been wearing a mask the second they're not in front of cameras in those intervening months. They don't want to die. Lindsey Graham does not look like the picture of cardiovascular health. That is a guy who has recently consumed gravy at breakfast. Yet all of them lined up behind Trump when it was him versus the health of the public: masks were wrong, dumb, liberal scaremongering, etc. And that horse is out of the barn. A lot of people will never wear a mask now if they can possibly help it. It's become an issue of symbolism, and, as Baldwin was saying, there's virtually nothing more important to people.

Tonight I listen to Kacey in the late twilight, heat still radiating from the dry ground even after the sun has gone. I miss everyone, but at least the air is cooler. "It is what it is," she sings, with sad beautiful clarity, "till it ain't / any more."

August 6

"Floods" of evictions expected, as one Florida lawyer toplines an article from the *Tampa Bay Times,* "after Governor DeSantis quietly changes Florida's COVID-19 eviction moratorium wording, making it easier to evict."

As if it weren't strange enough to watch someone you met a few times when you were 20 undertake the wholesale massacre of a state full of people, up from the fetid consciousness of Trump's mind comes the pronunciation "Thighland" for Thailand. I'm agog, until I realize it's exactly the kind of trick DeSantis is likely to have *told* Donald Trump about playing. They probably laughed about it on the golf course, traded stories. Locker room talk. Now people are rushing to mock Trump, and others are rushing to mock the mockers. So it worked. "I'm highly amused to see supposedly sophisticated media types snickering at @realdonaldtrump for saying 'Thighland,'" writes convicted felon and conservative thought leader Dinesh D'Souza. "'Tai-land' is the crude lingo of people who have never been to 'Thighland.'" As many people point out, D'Souza is incorrect. As others point out, it doesn't matter.

August 7

Canadian ice shelf area bigger than Manhattan collapses due to rising temperatures, per *The Guardian*. I click, expecting it to be a sad but relatively commonplace story, but no. This particular ice shelf was "the largest remaining intact ice shelf" on earth. "It's disintegrated, basically," according to Luke Copland, a glaciologist (didn't know that existed, cool job) at the University of Ottawa.

My friend Peter, who's in his 70s and in iffy health, told me not long ago that he's optimistic about climate change, because humans are so ingenuous, in the old sense, when they're in a corner. I sometimes have a hint of that hopefulness. But things are going much faster than perhaps he expected when he told me that a year or two ago, perhaps even than the real pessimists expected. Summer in the Canadian Arctic this year was not 3 or 4 but 41 degrees hotter than the 30-year average.

I think of ice as just being ice, but Mark Serreze, director of the National Snow and Ice Data Center, speaks of the polar ice caps the way I think of (the real) Manhattan. "We saw them going, like someone with terminal cancer," he tells *The Guardian*. "It was only a matter of time. When I was there in the 1980s I knew every square inch of those ice caps. You have the memories."

August 8

It's a dim blue late evening, the only tolerable time of the day now. I take my walk in the last light, fading farther and farther east into shades of white, until all at once it's dark, and I'm passing the French restaurant on Vermont more closely than I meant to. The candlelight with the sounds of glassware and conversation and music makes it seem almost exactly like life. It reminds me of Diet Coke: an impression of okayness, and then something bad behind it as I move swiftly on, really bad. I realize this is the longest uninterrupted run of good health I've had in years. I would give anything to be sitting out at the bistro, even with the strange plastic dividers between the tables, even with the servers in their trim French aprons wearing welding masks. But I heard a story yesterday of someone with my own particular banal condition dying of covid, and while it could happen to anyone, at any time, this combined with the spiking numbers in Florida and beyond—soon here, given how flocked that restaurant was?—have put the chill back into me of March and April. I shouldn't even be going out to Wulf's stupid lawn.

August 9

Sinking in work.

Germany gave every artist in the country €9,000 in March, with no strings attached. Presumably even shitty ones, like myself! Meanwhile, here, we debate whether a 3.5% tax increase on millionaires will be such a disincentive to them that they all quit working forever. It's too hot out. I don't want to work either, just like the mad millionaires. I can only listen to the soft consoling Sam Cooke, I try to break through, but nothing else will do.

I text with my friend Jess for the first time in months, since the start of quarantine. She's single and lives alone in Brooklyn. I feel guilty for not having kept in better touch with her, she seems lonely. She says dating has been a nightmare. She's 37 and says she feels guys realizing, as they sit outside together on park benches or whatever, that there's nothing stopping the person opposite them from being 27. I tell her she's just imagining it, and even if not, 27-year-olds still have a lot of shit to deal with usually. She says there are more college-educated single women than men in New York. She says she hates the word feminism now, she thinks it's been twisted into meaning that you have to work the same miserable fifty-hour weeks as men to be "equal" and then on the weekends you have the right to sleep with someone but it's uncool to even wonder about them emotionally until you've slept together a *bunch* of times. Plus it's hard to conceal that yes, you do want kids, and you have lost the time to say "in a few years" with credibility. She's going to delete the dating apps soon. I think about Wulf, who's seeing an almost aggressively unsuccessful actress who lives alone in her parents' mansion in Toluca Lake. I tell Jess she'll find someone the second she stops trying, and she sends a laughing emoji and says maybe. We move on to talking about other things, but the exchange remained irradiated with her unhappiness. Later she texts to say that feminism *is* a great idea, they just messed it up. Because where it's landed is, to her, only corporate interests camouflaged as women's rights, and guys you barely know trying to get you to do anal. I reply with my own laughing emojis at this, though as if to cover she immediately begins asking me to recommend a book.

Marx doesn't really talk about the fact that women have been working billions of hours a year for absolutely free since the concept of exchange came into being. Engels did, to his credit, but he wasn't as earth-shatteringly brilliant as his less interested friend. Alas.

August II

Kamala Harris will be Joe Biden's running mate. She's a good candidate. He vowed several months ago to choose a woman. I would have liked it to be Elizabeth Warren or Stacey Abrams, and though Abrams never had much but an outside shot, Warren seemed close. She was always my candidate—the best candidate. Warren grew up in Oklahoma, with a father who worked as a janitor. When she was a teenager the family car was repossessed, and she waited tables to help. She studied speech at the University of Houston, hoping for a stable career, then changed her mind, went to law school, and proved so brilliant that she changed legal scholarship permanently and got tenure at Harvard Law. As with Herman Cain, that journey across class lines alone was enough to make her life remarkable before she got into politics. Unlike him, she was right to do it.

She started by shocking a lot of complacent people into leftist consciousness with an inspiring off the cuff speech in favor of a strong centralized government that helps people. Then she fought with Obama, trying to pull him left. Then she became the most liberal member of the Senate (along with Bernard Sanders of Vermont, who, to his undying credit, had staked out these positions in that chamber a long, long time ago).

I liked Warren because she struck me both as an idealist like Sanders but also someone who has been ceaselessly effective within complex systems, working at the disadvantages of her class and sex. I've seen those law school professors up close—they're like demigods, wandering the Ivy campuses. Warren's JD is from Rutgers, which must have made her one of the extremely few people without her own Ivy League background to end up teaching there. Give me that woman. Anyway, Bernie would have been wonderful too, and Biden and Harris right now would be nirvana. The various candidates don't matter any more. Harris is qualified and smart. What remains to be seen is if she can help Biden win, the only thing that does matter.

August 13

Listening to Kacey, I have a usual thought, which is that if I had an ounce of courage, I would buy a trailer in Palm Springs, keep $50,000 in a checking account (is this number low? high? How out of touch am I?), and give the rest of what I have away. Even that would probably make me one of the most comfortable people in the trailer park. I could write there. I guess I'd be worried about people having guns. I can't tell if that's prejudiced or pragmatic. The real point is that I am not *better* than that, which I have finally internalized only now in what might be the last days of our country. No book I've read or opinion I have about clothes or factory farming makes me different than a person in a trailer park, we're the outcome of too many factors for that. Pride is maybe the laziest sin, because it's so easy to talk yourself out of it if you have a heart.

And that money could really help people. When I think of them these days, the billionaires seem like mass murderers to me, one and all, Carlos Slim, Tim Cook, Sheldon Adelson, even the supposedly generous ones, Warren Buffett, Bill Gates. It's not generous. Just give all the money away, Bill. Don't let it sit there moldering as you decide like some pharaoh how you personally think it should be disbursed—as if that money has anything to do with the little tiny particle of existence that is *you*. The mistake that has gone on for so long is believing that any single person should be associated with a sum as ludicrous as "sixty billion dollars," which is supposedly around what Michael Bloomberg has, for instance. He no more made that fortune than he made the sun rise this morning. He was nothing but a victim of inconceivable luck. A lot of people in the history of the world have started out their adult lives trying to make a lot of money. Many succeed, many don't, and no doubt tens of thousands just as gifted and motivated as Mike Bloomberg are on each side. He just happened to be born during a time when a small handful have by transhistorical chance exceeded the farthest reach of their grasp, and rather than their hard work earning them comfortable lives, it has given them control of more money than most *countries* have, control of *us*. Michael Bloomberg is 5′8″ and has an annoying voice and salts his pizza and burns up fuel flying privately to Bermuda all the time and made sexist jokes to his executives. He's not magic. He's just a person to whom something incredible *happened*. Some people become movie stars, too. Congrats, Mike, you invented a computer terminal and changed the law so you could buy a third term as mayor of America's stop-and-frisk capital. Your own role in your success was perhaps an extra few inches of effort and smarts here and there, which millions have given without quite such lush results. To give Michael Bloomberg credit for his fortune is to show that you understand nothing about numbers. Millions of children in this country are food insecure. In a just society, including a just capitalist one, Bill Gates's dedication might have earned him a nicer car or a ritzy second house. A third house even, what the hell, let's reward that entrepreneurial spirit! But in ours, he wields more money than the poorest hundred million people in this country combined, easily more political power than all those millions of food insecure children put together, a fact with which he can apparently live.

This is why every billionaire is a Hiroshima. The logic of Bill Gates's enterprise—if we can make the world better in the long term, fewer people will suffer, and he, Bill Gates, will get to do cool stuff—has a certain utilitarian logic if you squint really hard (even then I see no real defense: it's been proven again and again that *giving people money* is the best and fastest way to help, they make incredible decisions) but it's so scattershot, like he randomly gets interested in toilets and a thousand people scurry into motion. He's another beneficiary of divine timing: Born in exactly the right year to extremely rich parents, he went to a high school that had lots of computers, an unbelievable stroke of luck for a kid interested in computers in 1971. Then he invented Microsoft, a company that makes indispensable and by broad consent terrible products. From the wild aleatory fortune that poured over him, he took on the briefs of malaria, poverty, etc., from government. To him the lesson of his success was not that he was a bright, fortunate kid who got lucky, but that he was Leonardo da Vinci. And Gates is the absolute best of these people! He might have immediately developed a God complex, but at least it was a liberal one. What a cursed age.

Besides the trailer park (and I have no doubt that I would hate it the second I was there, and indeed that lots of people who are *there* hate it and some number of them are hateful, some percentage of all people being hateful, and the condition of being poor not designed to minimize hateful qualities) I have another moving fantasy. It's to buy 100 acres of cheap land somewhere and plant trees, like the main character in the novella *The Man Who Planted Trees* by Jean Giono. (The plot's right in the title.) It's one of the best of modern fables. Nobody quite understands the motivations of the man who plants trees, and that, to me, makes the book in some occult but certain sense about art: the absolute unnecessity of it, combined with the intense inner necessity of the artist to do it. In that paradox we have missed some big lie about life, because nothing humans need to do as badly as they seem to need to make art can be as pointless as our society pretends.

I would like to plant hundreds of trees. At the moment I can only actually identify three kinds of trees on sight, eucalyptus (grew up near one), palm (obvious), and bonsai (little). I could learn though! I'd want to have a TV, obviously internet, hot water—but then, I start to probe at this little tenderness, and what I see is that all of it, the trailer park, the hundred acres, the airstream chronicles posted by young beautiful people on Instagram, the families spending a kid's seventh grade in Florence ("it's the last year before things really start counting for college!"), the adult summer camps some of our friends go to—they're pathetic little wriggles toward some idea other than the City and the Suburbs, the fretting of people like me, with enough saved up not to have to worry about food or shelter, complaining from the inside about a bourgeoisie that should be incinerated.

August 18

The moon is yolk yellow, the night is sick, a city too hot to be masked, a wall of windless heat. Sam Cooke singing. I sweat no matter what time I walk. It's so hot that the homeless people without tents are exactly their own shape, sleeping on the sidewalk, no blankets or coverings, the rebuke sharper even than usual because you can see their outlines so plainly, each one of you just a person.

A few mornings ago I was walking at 5:30 or so, around when the sun was coming up, and passed the homeless encampment on Hollywood. It's expanded massively in the last month. It's about a hundred feet long, with proper doorways and taut blue tarps stretched over the entire thing, from a distance giving it the appearance of a public sculpture. As I walked past it, I saw fifteen or so men, mostly in their 20s. They were all wearing fluorescent vests, some of them looking at their phones off to the side, some trading jokes in Spanish, a handful putting on boots. It took me a minute to realize they were all getting ready for work. Two were smoking together. Another played a radio and sat by himself on the curb. They all had lunchboxes, small red and white Igloo coolers. A woman was picking among a chaos of bicycle wheels and electronics carefully bundled against one section of fence and came over to a tall, handsome man, gave him a hammer and a pair of earphones, and kissed him goodbye for the day. People went back to their tents for things they had forgotten. By the time I made my way back, they were gone, and the tarps were closed again, though a woman remained in the street, playing with her daughter.

All-time record high close for the S&P 500.

August 19

In Wuhan, an EDM concert at an outdoor water park sees "thousands in attendance." Wuhan hasn't had a case of covid since May, if you believe the Chinese government. Meanwhile here in the United States we are past 5 million.

Do I believe the Chinese government? In his journals from 1940, Orwell recorded his disgust that people in America were being issued gas masks—America, across the Atlantic from Hitler—while the English, the Germans' immediate targets for potential gassing, were not. That's the kind of organization we used to have in this hardworking country, before capitalism wrested control of the government from us. Now China is that country: masks, gas masks, it's not even a subtle analogue. It's 2020 instead of 1940, China is us, and we are England, and England is run by an old Etonian who looks like a munitions company designed a pig that acts like a human.

So it seems unfathomable—as we sit inside, with no end in sight except a vaccine—that Wuhan has beaten the virus back so comprehensively, and at the same time plausible. On the other hand, imagine having to go to an EDM concert.

We're on the third night of the Democratic National Convention, which is opened by the governor of Wisconsin, who ends, "Holy mackerel, folks, let's get to work!" like he's running for dog catcher of Lake Wobegon. Meanwhile, Mitch McConnell is probably skinning a rat alive to keep his instincts sharp. I've been thinking incessantly about the Edward St. Aubyn line, until in the sleepless middle of the night I go rummage pages to find it. "In the end, it was even harder to behave badly than to behave well," he writes. "That was the trouble with not being a psychopath. Every avenue was blocked."

August 20

Ha, Biden just jogged confidently up a ramp at the convention. Can't be a coincidence. His speech is fine. Credit to him: he ran on unity when he started, he ran on unity after he finished 4th in Iowa, and he's running on unity now. I like that he still has a little old school RFK left jab in him, quoting poetry and philosophy. The best compliment I have heard Biden given—and it's not a minor one—is that he's always at the leftmost edge of the center of his party. The platform of this convention reflects that. We could have a completely new climate strategy in place in six months, designed by Elizabeth Warren and AOC, student debt relief, voting rights, even a basic income. It's at least possible. Little green shoots of hope.

August 28

The whole Republican convention, every speech and gesture and carefully decorated setting, feels like it's leading up to a one-time opportunity to buy a timeshare next to a swamp full of crocodiles. The highlight is Don Jr. and his girlfriend Kimberly Guilfoyle, a former Fox News host. In their speeches they seem either electrified by the spirit of the moment or (as Twitter deems more likely) on a lot of cocaine. Guilfoyle, with the eyes shining out of her head like headlights on a country road at night, concludes her speech by screaming, with odd flat exaltation, "THE BEST IS YET TO COME!"

The best has to then go on waiting despite this introduction, because she's followed instead by Don Jr., eyes leaking uncontrollably, face mottled, beard heavy with salt and spittle, voice ranging wildly in tone and affect. His speech is so fervent in its praise of his father that it starts to get uncomfortable to watch. Nothing this kid can say is going to make his dad love him. Biden passes that sad test: He very obviously loves his children. Near the White House there's a fireworks display that almost certainly violates both the Hatch Act and District of Columbia noise ordinances. In short, an evening with all the panache and grandeur I associate so closely with the work of former *Apprentice* co-producer Chuck LaBella.

———

North Korea's leader, Kim Jong Un, who dies about three or four times a year, may be dead again, according to a Reuters report.

One of the faces of evangelical Christianity, meanwhile, the preacher Jerry Falwell Jr., has resigned as president of Liberty University in the aftermath of sexually suggestive social media posts. "It's a relief," he says. "The quote that keeps going through my mind this morning is Martin Luther King Jr.: Free at last, free at last, thank God almighty I'm free at last." Sure, Jerry. I don't see how anyone could object to that comparison.

The pandemic is wearing on me, on everyone I suppose. There were a few weeks in there when life felt okay, but now I'm smoking too much pot, nearly every day, often just after lunch, and the frequency and amount are trending upward, and I'm simultaneously working too much and not enough, somehow. Same as everyone. Back in New York, Ben and Rachel and Nathan talk about the impending fall in sad tones, the colder weather, school at home again, in Nathan's case new infections, and I remember how hard quarantine must have been at the very beginning in most of the country, the dirty hardscrabble March snow, bitter temperatures to get to a grocery store full of steamy breath and anxious people sweating in overcoats.

The actor Chadwick Boseman died today, of an illness that he had disclosed to very few people, working right until the end. I haven't seen many of his movies, but *Black Panther* made him one of the most famous and beloved people in the world. As with so many celebrity deaths in the past few months, it becomes a chance on social media for people to express grief—their real grief for the actor, and all the unspent feelings they have, everything and everyone they miss.

August 30

In the face of consistently bad polling, Trump has been writing more explicitly anti-democratic tweets about the election recently. "With Universal Mail-In Voting (not Absentee Voting, which is good), 2020 will be the most INACCURATE & FRAUDULENT Election in history," runs one. "It will be a great embarrassment to the USA. Delay the Election until people can properly, securely and safely vote???"

His great sleight of hand is that he can write about any subject without changing register. Most of us at least simulate seriousness in serious moments, sadness in sad moments, and so forth, but he has no emotions that I can detect except self-love, self-pity, and rage. His admirers identify this as authenticity, which it is, of a kind. That's why all his lying is irrelevant to them: he's ultimately a straight talker, in the sense that he rarely pretends to care about things other than himself.

A conservative on Twitter says "a hurricane" is coming in November, and in the snarky replies, liberal twitter relives the immortal moment when Trump said of Hurricane Florence that it was "one of the wettest we've ever seen, from the standpoint of water." I'd forgotten that. Really everything at the moment is summed up by his follow-up comment on Florence's historic wetness: "Rarely have we had an experience like it, and it certainly is not good."

SEPTEMBER

September 2

Pictures all over social media of children returning to school—lots of them on laptops in kitchens, thumbs up and smiling. Some are back in class in person, masked but looking happy. Their pictures sweeten the day, the purity of their faces, the smiles, the tucked shirts. It seems like a cosmic act of grace that kids are largely impervious to covid. I know about seven unique adults, I think, looking at the pictures, but *every* child is unique. A lot of them aren't great, fine, but they're something different from what has ever been. Their faces have no experience in them yet; only astonishment, even the older ones, pretending, the teenagers. It's so easy to forget when you become an adult how galling and exciting it was to be five or fifteen. We are magic talking to itself, Anne Sexton said.

September 3

A bombshell today, judging by the media reaction: In 2018, Trump skipped a visit to an American military cemetery in France, after calling the dead soldiers there "losers" for getting killed.

In addition, at another military cemetery, he reportedly said to his chief of staff, John Kelly, a four-star general whose own son died fighting in Afghanistan, "I don't get it. What was in it for them?" Trump denies both stories, but aside from the word of numerous senior officers (and as people point out, say what you want about the army, it's not that easy to become a general), the claim has the undeniable ring of truth. It sounds like him.

This is a good final test for at least the pretext of supporting the troops, which with "lower taxes" has been the central identity of the Republican Party of at least the last 75 years. For decades they've saluted with serious faces—all the draft dodgers, Cheney, Trump, W. Bush—at the solemn laying of wreaths, and then explicitly claimed the moral high ground because of their supposed respect for veterans. The Fourth of July, right boys? The flag? Was any of that real? Two percent? Probably none of it was, I suppose. It's almost sad. The two genuine heroes the national parties offered us this century, John Kerry and John McCain, both got mocked for their service and then thumped in elections. Maybe no one wants to be reminded that most of us have nothing to do with the military—that its enlisted membership consists of the financially desperate and uncomfortably zealous. Maybe we elect draft dodgers because we're a nation of them.

September 4

Northeastern expels students who broke social distancing rules after just a few days of the semester, but keeps their tuition money. The basic psychological stupidity of sending college kids back to school and expecting them not to infect each other defies belief. Literally all people that age want to do is have sex and talk loudly in enclosed spaces.

Northeastern is a venial sinner. My own college, Yale, has $30 billion, enough for everyone to go there for free forever, and yet year by year, for the sake of acquiring more money, they get cozier with, just for example, a freeloader named Stephen Schwarzman, a staunch Trump ally who once compared Obama closing the carried interest tax loophole to the Nazis invading Poland. Yale can't stop in its rush to name things after him.

If I had to tell the story of late capitalism in America as briefly as possible, I would say the two great dreams of American life after World War II were owning a home and a college education for your children; and that as a pair, those hopes have been so ruthlessly commodified, collateralized, and mutilated by money that they have been our downfall. Student debt is an anchor around the ankles of tens of millions of people. As for owning a house—well, it seemed great but the casino stalled in 2008 and for a few years people were getting evicted and skipping meals and living in vans while the rich people got things up and running again; themselves sustaining no real losses, obviously. Just the people who bought the houses. Just the people who tried to go to college for long enough to die less soon and broke, knowing more. What a catastrophe.

September 5

A friend who works at a hospital in a chic part of town was at a meeting today with the administrators, in a boardroom named for a famous actor and his family. They took relentless questioning about why the hospital hadn't prepared better, protected their doctors and nurses better, offered more for overtime pay, etc., while the administrators, who do no clinical work at all, were making so many million dollars. At the very end, my friend's boss, one of the hospital's few real rainmakers among the practicing doctors, stood up and said, "I could have worked in finance, but I went into medicine. Now I feel as if there was never a difference." There was an instant standing ovation that kept going and going, as if all the working doctors had to make noise at once to get through to these old white men empaneled in front of them, words wouldn't work on such complacency, how fervently they agreed. The applause went on and on, and that was the end of the meeting.

The last product still not on shelves seems to be Lysol. Masks litter the street, and hand sanitizer is so ubiquitous that you have to be discriminating.

In this hard year, perhaps the hardest news yet—at a "Trump Boat Parade" in Texas, the Travis County Sheriff is responding to "many boats in distress" on Lake Travis. Our beautiful boaters! Meanwhile, a friend texts, "Donald Trump snorted some Adderall or Cocaine before his press conference, and some of it flew out of his nose." So a lot's happening.

September 9

"The President never downplayed the virus," according to press secretary Kayleigh McEnany. We have always been at war with Eastasia. Scott Atlas, a neuroradiologist, has become the White House's chief pandemic adviser—in Nathan's words, "a clown." He supported lifting restrictions and letting the new coronavirus spread so that America would develop herd immunity, which every non-partisan doctor agrees would mean the death of millions. Trump has stopped talking to Fauci. His followers, including DeSantis, are leaving their states open. A terrible toll is coming because of these people, not necessarily here, but in this country, and you can feel it in the public conversation about covid. Meanwhile a happy late summer in the states that will be hit hardest, Florida, Texas, provided you can keep your boat upright.

Bob Woodward has Trump on the record calling generals "pussies" in an interview, according to a CNN leak. The President himself describes how hard he's working: "I watched Fox Business. I watched Lou Dobbs last night. Sean Hannity last night. Tucker last night. Laura. I watched *Fox & Friends* in the morning." A bizarre and olympian schedule.

A hundred degrees again. I can't remember what rain is like. I'm certain it's wet. In terms of wetness, some of the wettest stuff we've seen. The pandemic has lasted a hundred years. I don't want to read any more or think any more. There hasn't been a single good show in ages that isn't about baking. I listen to *Tramp* by Sharon Van Etten, a long savage angry moan, and take walks later and later, until I see no one, I can take my mask down for once and let my breaths deepen.

September 11

"I've never seen a man that liked a mask more," Trump says about Biden, as if his life had heretofore been given over to the single-minded search for the living man who most loves masks. This was at a rally—the rallies are fully back, the most overtly fascist element of the Trump era. "Look, I'm all for it, but did you ever see a man that likes a mask as much as him? And then he makes a speech and he always has it, not always but a lot of time he has it hanging down because you know what, it gives him a feeling of security. If I were a psychiatrist—right?"

This is middling Trump. He can't get a hold of an insult on Biden, probably because he doesn't feel superior to him, the way he automatically does to any woman, Hispanic person, etc. He's punching at Biden more than dismissing him. That feels like a win for our side. It also feels like a huge loss to be thinking of that as a win, but, you know, may you live in interesting times.

September 14

Pandemic fatigue in the timeline. It's a low, unhappy moment for me too. My freer attitude toward smoking pot became too free for a while, then more disciplined, then freer again, and then the "freer" metric developed into an unhappy minimum. I don't like it but I can't cope otherwise.

All I really need to do is take three days off from smoking and clear my head, but I can't bring myself to do it. I have work, most of it past due. Yet there are days when I give up at eleven in the morning and stare at the sky listening to Pusha T and Maren Morris in alternation for hours, immured in my thoughts. I feel no guilt. Or, I didn't, at first, in June and July. In the past few weeks it's started to return. I feel alternately more connected to people and more alone than ever before. I walk around hacking every so often since I started smoking and it's humiliating, sometimes even coughing for longer than a minute, eyes watering and nose running. During a pandemic such as this one it's almost designed to alarm people, so I try to slink onto a side street when it starts if I'm in public.

I haven't been healthier in a long time, strangely. I didn't even buy a Peloton in March, though I've done some kind of exercise every day since quarantine started I think, out of boredom. There are coyotes running down Hillhurst every night, in ones and twos, scared of humans. I smoke while I walk and shout at them if the street's empty. It occurs to me late, out walking with a joint, greeting the fellow Allen Ginsberg—beautiful judgment-free patrons of 7-Eleven as I buy some hostess cupcakes and a bottle of water for my walk, how similar the hacking in my chest is to the feeling I had when I was throwing up so often, first when I was nine and ten, then in various relapses over the years. Last year, in a terrible desperate fifty-hour crash for my body, though I don't like to remember it. It's something you can't shake, throwing up that much. I hated it, and worse there were parts of it I loved, the relief after throwing up, your sternum and throat burning. I wonder what my body knows and wants that I don't. Perhaps that exact kind of wrong is where my chest feels comfortable and unharmable at last. But these strange sober lucidities fade by the next day.

The alibi for a Trump loss is being laid down like covering smoke in Vietnam. It's effectively certain that he'll lose the popular vote, probably by millions of votes, but nothing is considered more laughable on the right than the popular vote. They have narrow pathways planned to contest every state. I don't know anyone decent who's not worried about it to a point of almost maximal anxiety every day. Millions of worried, well-meaning posts waterfall down into our social media. Every Republican is suddenly a grad school–level expert in ballot irregularities, even though they don't seem to exist. "NORTH CAROLINA," blares the President of the United States, "to make sure your Ballot COUNTS, sign & send it in EARLY." He's vehemently against mail-in voting except in the states where it helps him.

On a local ABC broadcast, Shauna Kinville of St. George, Utah, "compared George Floyd's murder to her struggle wearing a mask." I watch the video. There's hate behind the words, nothing behind her eyes. It's like watching an interview with someone who just spat at Ruby Bridges, except in high definition. I don't know what brought Shauna Kinville to this pass in life. I went to St. George once for a wedding. It was impossibly beautiful. It looks exactly like Mars.

September 18

Ruth Bader Ginsburg died today. It's both a loss and a calamity. The next two months will be a fight to fill her seat, which the Republicans will win. Or Trump might wait until after the election to make the appointment, which would juice the country-club, tax-cut Republicans who might otherwise tolerate Biden. So we might have lost Ruth Bader Ginsburg and the election and the Court at one fell stroke. *Roe v. Wade*. Voting rights. LGBTQ rights. All of it, gone, possibly for good. Six to three. Even with Roberts breaking ranks occasionally for the sake of seemliness (its last adherent, he roams the halls of the Court looking at portraits of previous justices, apparently, a dry Nixon), 5–4. That's the ball game.

It was a great American life, a pioneer life, in that it involved calm, nerve, intelligence, and the grueling breaking of ground. She was one of nine women in a class of 560 at Harvard Law. She became the first tenured female law faculty member at Columbia. She became a judge. And then she became a justice on the Supreme Court. She sat there for decades, and she was, in my amateur opinion, the brightest person on the Court in my life. She was both emotionally imaginative and extremely clear as a writer, which is not a common combination. To call her a feminist icon is facile; every step she took from the age of 25 or so onward was more or less the first time a woman had taken that step. She was a feminist *leader*. Every year she served on the Court was a standing indictment to the generations of men who had kept women off of it. In that sense she was a moral leader too. She was brave in her illness. She died in her stirrups.

Republicans are reacting to the situation with maximum glee even though they refused to have a vote for Merrick Garland with nine *months* to go in Barack Obama's presidency, even though the President is a mentally ill proto-fascist. There are involved debates on Twitter about procedural tactics that could be used to stall the vote, but it's already over. We have a front-runner, Amy Coney Barrett, whose proxies are busily refuting the word that she was in a Catholic cult, where her rumored title in this outfit was, unsubtly, "handmaid." It's so hopeless. The jackboots will be on the streets soon. I look at people in their masks, wondering whom I could trust if society really broke apart, testing the flexibility of that knife. If only it could have been a day to feel shitty for the reason that we lost someone who mattered so much.

In a protracted, cagey military skirmish with a candle (a three-wicker) Emily picked up for me at Target, which in my view is INTENTIONALLY shaped so that the candle will run down quickly. I learned this the hard way on the first of the two candles she got me. In retaliation, I have painstakingly been integrating the old wax into the hot new wax around the flames of this candle. It takes about twenty minutes a day. The candle's visually a mess, but the space around the wicks remains clear and I would vouch for the soundness of its architecture with all my honor. "Those candles were eight dollars," says Em, which as I reply shows she doesn't get it at all. She gives me a hug and I go out to do battle. I smoke, put on Amy Winehouse, light the wicks, and go to work. The only way out is through.

September 19

And on the heels of the death of Ginsburg, the story that should be the defining news of the election—that should end a presidency— today.

In Georgia, a nurse named Dawn Wooten has stepped forward as a whistleblower: The ICE detention center in which she works, she says, has performed forced hysterectomies—sterilizations—on dozens of women. Per Priscilla Alvarez of CNN, Wooten describes detainees who "didn't fully understand" the medical procedures they underwent. "These immigrant women, I don't think they really, totally, all the way understand this is what's going to hap-pen depending on who explains it to them." The complaint is signed by Georgia Detention Watch, the Georgia Latino Alliance for Human Rights, and the South Georgia Immigrant Support Network. An Episcopal priest working for the last of the three organizations, a woman named Leeann Culbreath, said this news "affirmed her worst fears" about what had been happening. The women she was able to speak to had undergone gynecological procedures with "alarming frequency," she said, or in Wooten's plainer words: "Everybody's uterus cannot be that bad."

Does it need to be reiterated that the final solution started with sterilization? Even late into the war, there were only ("only") mobile killing vans and squads in Poland (never Germany), and the medical centers that began to perform first sterilizations, then euthanasia on a variety of people. Where it went from there—how quickly the Germans were prepared to scale their exterminations in 1943 and 1944—we all know. What's less commonly remembered is that, in the words of the historian Henry Friedlander, "The killers who learned their trade in the euthanasia killing centers of Brandenburg, Grafeneck, Hartheim, Sonnenstein, Bernburg, and Hadamar"—the six killing hospitals the Nazis operated—"also staffed the killing centers at Belzec, Sobibor, and Treblinka."

These were among the deadliest of the camps. If they are less remembered than Auschwitz, it is for one reason: they were worse. The Nazis sent 1.3 million people to Auschwitz, and of those something like 200,000 survived. They sent 600,000 people to Belzec, where the well-educated doctors who had been the regime's earliest practitioners of sterilization and then euthanasia worked. Of those 600,000, the number that survived was 7.

It's possible that in two years the doctors who were performing these hysterectomies could be doing the same work in camps. I sit up almost the whole night thinking about this story, unable to sleep. It's an awful haze of a night. It doesn't have to end like Nazism to be like Nazism. The heat is baked into everything I can see. I smoke and smoke and can't get high, only more confused feeling, until I'm hacking, coughing, not in touch with anything inside me that I recognize. No music sounds good. *My mind's not right,* as Robert Lowell abruptly breaks off, mid-poem. There's fear and stress in both attention and inattention to the news. I haven't answered a text in days, because it's so hard to imagine that anyone wants to hear a word from me. I owe everyone work but I don't give a shit if one of them gets it or if they decide never to talk to me again. I'm through with thinking about any of that. I haven't been anywhere in so long. I want to be back on the east coast. I wish I could be with my mom, my brother, my sisters, my friends. I wish I could see pine trees or a Duane Reade. I'm too far away from the real part of the world. It's been two years since I rode on Amtrak. Between school and having parents who were divorced and my grandmother in Washington D.C. I probably rode that northeast corridor train 500 times in my life, alone starting when I was eight, and now I'm sitting in a state called California that I don't even think I believe in. I resigned myself to death at the start of this, and five months is a long time to wonder if tomorrow you get the disease that kills you. I want it to be over. I want to stop being myself for ten minutes. You have to just keep being yourself in this pandemic because you never see anyone, nothing is inflecting you now—nothing but the internet, whose qualities we know.

It sickens me because I have had enough luck for twenty people's lifetimes and a woman is sitting in Irwin County, Georgia (always Georgia) and realizing, at 23, that she will never be able to have children. That happened in our name, with my money. We've been asleep for too long; we've been awake too long this year.

Long past midnight, I get up and stagger to walk up the street a little, to tire myself out, no mask on, too late to matter, the streetlights sallow and mean, the strange inner sense you get here of waterlessness, that people weren't meant to live in a desert. I decide to take a week off from smoking. We'll see if that plan survives the morning. In bed, exhausted, I read, "The allegations raised by Wooten are similar to those surfacing around the country"— *around the country*—"from immigrants held at ICE facilities, according to court documents, lawyers and other whistleblowers."

September 21

200,000 deaths in the U.S.

September 22

Some days you wake up feeling like a different person than the day before. Not very often for me—mostly it happens behind my back. But I woke today and found a note written to myself in the middle of the night after an unusually long walk. It said, in stoner scrawl: *Listened to Beatles for first time since age 10.* But I remembered already.

I have listened to the Beatles a lot since I was 10, probably more than any other band. At boarding school I used to drop my backpack on the floor of my room the second the school day was over, put "Abbey Road" on my CD player, then fall on top of my covers and go to sleep, as the wintry Massachusetts day faded in the empty trees clicking against each other outside. I wrote a book listening exclusively to "Revolver" and "Rubber Soul." I've seen Paul McCartney live twice. Once was in Grand Rapids, Michigan, where I drove four hours to see him by myself and feeling stupid the whole time I drove. Then, after about eight minutes into the concert discovered to my shock that my arms were raised and eyes were closed, and realized with a start that this must be how religious people feel. The other time was at Dodger Stadium right before covid, and Ringo came on at the end, and you could feel people's hearts bursting. (We sat near Pierce Brosnan. "He looked great," my mom reported to her friend Camilla.) The last two Beatles on stage, right in front of us; everyone understood it was sacred. Those boys were on the upper deck of those buses in Liverpool together fifty years ago.

But I know their songs by heart not because of any of that, which has been an afterthought, but because I listened to them so much when I was young that they became part of my deepest circuitry. I was a child of the humble cassette tape era, and I would say I flipped every one of their tapes a thousand times, some ten times as often as that. They'll be in a brain as long as there is my brain.

Yesterday it was a cool evening at last after this blazing month, and I was walking in Griffith Park. It was cloudy, the wind measuring everything, swaying the tennis nets. Discarded blue surgical masks fluttered around the street, and walking the empty hillside felt good, my body limbering and loosening.

Even before I got sick, my life was, like everyone's, complicated. The place in my house I was happiest when I was 7 and 8, my cassette tape days, was an armchair in the corner of our living room. No one passed through it unless they wanted to, because of the unusual configuration of the stairway and the kitchen, and I could be alone there. I'd set up camp in a big armchair my mom and I had had since our solo days, with a pretty pattern of lilies, and I'd stay there with my tape player and listen to the Beatles for hours while I read.

There are millions of bigger Beatles fans than I am, but I feel stubbornly certain in my heart that no one can love the Beatles *more* than I do. They were incredibly alive to me from the moment I heard them. My mom gave me their earliest tapes first, so over a few months (before I had learned all the songs) I grew up parallel to the band, listening to them change and grow, intent on the phone as my Uncle Will expatiated on the greatness of the three dozen songs the band wrote in India while also expressing some dubiousness about the maharishi himself . . . I accumulated secondhand stories—there was no internet—and the books I had about the Beatles and the songs into almost a private mass. It was a role that reading would later assume in my life for a long time.

Looking back, I think it was their joyfulness I found so mesmerizing. Even their saddest songs have an undercurrent of happiness. (You're never too far from a 7th chord with the Beatles.) I think it's because they were four working class kids whose crazy plan had actually *worked*. Especially in their early pictures they look dumbstruck to be so famous and gifted and rich and happy. It's there in their first perfect song, *Please Please Me*. A minute and a half in, John and Paul mess up the lyrics, then sort of cover it as they launch, with John laughing—but not to the listener, just caught up in the happiness of the playing with Paul, this other fucking *genius* he found in *Liverpool*—and then covering the laugh with the start of the chorus. (George and Ringo were geniuses, too. For that matter George Martin was a genius! Nothing in his career had prepared Martin to produce the music of a band like the Beatles, but as soon as they finished that take of *Please Please Me,* he said, with the good breeding and adventurousness of spirit that the handful of really good members of the British upper class do have, "Congratulations, gentlemen, you've just made your first number one record.")

That joy in life, that freedom, is what makes their music different from all other music. There's a reason it's the Beatles that Soviet kids were trading on the black market. In the middle of the century that gave us television and airplanes and the bomb, they were a distillate of all the fearful, wonderful, vertiginous freedom we suddenly had. "Even in the most sublimated work of art there is a hidden *it should be otherwise*," said Adorno. I've prodded the thought for soft spots, because aphorisms can be cheap, but I think it's brilliant and sad. I also think there's an exception: the Beatles. Even at their most grizzled, they were on a grand adventure. "When you get to the top there is nowhere to go but down," Larkin once said. "But the Beatles could not get down." None of them was even 30 when the band broke up.

As I walked back down through Griffith Park, I thought about the last few days, which I've spent writing a long descriptive passage of when I first got sick, the first time I've written about it. I thought of the way I should really have put it, which was to say that ultimately there's just one of those "two types of people things I believe," and it's that there are those who have been sick and those who haven't. Neither side is special, and by "sick" I don't mean any specific thing, I just mean there are people who have been at war with their bodies. Not pain, but a contraction of your whole existence into nothing except pain. Everyone has to answer for themselves whether they know what that feels like.

Then, while I was walking in long pissed-off strides, thinking about all the things I should have said, I realized that Spotify had tossed out a Beatles song at random. I kind of avoid them on Spotify—too tender, too real. It was *I'll Get You,* which is really a true 50/50 Paul and John song (in later years they usually wrote separately and then helped each other in the studio, despite maintaining the "Lennon-McCartney" credit) and as I listened, the song slipped behind my defenses so easily that it took me a moment to realize what was happening, that I was hearing it, first in indistinct glimmers, then completely, with the same ears as I had when I was little.

It sounds so slight the day afterward, like most such experiences. (It's all in William James.) But it wasn't. When the song ended I put on a random Beatles playlist, practically in a trance. I didn't even want to look at my phone for long enough to get distracted by a text, I didn't want to lose the feeling, and walked for hours through the night, listening. I put so much of myself inside those songs for safekeeping back then, I saw. I listened and if I was someone who could cry, which is an aspiration I have, I think I would have cried; at least, my face was warm, and I had a feeling of disbelief which is what I think crying must be like, when your inner life and the world are so different that you can only reconcile them by crying tears.

I listened to all of it. In my head I tracked the other songs in which various band members laugh (*I Should Have Known Better, It's Only Love, If I Fell,* etc.) and observed with intense satisfying scrutiny just how weird and sad and good John's parts of *A Day in the Life* are, so much of each that it's hard to believe it's a part of mainstream culture, until you remember that one of Paul's transcendent gifts is to lift the sensation of hopelessness from a song without rejecting its presence. I listened to *The End,* which is a completely perfect short song and really was—well, the end. The most emotional I got, to my embarrassment, was hearing them sing "Everybody had a hard year." I nodded, in the misting dark, as I headed home. In my defense it was very late by then. Everybody had a hard year.

Paul was the more preternatural of the two leaders in the group. He was like Ray Charles or Taylor Swift: no waiting period, straight to genius. They leaned on his sheer melodic brilliance occasionally (chords changes you wouldn't ever expect which not only suddenly seem reasonable, when you hear them, but indisputable) to carry their bad songs, all four of their bad songs. That was one thing I learned from the cassettes. Another was that John was more curious. Of all the Beatles, Paul's range of emotion might be the most limited; he can write well about euphoria, absurdity, sympathy, and love, but beyond those subjects (both in the Beatles and later) he generally gets either mawkish or banal. Still, if you had to select a pop star's gifts, those are good subjects, and John felt everything, moved between every emotion, so exhaustingly, that the band actually benefited from Paul's simple heart and genius for pop melody. John had musical genius too, but he was more like a writer—a loaded compliment.

As I arrived home, completely sober, completely exhausted all at once, and listening to *Hello, Goodbye,* I said hello to these four old friends of mine, and I very cautiously said hello to myself when I was eight, a person whose characteristics and dreams I think I have largely forgotten. But that was me, as definitely as I am myself now.

The Beatles' first single after their manager Brian Epstein died—he was there from the start and in an important way like their father, though he was a gay bachelor less than a decade older than they were—was *Hello, Goodbye.* (Its B-side was *I Am the Walrus,* which pissed Lennon off because he worked really hard on it.) It was with Epstein's death and *Hello, Goodbye* that the Beatles lost their initial illusions, and their music from then on became more interesting, and it also became inevitable that the band would end. (Typically brilliant of them to give us an album from their 25th year together first, without having to get there, which I think they knew they wouldn't: "Sgt. Pepper.")

Am I alone in having gone into different parts of myself during these last few months? I think no, it's the other way: that none of us had to think about ourselves and how we move through the days of our lives this deeply before. All of us went inside as certain people in March; it will be interesting to see who walks out. Whatever it was, the music as I walked felt like water flowing down dry riverbeds. It occurred to me that in this year of change, it might be possible for me to change. I went to bed at a rare peace with everything—or really, truthfully, with the deep past, I suppose, which has always been so present in my adult life, never cleansed of its meaning, rushing farther away and closer every minute.

September 23

Doctors tell us with a new finality in the past few weeks that a vaccine is the only way out of quarantine. It seems naive in retrospect that we thought anything else was possible. Since Trump started by downplaying the virus, that has been off the table. No water parks. No EDM concerts. No brie by the Seine or, no street food in Seoul.

Indeed, because half of the country won't take the precautions you need to do that stuff, there's going to be another surge here at any time—all the doctors seem sure of it on TV, Fauci, Nathan too, that flu season, and the reckless reopenings by red state governors like Greg Abbott of Texas and Ron DeSantis in Florida have set us up for hideous new rates of death, so high that we may potentially be back to the rationing of ICU beds and ventilators, even with all the preparation that has been done in hospitals since March, even with all we've learned.

As for promising news on the vaccine, Nathan's reluctant to get too excited about it "until the data has been unblinded." His brisk tone when he tells us this reminds me of the spring, when he was getting so busy in the covid ward, treating those very first cases in America. He has no illusions about the cascade of new ones that are coming. The steroid is good, but not that good.

September 24

Six months after Breonna Taylor was killed, a grand jury in Kentucky indicts one police officer on criminal charges. The three officers who entered her apartment, looking for her boyfriend, had a no-knock warrant, and it's proved difficult to figure out a way to charge them with a crime. They returned fire, possibly "with abandon," but they were there legally. People on Twitter are demanding their arrest, but it's unclear whether it will happen. In fact, as a friend says, it would be nice even to hear that these three particular cops *were* definitively scumbags and not just executing a warrant and panicked, which is what makes the whole thing so precisely Kafkaesque: everything within a generally well-respected system of government can simultaneously be legal and designed to result in the death of a person like Breonna Taylor. That is a version of hell.

Of all the faces that populated the signs at the Black Lives Matter protest, it's Breonna Taylor's that to me has the most hope and initiative and excitement in it. Of course, pictures don't mean anything, but you have to admit your true reactions at least to yourself, and I liked Breonna Taylor. I would have liked her. I don't know—I don't know her, it's ridiculous even to have an opinion. It's only possible to look at her pictures because she's not here and I am. I feel the weight of knowing that anybody could have predicted it, looking at the two of us.

September 26

Wulf sends around a stat: "A president who lost the popular vote by 3 million votes gets 3 Supreme Court picks, confirmed by a Republican Senate that represents 15 million less people than their

Democratic counterparts." Sometimes you need it rephrased to realize how far outside democracy we've strayed through the bent infinite maze of rules. Republicans lose the popular vote every single election and get to be president about half the time. Actual madness.

A new set of polls from Fox News shows Biden getting only stronger among likely voters:

Nevada: Biden 52%, Trump 41%
Ohio: Biden 50%, Trump 45%
Pennsylvania: Biden 51%, Trump 44%

Ohio is red enough that if Biden wins it, it will mean the night has gone so decisively against Trump and his GOP that the Democrats will probably have 55 senators, a broad mandate for a grand reformation of the nation based around climate change and economic equality. No one on the left is entertaining dream scenarios, though. Grim and ready, that more sums it up.

I keep thinking about Matteo's comment about the boomers, that they just won't get off the stage. Fifty years after Woodstock, we have to watch two old white men try to convince us to let them be President. About half the people in the Senate are over 70. Half! And all of them are white. California, the most populous state in the union, has effectively one senator, Kamala Harris, and she's currently running for vice president; Dianne Feinstein has "lost a step" mentally, per various gingerly-phrased reports coming out, and there are worries in the party that she won't be able to handle the Supreme Court hearings. And she's thinking about *running again*. She's 87 and has a net worth of $58.5 million. Jerry Nadler (it brings me no joy to report) almost certainly *shit his pants* during a live press conference and then shuffled very slowly but urgently left and out of picture. The most powerful Republican is a decaying corpse named Sheldon Adelson. Chuck Grassley, the Iowa senator who at 87 is *also* planning another run, is President Pro Tem, third in line of succession, and chairs the Senate Finance and Judiciary Committees, arguably the two most important jobs there. Anyway, seven days ago, he tweeted, "If u lost ur pet pidgin /it's dead in front yard my Iowa farm JUST DISCOVERED." Though that (pidgin!) doesn't hold a candle to Grassley's best tweet, from a few years ago: "I'm at the Jefferson Iowa DairyQueen doing 'you know what' !!!" Not sure what, no Chuck.

And so on. The word "gerontocracy" is coming into common Twitter usage. "I deserve the most mentally ill president imaginable," Dril tweets. "99 year old babbling doofus. Send us into the volcano sir."

We thought we'd moved on from that generation with Obama, but Trump is like their Balrog's whip from *The Lord of the Rings*—just as he's falling to his death, the monster lashing out one last time and catching Gandalf's ankle, dragging him, too, down into the abyss.

September 27

I get high for the first time in almost a week, and I feel angry again for having robbed myself of the relief of it for this long. There's a pandemic (I argue to I guess myself), and I already proved I can live without pasta, which I have been eating for decades practically without interruption, and I proved I can live without smoking, but who am I proving anything to anyway?

Opening TikTok, I see a video with tens of millions of views of a guy on a skateboard, listening to *Dreams* by Fleetwood Mac and drinking Ocean Spray cran-raspberry juice. He is taking it inspirationally easy.

I don't know where that night listening to the Beatles came from or went, and I don't think I'll ever be able to explain it in a way that doesn't make me sound weird. But I still wake up every day and feel instantly glad about it. Who says that change has to be one thing—one way. "At bottom," Rilke says, "the only courage that is demanded of us is to have courage for the most strange, the most singular, and the most inexplicable that we may encounter. That mankind has in this sense been cowardly has done life endless harm. The experiences that are called visions, the whole so-called spirit world, death, and all those things that are so closely akin to us have, by daily parrying, been so crowded out of life that the senses by which we could have grasped them have atrophied. To say nothing of God."

Text with my friend Sarah about *Tusk,* our tone indignant, as if Fleetwood Mac were a band from our corner bar and everyone else were just discovering them because of this viral TikTok. She does own a t-shirt that says "Silver Springs Should Have Been on *Rumors*" in small lettering. I think the key to Fleetwood Mac is that they started as a hard blues-rock band in England, then maintained the same rhythm section, but teamed up with these weird elfin Bay Area nymphs, Lindsey Buckingham and Stevie Nicks. (They only wanted Lindsey, but to his credit he wouldn't go without Stevie.) The magic of the band is in that fusion of blues and druggy folk. Nothing else is really like it. There's a reason that every five years a new generation rediscovers and falls in love with that band. Doggface, the cruiser on the skateboard sipping juice, becomes famous outside TikTok by noon.

September 28

After four years, Trump's taxes come out. There's so much fucking news! Jesus! He paid nothing—of course. Not of course; I was actually shocked, even if briefly, that it was actually *nothing,* that year after year he paid nothing in taxes. I assumed he would have all sorts of odd corporate hustles going, but I didn't expect him to have simply paid nothing. Though what has stuck in people's minds is not that, but that in two consecutive years, 2016 and 2017, he paid the same sum, $750. It's the more eldritch, nightmarish figure; for this buffoon who inherited tens of millions of dollars to have to actually sign a check for that laughable amount, sitting in his golden apartment, less in taxes than a teenager working in a fast food restaurant to save up for college pays—for that to happen, $750, it's too much.

$750, and no one on planet earth whines more about how badly he's treated.

September 29

The first presidential debate is tonight. The question is whether Biden should attack Trump on the taxes, which might backfire. When I canvassed door-to-door in the St. Louis suburbs for Claire McCaskill's (losing) Senate campaign to a freak named Josh Hawley in 2018, the neighborhoods I was in were working class, and the most stubbornly durable idea I encountered was that Trump, whatever his faults, was a great businessman. Even the Democrats

I talked to thought so. So theoretically Trump could benefit from the perception that he's a tax dodger ("a shark, but our shark") as various forty-person panels on CNN discuss at length.

I used to watch these debates reverently. Even the ones with Bush, who I hoped was an aberration. There's still an edge of credibility to the event. A lot of people watch the debates, and maybe something tonight *could* tilt ten thousand voters in Sheboygan. The Electoral College is that stupid. And everyone can see the path to Biden losing the night's news cycle—Trump could manage to hold himself together, Biden could make a blunder or misread a moment, giving birth to the dull cycle of memes we've tricked ourselves into thinking is funny; and then the election math will shift.

I think things are so tribal that the debates are unimportant, and we're passing the time until we see whose tribe is biggest. But I am also no one, and know nothing.

The honest truth few want to say is that Biden is maybe a tenth of a step slower than he was as Vice President. He's still sharp and impassioned, but many Democrats seem quietly at peace with the idea that he will be a steward for the party and the government itself, a figurehead (who also somehow radically changes government forever, primarily by delegating—it's complicated). That tenth of a step makes someone as aimlessly ruthless as Trump scary for Biden.

So many things are called Shakespearean, but Biden's story is the one that deserves the description to me. I was obsessed enough with Shakespeare to accidentally do a master's degree and part of a doctorate about him and his contemporaries, and he would have loved a figure like Biden, striving his whole life to be ruler and just failing, then, after two personal experiences that would have leveled other human beings into dust, forty years apart—the loss of his wife and baby daughter in a car accident in 1972, the death of his son Beau from cancer in 2015—an opportunity to try once more, and improbably it happened, he won. But he won as his powers are on the wane, and knows, I'm sure, that much of the hard fighting, which for so long he would have relished, is to be deferred to other people. Shakespeare's sense of irony is so *probable*. I go into the debate hoping Biden destroys Trump.

September 30

Reverberations from last night's debate run throughout the day. Mostly they emanate from a single moment, when the moderator, Fox News's Chris Wallace, asked Trump about right-wing violence. Specifically he asked about Kyle Rittenhouse, the pro-Trump teenager who shot two people in Kenosha, Wisconsin, last month.

Trump responded, "Almost everything I see is from the left wing," meaning the violence. After pushback from Wallace and Biden, he added, "I want to see peace, what do you want to call them. Give me a name."

Biden spoke up. "Proud Boys," he said, referring to the highly visible white supremacist gang, recently designated a terrorist group in Canada.

A strange contortion passed over Trump's face, a devil's calculation, and he said, holding his hands up to show that he was doing it, he was giving in, said, "Proud Boys, stand back," making good on his word to the two men in the debate hall with him. But then he added, "and stand by."

After the wrath he faced today for those three words, those

blood-curdling words, Trump claimed not to know who the Proud Boys are. A bald lie. He did the same thing when the popular former KKK leader David Duke endorsed him, even though the networks immediately dug up clips of him talking about Duke.

Trump's words are being received on the left and in the mainstream media as an ugly dog whistle at best and, toward my end of the echo chamber, as the recruitment of his own army of brownshirts. If this moment ends in mass death, something that works at my nerve endings for at least a few moments every day, this will be a moment to look back on. Mild calls for impeachment from a few really wild-eyed liberals on Twitter, e.g., myself, but no energy evident for it in the Democratic Party. I hope they're right and that "staying on message" means we win the election, though that involves hoping we have an election at all.

OCTOBER

October 1

Having finished the book I had due to my publisher, I'm in the time-consuming but gentle process of edits. The hardest part is over, the writing. It's good timing, because I am excited to devote the 34 days until the election to worrying. I catch up on the news neurotically often. Hope Hicks, one of Trump's advisers, has just tested positive for covid, setting off a frenzy of speculation that the President and his inner circle may have been exposed—he'll skate by, as usual—but even after that have time left over in the day to manage to watch a few movies and read books again for fun.

In the afternoons, if I've finished the number of pages I can revise in a day—about 20—I sit outside in the yard, and, after a few months without much time to spare to it, research my next book, the novel about the graduate student collecting sorrow songs in the south of the 1930s. Something widely known but more striking the more you read about the time after the Civil War is how far from inevitable the separation of the races through Jim Crow was. The public schools of New Orleans were fully integrated until 1877. As late as the same time in South Carolina, black people were served at bars and soda fountains and admitted to public lectures. Every session of the Virginia General Assembly from 1869 to 1891 had black members. Think about how long it took to win those rights back—most of a century, John Lewis's century.

As late as the 1890s, a southern liberal wrote Jonathan Swift-style satire of the idea that "black" and "white" people could ever be disentangled: separate transportation, separate bathrooms, separate restaurants, and so forth, the whole farce.

By 1900, almost every word of that had come true. In Louisiana, where just twenty years before schools had been integrated, there were eventually, thanks to Jim Crow, separate white and black bibles for witnesses in court to be sworn in on. That was how hysterically granular the attention to racism in this country was.

It was the outcome of a huge, highly romanticized white supremacist movement in the south, as confederate veterans died off and were eulogized, and more to the point as white and black workers began to compete for the same jobs. It was in the 1880s and 1890s that the backlash was most brutal. Lynching became not just a common occurrence but an epidemic.

At the same time, and for the same motives, there was a concerted, widespread effort to disenfranchise black voters, the aristocratic white southern class's less directly violent equivalent to lynching. That era was the height of the respectability of the study of eugenics, and the southern intelligentsia (ha) came to consider it both their scientific and moral duty not to let black people vote.

(The eugenics aspect of this argument wasn't the opinion of a small southern minority—in 1907, Indiana enacted America's first sterilization law, and by the 1930s about half the states had done the same. Sterilization of the handicapped was made compulsory in Virginia in 1924. The case drew enough objections that it reached the Supreme Court—which upheld the law. Among the groups being sterilized were epileptics, the "morally deranged," and the "feeble-minded" as judged by the risible IQ tests of the time. The sterilizations at the ICE detention centers are far from the start of America's history of legal medical violence.)

The men driving the disenfranchisement movement, both through violence and the pen, were unequivocally successful. In 1896, Louisiana had 130,334 registered black voters; eight years later, in 1904, there were 1,342. The same pattern occurred in states all over the south. Georgia was the home of the most vocally white supremacist press and the state that had by far the highest number of lynchings. Hoke Smith, the editor of the *Atlanta Journal* and one of the most influential men of the period, ran for governor and won specifically on a platform of disenfranchisement. The efforts to suppress black southerners got infamously shoddy legal scaffolding from *Plessy v. Ferguson,* the 1896 decision that enshrined the phrase "separate but equal"—the equal part was not enforced much—in the law. Though it was actually the coinage of a different, earlier Atlanta newspaperman, one of Hoke Smith's Georgia forebears in the press. Always Georgia.

Starting in 1900, after these more systematic efforts at oppression began to work, the number of lynchings in the south declined. (They didn't stop. During World War I, multiple black men were lynched while still in uniform.) It was because the lines had been drawn starkly: no voting, no property, no "sass," and it increased your chances of avoiding murder. Black people had no recourse from these choices. No protection arrived from the federal government in the north. The migration to St. Louis, Kansas City, and Chicago had not yet begun in earnest. Instead, black people were largely restricted to the backbreaking work of sharecropping and domestic service, which would remain almost their only channels for survival for generations. That's the period I want to write about.

What kills me is that the story isn't even *over*. What voting protections black people have now—minimal compared to those of whites—have been won back at the cost of literal blood, in many cases. Yet if we lose in November, it will probably be because a few thousand mostly black people in Philadelphia or Milwaukee have their ballots thrown out by a court of law. By Amy Coney Barrett, probably. In 2020.

Strangely, the less brutal stories I read are sometimes more persistent in my mind, perhaps because they hint at the millions of lives of which we have no record, because they merely began, passed, and ended in circumstances of misery, rather than in any notably violent way. For instance, black men in the south during that era could be sentenced at any excuse to hard labor. The resulting labor prisons were forebears of the modern gulag. The life expectancy even for healthy young men at the labor camps was no more than a few years, the conditions were so dire—besides which it was really a way to round up cheap labor, and sometimes on the most heartbreakingly flimsy pretenses: having a turkey, looking at a white woman, not removing a cap.

In every book I've read, music comes up again and again as a chief counterweight to the unbearable weight of these experiences. What W. E. B. Du Bois named "sorrow songs" date to long before emancipation, when music helped pass the work hours on the plantation and provided the entertainment most evenings. That song got some formal shape over the years from traveling black musicians. Eventually, in the early 1900s, W. C. Handy and Gertrude

Rainey made it onto the radio in Memphis and New Orleans, and a whole different story began. But a dense and fascinating study I'm reading by Samuel A. Floyd Jr. convincingly theorizes that much older African musical traditions were passed directly through slave culture to early New Orleans jazz and blues, and from there to the world—straight to Taylor Swift, Led Zeppelin, the Beatles, the real origin of this music lying in traditions several centuries old, from a different continent, brought here on slave ships. As I'm imagining my book, the most engrossing part of writing for me, I realize that the more I read about my subjects, the less claim I have to write about them. But a novel can be about that too.

October 2

Trump has covid! Chekhov's rustiest gun fires off. I'm thrilled. Fuck him. Let him take his turn at the roulette wheel. If he couldn't be bothered to reach out a few fingertips and save others from it . . . no, I don't know if I want him to die. But not knowing is itself a void. I once asked my friend Sasha, a Bosnian, whether it was wrong to feel indifferent if someone like Trump lives or dies, and he thought for a moment and said, "Remember, they want you dead."

The virus is everywhere in the White House. Other people who have it include the bird-brained and deeply malevolent Stephen Miller, author of Trump's most overtly racist policies, Chris Christie, who with the greatest detachment I can muster I would guess weighs 440 pounds, placing him outside the ideal male physical body type for surviving the coronavirus, Bill Stepien, the new, "savvy" campaign manager hired for this endless stretch run, Ronna McDaniel, head of the RNC (who in a Stalinesque detail stopped using her maiden name, "Romney," at Trump's explicit demand, because he hates her uncle Mitt Romney) . . . but it goes on, Thom Tillis, Ron Johnson (one of the very worst senators, a lizard-like Wisconsinite), Kellyanne Conway, the President of Notre Dame, who you'd have to hope will be out of his job by this time tomorrow for setting such a poor and childish and vain example.

A forensic photo layout in the *Times* shows all these schmoozing idiots talking to each other so closely you'd think it was a middle school slow dance. They were maskless, as barely needs to be said. No one I know would dream of talking to each other without masks on or six feet apart at a gathering of more than five, let alone dozens. Fitting that this grotesque carnival of contagion was the announcement party for the diabolical Amy Coney Barrett, who stands at the center of all the pictures like the blood celebrant of a Satanic ritual.

Even with these dozens of great leaders ill, the world is carrying on in its hobbling way. I learn from scanning the tabloid rack that Lenny Kravitz has "wowed" fans with his new quarantine body. Anne Hathaway will play the lead in an adaptation of *The Witches* by Roald Dahl. Pumpkin spice season is "here at last."

I love *The Witches,* but I like *Danny the Champion of the World* best, after that *Matilda*.

October 3

It's one thousand degrees today, which must be a record. Every time I'm outside for more than one minute I start to look and feel like a character in *Trainspotting*. As the nights get incrementally longer, though, the evenings do get sweet again; a slender line of pink to the west beneath a vaulted immense sky of pure evening blue, majestic over the quiet rooftops of people who are home, because the numbers are getting higher again.

One month until the election. No movement in the polls, even after Trump's Proud Boys comment. The electorate overall is burnt stiff with conviction, taut as a sail in a strong wind. As for Trump's covid, we all kind of wait, a little rudely, until the window opens when he's most vulnerable to death. Then we'll see. It's in a few days. But surely this personal irresponsibility, I think—his efforts to distance himself from covid—surely, when it comes time to the election—these pointless fantasies about the electorate take up so much of my time, the idea that we could sweep all these races, Susan Collins losing in Maine, Lindsey Graham in South Carolina, hell, even Amy McGrath beating Mitch McConnell in Kentucky, a national repudiation of the last four years, a license to give health care to everyone and start dealing with racial justice and climate change . . .

My favorite song by Kacey Musgraves is probably a concert version of *Follow Your Arrow* in Austin, Texas. It's already one of my favorite songs, but this version has an awkward and short introduction by Kacey, except that then a minute in she realizes the whole crowd actually knows every word of the song, *her* song. It was before she was as famous as she is now. Her band is sounding great, her voice is at its best, already, but after that it goes from good to great, she comes alive and the crowd sings back at her, a communal song suddenly, and Kacey drops in some quick between-lyric stage

talk that's funny and natural, and the whole band and Kacey herself and me (small me, alone in my headphones) are there at once.

October 5

On CNN, Dana Bash reports that Chris Christie has "checked
himself into the hospital as a precautionary measure." Sure, that's
how it works. You just check yourself right in. The entitlement
of these people! They'll be the first in line to get the vaccine if
we get one, too, after denying the virus was different from the
flu for a year, unnecessarily killing tens of thousands, hundreds
of thousands of people in the process. Meanwhile, a doctor identified as "Cmdr. Sean Conley" praises President Trump's health,
then gets flustered and mentions HIPAA when a reporter asks
if Trump's lungs have been damaged. So we know his lungs are
sponge cake. He might really die. It would be the longest suicide
I can remember.

Gigantic pink banner hanging off a bridge above the 10, slowing
down traffic: "JESUS IS COMING." Tmi.

October 7

As we continue the wait to see if Trump will die of covid, we
had tonight what I think will without any plausible foreseeable
challenger be remembered as the best Vice Presidential debate of
all time. I can't remember a word either candidate said, but that
quibble diminishes considerably in significance when you consider
that roughly an hour into the debate, a huge black fly landed on

the forward part of Vice President Mike Pence's snow-white and impenetrably hard hair (one of the countless martian-like glimpses from behind his broad attempt to be a casual-normal-guy) and then stayed there for not a period of a few seconds but for *minutes*. It was completely electric.

Pence "never reacted to the fly's appearance on the right side of his head," *The New York Times* reported in the aftermath of the remarkable events.

That Pence didn't notice the fly seems somehow morally indicative, like the fly actually landed not on his hair but on the insectile carapace of self-assurance in which he's encased. Pence is the kind of Christian so sanctimonious about his religion that it honestly never occurs to him that (for example) it might be wrong to lock up children and parents separately because they're seeking asylum in the United States of America, help from us. His side, the correct side, is fine with whatever issue they present him to talk about. He is so implacable because he thinks so little; he is Winston Smith after the conversion. The indelible picture I have in my mind is of him staring away from a pen full of people on his "inspection" of the facilities housing children separated from their parents, where 10-year-olds were left to care for infants and children slept in piles under those metallic space blankets. His square jaw, the studious way he was presenting a credible simulation of someone inspecting the migrants' abject living arrangements, while having as little awareness of the inner reality of the people themselves as he did of the fly.

Obviously more important things came up, namely the fly, but I do wish that moderator Susan Page of *USA Today* had asked Pence about Eric Trump's remark a few days ago that his father has "literally saved Christianity." Huge if true.

October 8

Back on Zeppelin, which means that even my improved state of mind since the end of summer—since the Beatles, really—is not impervious to the news. Covid, the election. I knew it was time to go heavier when Spotify started recommending Billy Joel to me. It's the second Zeppelin album, which has none of the soft acoustic bullshit on it. The soft acoustic bullshit that in different times, when just for instance there wasn't a FUCKING PANDEMIC, I loved. I can't take the Billy Joel reclamation. If you like him, fine, but I will not have it impressed upon me that I must regard him as like a Bob Dylan or an Aretha Franklin or whatever. I refuse. His second best song, *Vienna,* has an accordion solo in it. I have nothing bad to say about his best song, *The Longest Time.*

High and sitting outside in the golden light, I think, I could just never open my laptop again. Nothing would really happen. A month or two of worried and annoyed e-mails, maybe some calls, perhaps not even that much, and then silence, for as long as I wanted. Forever.

We're always talking on Slack, but tonight my four friends and I, all burned out again, convene on Zoom. It's cathartic to see them, exactly like the start of the pandemic again. Patients are asking Nathan for convalescent plasma, a dud therapeutic that the Trump administration hyped up, like hydroxychloroquine. Rachel and her family are in the process of moving from the city to the suburbs. Wulf is writing a pilot, he tells us, sitting back with a glass of red wine ("spicy pinot," his accustomed request at restaurants), just a few miles from me. I know some of this intel from hanging out here around the firepit last week, but I let him break the news. (Amazing friend.) The part of the Zoom I lean forward for, though, is to hear about my friends' kids, whom I was just getting to know before this started. Sometimes I pause and think about how they might remember this time, whether as a curious blink or as their defining childhood experience. Will these kids be writing novels about growing up in quarantine? I ask the Zoom. Of course, everyone says, and it only sinks in then, I think, how much we've all been through together—not how much we've been through, but how much we've been through together. It's not common to have a complete shared experience in a society.

Just before the end of the Zoom, we all let ourselves imagine for a minute that Trump loses.

October 14

After naming four of them during her confirmation hearing to replace Ruth Bader Ginsburg, Amy Coney Barrett can't recall the fifth of the freedoms protected in the First Amendment: the right to peacefully assemble in protest. Came up quite a lot in June, Amy, as it happens!

They may not even need her help to steal the election. According to Trump loyalist Corey Lewandowski, based on "grass-roots, law enforcement, + increased African-American support" it's become "mathematically impossible" for Trump to lose. This is the groundwork: Get law enforcement on their side, spread the idea that to lose is outside the realm of the possible, could only be a fiction perpetrated by Democrats, and hold power at all costs.

Lewandowski is big, dumb, and mean, one of those Carl Hiaasen figures surrounding Trump who has improbably made his way to the very center of our national power structure, rather than scamming drunk tourists into buying fake boat tours, which is about his level. He's the one who grabbed Michelle Fields, a reporter for the far-right outlet *Breitbart*, so hard that she had bruises on her arm. This is the level of person we have succumbed to, are assimilating. Lewandowski taught at Harvard as a fellow after he left the White House two years ago.

Senator Feinstein: "You don't have a magic formula for how you do it and handle all the children and your job and your work and your thought process, which is obviously excellent, do you?"

Amy Coney Barrett laughs: "It's improv."

Not sure how any of us are going to make it through the next twenty days.

October 15

I have six thousand important e-mails to write, so I'm listening to Maren Larae Morris on repeat in the yard and jotting down a list of which candidates up for election next month I'd most like to lose, if I had to rank them. I come up with:

1. Donald Trump (R).
2. Mitch McConnell (R-KY). Arguably should be number one. If he loses Trump will have lost, so he even has a tactical argument (as usual, fucker) for the top spot. But Trump has to go. He's too dangerous. The variance is too high. Mitch McConnell, by contrast, will fuck us from anywhere he is, in or out of office. Our best investigative political journalist, Jane Mayer, took her swing at him not long ago and came up

without much. He is the epitome of what I think Dungeons & Dragons, though I've never played it, probably means by "lawful evil."

3. John Cornyn (R-TX). Pale, doughy uncle in a cowboy hat. No conscience.

4. Lindsey Graham (R-SC). Committed, by enthusiastically supporting Amy Coney Barrett, the most open act of hypocrisy in the recent history of the Senate, a Katie Ledecky–like achievement (except the opposite, because bad). Specifically, it goes back to when Obama nominated Merrick Garland to the Supreme Court, many months farther away from the election than we are as of today, and Graham said: "I want you to use my words against me. If there's a Republican president in 2016 and a vacancy occurs in the last year of the first term, you can say Lindsey Graham said, 'Let's let the next president, whoever it might be, make that nomination.' And you could use my words against me and you'd be absolutely right." Everyone does, but he is of course still part of the leadership rushing the Coney Barrett vote to the floor, and women's health rights will be set back to the era of Jim Crow. It was that easy.

5. David Perdue (R-GA). Responsible for nearly one third of all trades made by members of the Senate in 2020. There are a hundred senators and one in three times one of them did an inside stock deal this year, it was this vampire David Perdue. Be gone.

6. Kelly Loeffler (R-GA). Richest member of the Senate; in itself disqualifying. With her husband, the head of the NYSE, "dumped millions of dollars in shares after she attended a closed door Senate briefing on the coronavirus in January," per NPR. Then in February accused Democrats of alarmism on Twitter

while actively trading further shares, according to *Vanity Fair*. Scum of the earth.

7. Kevin McCarthy (R-CA). Dumb, mean, biddable, with regrettably decent political instincts.

8. Madison Cawthorn (R-SC). The MAGA 25-year-old who posted a picture of himself at Hitler's "retreat" and wrote, on Instagram, "The vacation house of the Führer. Seeing the Eagles Nest has been on my bucket list for awhile [*sic*] and it did not disappoint." How long can someone who's 25 have dreamed of seeing Hitler's summer house? Unbelievably creepy.

9. Susan Collins (R-ME). I never want to have to think about her again.

10. Mike Pence (R). Last place in everything.

Conspiracies rife on the right that Trump is going to suspend the election, or that if he loses, the electors will be able to overturn the election results.

A *Vice* reporter publishes a piece about Trump's taxes which indicates that, as MSNBC's Kyle Griffin puts it, "Deutsche Bank and other lenders have forgiven about $287 million in debt that Trump failed to repay" since 2010. People get evicted over a few hundred dollars every day in this country. But that's mighty white of the boys at Deutsche Bank to let that $287 million fly for the President. Mighty white.

October 23

"Stop wiping down groceries and focus on bigger risks, say experts on coronavirus transmission." In March and April, this news would have been monumental. But most people stopped disinfecting their groceries months ago, including me. I have admiration for the ones who stuck it out. Seeing the alert reminds me that the artist Marina Abramović lived at home until she was 29 and her mother made her wash everything with detergent, "even bananas," which I had somehow forgotten until today, through this whole wearying pandemic.

When people talk about covid these days, the heaviness is right there in their tired faces and slow way of talking, mammals keeping back what little reserve they have. No doubt I'm the same. But by the end of the Zooms people are usually laughing, and a memory of the time before covid, the promise of a time after covid, is rekindled. The virus occupies the second part of our brains because of the election, but rarely has a second priority seemed so ridiculously defining of life. It's just that you stop thinking about your health problems when a rhino is chasing you. That's November 3rd. But we set a new record for cases today. The surge is coming. It's all starting over. Even the most optimistic doctors on TV say that with reinstated distancing rules and lockdowns we still won't be able to reverse the trajectory of new cases until the new year, and Nathan considers *them* foolish—says the worst month will be February, if anything. By then there will be so many deaths he thinks we'll consider the deadliest days of March and April our new, grim goal to get back down to.

October 26

Something that depresses the shit out of me in these last days before the election (not a difficult task) is the dozens of allegations of sexual assault against Trump. How did it slide down to *last* place of the things we care about. It makes me so angry. Maybe it wouldn't have meant anything, but I wish one senator had used their time with Amy Coney Barrett to read out loud E. Jean Carroll's precise, calm description in *New York* magazine of how Trump raped her—an account that hasn't changed in a single one of its details in 25 years, when she first told it to friends—then ask Coney Barrett how she could accept her nomination. I'm under no illusion that glassy-eyed Coney Barrett would do anything except deflect the question and probably impugn Carroll on the way, but if nothing else I would like that article to be spoken into the congressional record. I don't think anyone could actually read it and believe afterward that Donald Trump is innocent of the crime of rape. And in a week or so, we go to vote on whether he should be President again, and it's not even part of the discussion. That's how low we've fallen too.

Black people must "want to be successful" in order for his father-in-law's policies to help them, says Jared Kushner, per pool reports.

Kushner. I remember when one of his stated goals four years ago, besides the warm-up brief of bringing peace to Israel and Palestine, was to "modernize the government." I haven't heard much about it recently. Maybe they did it! I went to school with a lot of people like Jared. In his head, he thinks that if his father hadn't paid $2 million to get him into Harvard, he would have been able to do it on his own, despite his lack of any exceptional traits. That's the inner logic that allows him to live with himself, why he doesn't mind knowing nothing.

The ultimate example of this kind of person is someone whose reputation is slowly being laundered, George W. Bush. We deserve what happens to us if we let it happen. He was a stupid, incompetent, malicious president, and for pure arrogance I'm not sure even anyone from the Trump administration matches him: He knew nothing and thought he knew everything, had earned none of his outlandish privilege and thought himself better than everyone.

And then, in a lifetime of almost radical good luck, the greatest piece of all: being followed by an even *dumber* Republican, so that he looks statesmanlike in retrospect, at least at a casual glance. I'm sure he was nice to people around him in a way Trump wasn't, but young people have to know this: He was the antichrist. When he was governor of Texas, I remember, he made fun of a death row prisoner—a woman who had converted to Christianity, *his* fucking religion—after she asked for clemency. According to sources, he mimicked her, begging for a pardon in what apparently he considered a hilariously meek, "womanly" voice to his office buddies. Then he looked on with his little shit-eating smirk as the State of Texas killed her stone dead. George W. Bush is a force of evil in this world. Never let a single person you know forget it, or you have betrayed the dead. I really mean that. It isn't a joke. Millions of humans in Iraq *died* because George W. Bush's dad had the right lawyers in Florida in the fall of 2000. He incinerated the environment in what may have been our last years to save it, gave untold amounts of money to rich people from the pockets of the poor, and then retired into unalloyed comfort and a reputation of increasing decency. It's a sign of how mad our society has grown. He was the opposite of decent. He was hell. I swear it. Above all: It was under George W. Bush that the question of whether we, America, should *torture humans* was placed back into mainstream conversation. That was George W. Bush. He was disgusting. He is.

There were great people at the schools I went to. When I was new at boarding school, the same place where George W. Bush went, a grinning pale redheaded senior named Geordie and I once queued up the Rolling Stones song *Wild Horses* to start at the exact same time on two CD players across the hall. It was a chilly weekday afternoon, and when we finally got it right, and music flooded our snowbound dorm, he broke into a beatific smile. "This is the happiest I've been in a *while*," he said. It was the coolest I had in fact ever felt, though I did not say that. He got kicked out eventually (people got kicked out of our high school constantly) and the last time I saw him, moving out of his room, he half-implied he thought I might have had something to do with it. I didn't even know what had happened to him, or where he could have gotten that idea, unless someone was covering their own ass. I knew vaguely that it had to do with a girl named Sarah Carlyle, whose father owned "a thousand gas stations," according to campus lore. The closest I had ever been to her was to see her figure moving across the cold gray beautiful lawns, and for an hour afterward being in love. I wonder what sylvan beautiful person country estate she's spending her pandemic in, Sarah Carlyle. Anyway, Geordie, I speak this into the universe: I would have fuckin never.

October 27

Amy Coney Barrett confirmed.

The pictures of her swearing-in are from 9:17 at night. Very normal time to do it, not rushed or autocratic at all. Standing in the dark outdoors under stark white lights, she holds a hand up as Clarence Thomas presents a Bible to her. Trump looms over them with a particular orangeness under the blinding high school football field lights—occasionally his makeup-school skin tone, which we all accepted at some point, stands out with especially surreal vividness again. Throughout the swearing-in he has the alert and subtly anxious face of a dictator, controlling everything, understanding nothing. All three look ad hoc and furtive, vaguely conscious they're in the wrong, like people at a shotgun wedding.

How galling that two people named Brett and Amy are going to end the American experiment.

October 29

With less than a week to go, a whole crew of slackjawed former athletes (Brett Favre, Jack Nicklaus, "Jay Cutler") have endorsed Donald Trump. The rapper Lil Wayne too. The rollout is Trump's glitzy attempt at a closing, and who knows, it may work. Biden's team has a well-prepared closing pitch. Trump, by contrast, seems in his tweets to be frantically signaling to everyone out there that he needs help. He doesn't care whether it's from Russia or a hentai message board or a guy with an AR-15 who knows Nancy Pelosi's address—he just sees the polls and he wants it to stop. Every tweet is an incitement to violence, implicit or overt. Even his advisers are apparently asking him to step back, but he won't stop tweeting, each one more "destabilizing" than the last, "destabilizing" the preferred word among journalists. It's very hard to say in a reportorial tone "A crazy person's in charge of the country and we don't really know what's going to happen." So that's what "destabilizing" means.

With the election all but here, a frantic passivity overcomes everyone—constant motion, the race already run. A historic percentage of early votes have been cast. The fact is that if you believe in reality at all, the election is over and Biden has won. Even if the polling errors favor Trump more strongly than they did against Hillary, Biden will win easily. But there are obviously unknown factors too: voter suppression; the Supreme Court; not to mention the strange belief lingering from 2016 that there are huge undiscovered lands of American sentiment, that the right was nothing at all like we thought—could barely give a shit about John McCain being in the Hanoi Hilton for five years, or troops they're not related to, or . . . and it's not difficult to persuade yourself that Trump doesn't have a sort of transcendent parasympathetic understanding with those people. It gets back to the fact that while in all respects he is wrong, in every single one, in 2016 he was deeply right about the only thing that mattered: people's lives were fucked, and the Clinton presidency had a lot to do with it, and the well-earned sense of injustice in this country in some strange way exactly matched Trump's continual *rage,* his pure fury on his own behalf.

October 30

One of the best things Emily and I ever did was read *Remembrance of Things Past* together, over the course of a few years. We made plans to read *Middlemarch* together in March. She tried longer than I did, but gave up in numb old April. Maybe we should try again, though. I'm back in the mood for a long novel at last. And I've only read *Middlemarch* six thousand times or so. Besides which, I always seem to want to spend more time with Em, too, these days. I don't know if I expected that at the start of quarantine. I can't start to imagine what other relationships have been like this year.

Every minute of every day has become a matter of waiting. It's agony; we all want him to lose so badly, and there's simply no news. There may be promising signs in the early voting numbers in North Carolina, for instance, in Michigan for sure (we have to win Michigan), in Pennsylvania, and even in Georgia, a state where victory for the Democrats would mean a true realignment. But we're counselled to ignore them completely.

I have a secret faith in myself because I was the only person I knew in 2016 who was worried about Trump winning, as far as I can remember, and now I'm the only person who thinks Biden's definitely going to win. I don't even think it will be close. I remember very clearly when I thought Trump could win: there was an article in the *Times* a few weeks before the election about the Clinton campaign expanding to Texas, and I just spontaneously thought, oh, fuck, we're going to lose, aren't we. This time, it was covid. It was just so clear that Trump had met the one problem for which his cursed gifts had no real use. People were going to want someone who could get rid of covid. It was over then, I suddenly feel sure. I don't know if I let myself think it until today. Nor do I know if it's true.

NOVEMBER

November 3

As I go to sleep, it's late even for the west coast, where we started getting returns at four o'clock in the afternoon. There has yet to be a decisive call for either candidate, but after agonizing, centuries-long hours of watching the returns, things look promising for Biden—more than promising, in fact, because I haven't seen a single convincing counterargument to the math that says he will win Pennsylvania as the city vote is counted, and winning that state would end the election. He carried Arizona, as we hoped and cautiously expected, and the former astronaut Mark Kelly picked up a Senate seat there. For that matter Biden could even win Georgia, though we won't know for days. Not Florida (of course) but Georgia. That's a bright spot and probably a credit to Stacey Abrams, as usual.

The big news is good, then; the rest, aside from Kelly, a disaster. A wipeout. We lost the Senate—or at least are very unlikely to win it, with a couple runoffs still to come but *down* 50–48, when we'd hoped to land at 52–48, perhaps even 53–47, to our side. We lost ground in the House, though thankfully we held the majority.

But more than anything, we know that a huge tsunami wave of people woke up this morning and went out to vote for Donald Trump with their whole hearts. Biden may end up winning the national vote by five million votes, but something like 70 million people voted for Donald Trump. It was never a fluke that he won. And the aftermath of that affirmation for him is a scary thing to contemplate.

But who cares when there's this tremulous feeling among us all about the hell of Trump: What if it really is over? What if it really could end?

November 7

The major outlets have now all called the election for Biden, even Fox. He's accepting congratulatory calls from foreign leaders, and his transition team is beginning to plan appointments and hirings. On January 20, pending a peaceful transfer of power, which I personally don't think is in doubt, though others are fretting (to me it's simple: the generals seem to fucking loathe Trump), it will be over. Donald Trump will be gone. It would be so exciting if we didn't have to wait out these intervening months. It's so exciting anyway.

Trump hasn't conceded. Rudy Giuliani, once "America's Mayor" for a benighted period of about five years, seems to be taking the legal helm in Trump's lavish claims about fraud, which are pure nonsense, unconnected to reality. But the belief in these charges of fraudulence among Trump's really zealous supporters is absolute. They find videos of poll workers fixing equipment, which go viral, only to be proven innocent—by which time there are two more grainy videos, ten more rumors about Democrats stuffing ballot boxes.

Unfortunately for the "optics" of their side in this fight, Giuliani or his people today accidentally booked Four Seasons Total Landscaping in Philadelphia instead of the Four Seasons hotel downtown, which was where Trump had earlier directed his supporters in a tweet. Either that or that hotel realized they didn't want Donald Trump and Rudy Giuliani there. The press conference went bravely on, Rudy talking in front of what turned out to be a low-slung anonymous brick building flanked by a crematorium and a sex shop.

After four years of lifestyle stories about him driving me up the wall, I kind of want to know what Trump is thinking and doing in these moments of loss. Perhaps contemplating the two sides of Henry's ruminative plaint in *Henry V:* "What infinite heart's-ease / must kings neglect that private men enjoy!" So many words of Shakespeare's have entered English already, but I think we should make room for "heart's-ease." I would love to have some infinite heartsease. I don't need any more infinite jests. It was a long four years.

November 9

Earth-shattering news, the news: The Pfizer vaccine works in humans and should be easily approved for use. Holy shit. It might start being distributed as soon as *December,* as we hear from Nathan, and then shortly thereafter in the media. There's wonder in people's eyes when I go for a walk this afternoon, in their nods, their glimpses at each other. I feel shaken with hope; it's like caffeine, it turns racy very fast, I'm not ready. I can practically reach out my fingers and touch December, which is funny, because I remember

March, when three weeks inside seemed like an eternity. Now it's a blink. What an overwhelming six days, to defeat Trump and to cash in all of our coins of hope from the tin can bank and get the news of a *working vaccine* . . . it's a numb, exhilarated tone online—the idea of an ending too much to comprehend. Not a partial ending, not a reopening with risks, not this unending vigilance, but a true ending.

The good news is discordant: In L.A., the largest number of covid cases today in three months, a flashing red alarm that the "surge" could become permanent. But we have a vaccine. We can sit in our living rooms and wait this out at last with a real ending in sight, not a vague one. None of us on Slack can quite believe it, not even Nathan. In fact it's hard to conceive of life *after* this at the moment—walking maskless into a café full of people, the idea is so remote now, even the idea of getting a coffee at the drive-through without a mask is horrifying. There's no way. Is there? The prediction on med twitter is that people with my specific condition may be in the third or fourth group to be vaccinated, after medical workers and senior citizens. But it will be up to the states how they're distributed.

More than a few people have said that between Trump and covid it's like a war has ended this week. It has been, in a sense, more of a "war" as experienced by most Americans than anything that's happened since Vietnam. It's always a small number of people who fight a war for your country, in this case mostly medical workers, frontline workers, the minimum wage class; the majority of people's job in a war is to sit at home and save tin and string and worry, and in fact that's exactly what we did. So what is it like when a war ends? In this case it's like a slow untwisting, breath by breath, of some core inner nerve that has been corkscrewed to its highest intensity for four years. We can still be mad, but we don't have to be only mad.

The days are finally cooling off, and we're headed toward my favorite season in Los Angeles, winter, when there's a mix of rain and sun, mild days and chillier ones, the air clearer, and the mountains in the distance white and gray with snow again. It's a whippy windy night, the sky blank, a huge upward gray-white veer, like sadness. I sit out in the yard in a sweater and headphones and smoke, feeling the cool saline air from the Pacific as it blows through the trees. I have come to appreciate what it means to be at home more during this, instead of turning against it, in the end. What does home mean? "No need to hurry," as Virginia Woolf said. "No need to sparkle. No need to be anybody but oneself." The vaccine is 90% effective. They would have been pleased with 60%, apparently. It seems like a miracle.

November 10

In the aftermath of the election, there's increasing chatter on both sides that Trump will somehow seize office permanently before power changes hands. The slow purge of even Fox News from purist right-wing circles is accelerating. Trump fans prefer OAN and Newsmax, fly-by-night operations growing at gold rush speed, which sell unhinged whiteboard theories about how the election was stolen from Trump. It doesn't help that elected Republicans won't say that Biden won the election. At this very last test they fail once again to choose their country over the President. "What's the downside for humoring him?" a GOP source says to *The Washington Post,* anonymously.

I actually don't think that Trump and Giuliani have it in them to hold on to power, they're buffoons. They'll file a bunch of lawsuits and do press and Trump will stomp off and golf around Christmas and never come back. But in October, the FBI arrested thirteen people for plotting to kidnap Gretchen Whitmer, the governor of Michigan, and it's been in my thoughts. For some reason it was almost *light* news at the time, I think because their plans were so dumb, because they got caught, and because someone called them "Vanilla ISIS." But now the community of #MAGA diehards that produces these extremists is cut off further still, has fled Fox for having any facts whatsoever, can apparently only watch news that contains no facts. So what's worrying isn't quite Trump, whom the military and Microsoft will see out, if it really comes down to it, but his hold on his followers, particularly the idea of them setting their sights on visible Democrats, and a cycle like the deaths of the heroes on the left in the '60s beginning again. There's already an uptick in angry rhetoric targeted at Ilhan Omar, a Muslim member of Congress.

The person who could end this is Mitch McConnell, who knows perfectly well that Biden won the election. "President Trump is 100 percent within his rights to look into allegations of irregularities," McConnell says, however.

On *Pod Save America,* former Obama speechwriter Jon Favreau states baldly that our only recourse, if the election is stolen, will be to take to the streets in protest. I don't listen to the podcast regularly, but they've done a good deed since Trump was elected. They became the clearinghouse for the strategies and talking points that the people who saw Trump as an existential threat could rely on for regular, dependable information, both about what Trump was doing and what we could do in response.

And here at the last, Favreau's right: no point in saying anything but that if the election is stolen by the width of Brett Kavanaugh's fat fingers, our recourse is protest, and after that civil disobedience. In a way this is the darkest moment of all, this podcast, an institutionalist avatar of the left, stating that norms and laws may not, in the end, be enough. It was the risk we all realized last election night. If we make it through this, it's this I'll think of and remember: That was how close we came.

November 11

Early morning, and the wine bottles of Los Feliz rattle into the patient recycling truck.

Facebook reminds me that it's the one year anniversary of Trump's former press secretary Sean Spicer being eliminated from *Dancing with the Stars*. A hard first blow for conservatism at the time. Spicer was Trump's first press secretary, most famous for starting his first press conference by insisting with fiery passion that Trump's inauguration crowd was the biggest ever. It was an assertion so self-evidently untrue—one look at a picture of Obama's or Reagan's inauguration showed as much—that the press barely disputed it, because they were busy laughing at him on Twitter. They were right, it was funny, but they only won the battle; they've been fighting a rearguard war ever since against lies exactly as insane but much more important. Including this pretty big one now, about how many people were in a crowd for Trump again, how it's more than they're saying. As at the beginning, so at the end, or whatever it says on *Star Trek*.

Some people think that was the first lie of the Trump administration, but it wasn't. Trump said directly after his inaugural that the rain had stopped just for him, even though it hadn't, and everyone in the room knew it. That was the first lie.

I watch the clip again, in which Spicer, with a historically bad dancing score for the show, stands rueful and panting, but looking, despite being the subject of the judges' unadulterated moral and artistic scorn, utterly ecstatic to be there. He's wearing a ruffled neon-lime shirt with a plunging neckline, diamanté shoes, and skintight white pants. Every empire is humbled differently.

November 12

The election and covid are over without being over, and as the days pass I find myself in a very inside feeling mood, remote from life, hopeful but watchful, guarded. Borges thought the only metaphors that mattered were the oldest ones (life and river, death and night) to which I would add light at the end of the tunnel. There's light at the end of the tunnel. But we're still in the tunnel. I listen to *folklore* by Taylor Swift on repeat and do a 550-piece puzzle of London. Emily got me a dinky but lovable little firepit at the start of covid, and on these chilly nights I love to sit and watch the fire crackle, sipping iced coffee left over from the afternoon, listening and thinking, as if I were absorbed in something much more serious than simply, for the first time since Trump was elected, not thinking at all.

The covid spike has begun in earnest. There were more than 2,000 deaths in the United States today. That number was about 900 a month ago, and the curve is headed straight up and right.

In May and June, when we finally (what then seemed like

"finally") started hanging out in person again, outside and distanced, still novel then—cold, now, most places—there were 500 or 600 deaths a day. It seemed like a huge number at the time. We thought perhaps we could keep it there, at least. Clearly not. But the 2,000 now feels like fewer than the 500 then, which is how the numbers anesthetize you. As for Trump, he hasn't had anything on his schedule since the election. What minor pressure there was on him to assemble scraps of good news on the virus—at least to maintain the status quo—is gone. We just have to hope.

The lightning bolt quality of the virus is more sharply terrifying as the stories multiply in number and as the press has gotten excellent at reporting them. It can come for anyone, any age, any time, not just the old and the infirm. Marathoners in their twenties are dying from it, diabetics in their nineties surviving. It reminds me of the story Camus tells in passing about the medieval village where the one survivor of the black plague was the bearer of the corpses. Only the gods know how it ends, as the Greeks said.

Irony is built into all plagues—built into death, perhaps, because irony is based on partial knowledge, and death is the thing we do not know. The most famous story is of course about the man who saw Death in the market: Death looked him in the face, astonished, and the man whirled away at the awful look and rode as hard as he could for three days and three nights, to hide in the remote town of Samarra. The first person he met was Death. "I was amazed to see you," Death tells the man before taking his life. "I knew we were to meet here in three days, but never imagined you could be here in time." There's a version of the same fable in Orwell, who mentions a woman in the papers who moved from London to one of the uninhabited islands in the Hebrides to avoid air raids, and then became the first air casualty of the war when the Royal Air Force dropped a bomb on her island during testing.

November 17

Mood suddenly just slightly hopeful about the runoff elections in Georgia. If Democrats win both of them, the Senate will be tied, 50–50, and Kamala Harris will be the tiebreaking vote.

The Republicans have ruled as a minority in this country for the last thirty years, winning exactly one presidential election by the popular vote in that time and acting every time they have power, however ersatz, as if they had just swept every state except Alaska. If we win, it's our turn to do that, and not least because more people *want Democratic policies,* guaranteed health care, higher taxes on the rich, and so forth, a factor that has largely been eliminated from public thinking on politics in America during my adult life, but seems due a comeback.

If we have a swing at bringing one issue into mainstream debate, I would like us to pick reparations.

I remember the night I realized I supported the idea, which was in 2007. I was watching a Democratic debate, and the moderator asked Dennis Kucinich, the sole progressive candidate on the stage, an elfin Clevelander with a statuesque red-haired wife, if he favored the idea. Kucinich replied, not very eloquently, that he did. At the time I was intensely interested in politics—in fact, I worked on Howard Dean's campaign during the 2004 election cycle, and later John Kerry's, which is how they both became President—and I remember being surprised at Kucinich giving what seemed like such an "unpopular" answer, per conventional wisdom. And indeed, as I recall they tossed the question to the closest thing to a progressive in the rest of the field, John Edwards, a good-looking guy who has become a weird sad joke but at the time was a front-runner, having been Kerry's running mate. And he said something like "I think it's safe to say not many of us would go as far as our friend from Ohio," and the whole stage *laughed*. At least that's my memory of it. And I remember thinking, as Kucinich stood and waited out the laughter, but wait, he's *right*. I didn't exactly become a Dennis Kucinich fan that night as much as I turned on the whole apparatus. The argument seems so straightforward to me. Black people have far, far less money than white people in this country. Either that's because owing to slavery and racism in every generation they start with less resources of literally all kinds (this is the answer) or because they're stupid and lazy (not the answer, unless you're Jared Kushner or Fred Trump). You can debate the form of reparations, but to me the answer you pick from those two choices ends the debate about whether we should have them. We should. Are we going to keep acting like this country never had slavery? But I am dewy-eyed, I know. We'll be lucky if they let us keep Obamacare.

A zombie phrase reappears: it's time for us to *flatten the curve,* as we all walk back millions abreast in the direction of death. The Zooms are back. It's even raining again. It feels so much like March, April. How much damage can Trump do in the next sixty days? We underestimated him before. We go into the cold of the late fall as a country without any plan to fight covid and legitimate doubts about whether we can count on a peaceful transfer of power in the new year.

DECEMBER

December 14

300,000 deaths in the U.S.

December 25

On Christmas, I think about what I would do if I had been absolutely alone this entire time. Christmas matters, sadly, at least it has never stopped mattering to me. The war on Christmas failed. The movies matter, the stories, the image of a peaceful snowfall and a family around a tree, they still shine to us. No one signed up to care about this shit, but here we are. And if I were alone today, on Christmas, I think I would be hurting. That's the truth, though I wouldn't utter it to a friend in that position. Maybe I wouldn't be—maybe I would be just fine, pottering around, nothing but my own problems underfoot. But now, after Christmas with Emily for a surprising number of years in a row all at once, the familiar ornaments we bought together in Stockholm and St. Louis going up on our tree, playing hands of Monopoly Deal, drinking eggnog, I feel a sorrow for the people who have been alone all this time and are alone again today. It's a useless sympathy, but it's there. Sometimes I think about how the right makes fun of the term "safe space," and I think, well, but everyone does need a safe space. The world hurts.

Rachel, Ben, Nathan, Wulf and I always get together in New York at this time of year, but not in 2020 obviously. Covid is absolutely everywhere, the national maps of it flaming red. Unless you're a hermit, you know someone who has had it during this surge. The question is more, how many people, whether they've come all the way back yet or are "long haulers," and whether they lived. On the deadliest day in the spring, 2,116 people died of the virus; the daily number of deaths has been higher than that now for weeks in a row.

I knew deaths must mean millions of people overall have had it, but when I ask Nathan on Slack I'm still surprised to hear him say that they think somewhere between 80 and 100 million people in America have had Covid-19 (named for the year of its discovery, people sometimes remember to each other in conversation, 2019). That's one of every three people in America. I remember thinking in March that 10,000 people might die here, then revising the number up: maybe 25,000 even. Maybe 50,000. And then I stopped. I don't even feel stupid. No one was ready for this year, and if I was less ready than everyone else to understand it, so be it. I think if you had told any reasonable person in March that we were edging toward 400,000 deaths, they would have been shocked. It wasn't one of the guesses you even heard, anything that high. Also I do feel a little stupid.

In some incredible personal news, Spotify has told me that I am among the top 1% of all Taylor Swift listeners on the app for

2020. By chance, or more accurately by overwhelming statistical probability, I'm listening a lot to Taylor at the moment—but an album I haven't listened to in ages, in infinity, in fact, since it's the last album (*Lover*) I was into before coronavirus, during the brilliantly colorful superbloom days we had last January. So while the album is barely a year old it somehow is the oldest record I know—belongs to an unfallen world, when I walked without a mask, passed right by people on the sidewalks with a smile.

Researching my new book takes me further and further into the history of blues and pop music, i.e., Taylor Swift's direct ancestry. Most of the performers are black, but the whole south is and has been poor for a long, long time, and some of those poor people were white. Taylor Swift comes out of both those musical traditions, including the tradition of John Prine and the Carter Family and Dock Boggs and Jimmie Rodgers. Country was a music of desperation and yearning, too. If you listen to those singers, and residues of it are left even in these later Taylor Swift albums, you hear it. The tragedy—the great con—was that so many of the people from that part of the south were raised to think that they had more in common with rich white people than poor black ones. In her unforgettable poem "A Wife Explains Why She Likes Country," Barbara Ras riffs on her title kind of lightly at first; it's because she likes rodeos more than golf, because sometimes whiskey tastes better than wine, because in country you can smoke forever and it'll never kill you. Then she gets more serious. *Because I'm lost deep within myself,* she writes, *and the sad songs call me out.* It's a feeling I've learned well since March. *Because even you with your superior aesthetic cried / when Tammy Wynette died,* she goes on. And then she finishes so quickly and perfectly that it knocked the wind out of me the first time I read the line: *Because my people / come from dirt.*

—————

It's Kacey Musgraves who's my favorite. Kacey, if you're reading this, which you're not, you are my favorite. We should get high and talk about stuff.

December 28

Back yet again to smoking too much. I'll stop again after the inauguration, or at least, when I finish the book I'm working on. To compensate for the uptick, I walk farther and do yoga or run every day regardless of whether I want to, like a real adult, but I still feel a sadness or shame at needing a drug at all. And the sordidness of it—the smoke-singed fingers, the hacking midday cough—feels internally like an affront to anyone who ever loved me, or does now. It's been a lot: the pandemic, the touch-and-go safety of the protests, the election, the ongoing attempted verbal coup. The last four years have been so long; even until now I've barely dared to look at the election straight on, as if it were an eclipse. We won though. I'm almost sure of it.

2021

JANUARY

January 1

A new year. 2021. Everyone will have to roll it around in their mouth for a week or two. To me it sounds like the far future.

For a while I studied the medieval period in a haphazard way. I was tired of walking through churches and acting appreciative of an ancient stained glass window of unicorns bowing to Jesus holding a chalice, or whatever, without having the faintest idea what it meant. Even though I liked the churches.

One thing I learned was that the year 1000 is the subject of a lot of discussion in medieval scholarship, in part because the decades leading up to it were plagued by fear and chaos. There were millenarian cults, predictions of the apocalypse, and violence throughout Europe. Indeed it was such a bad period that in the century that followed, the monastic system spread and expanded massively— a series of enclosed, well-defended, self-sufficient, and above all safe spaces. They were non-worlds, monasteries—refusals. There were no women allowed, nor even visitors in general at some. (Women who were alarmed about the year 1000 had to fend for themselves, from what I can gather; the usual story.) Their great contribution to the culture was copying manuscripts and making beer. Seems light.

My own suspicion is that something similar happened around the year 1500. It was in 1500 exactly that Dürer painted the self-portrait that permanently reoriented art, and in their primes, a country away, were Michelangelo and Leonardo da Vinci; in 1517, Martin Luther (the namesake of Martin Luther King Sr.) posted his theses in Wittenberg. It seems uninteresting now, but it was like a *bomb,* as seismic culturally as Darwin or the internet, an event that changed the life of every single person in Europe, and which is the reason England and thus America exist in their present form. It was in 1519 that Magellan began his voyage around the world. And in 1526 Tyndale's bible appeared—the first translation of the bible from Latin and Hebrew into English, a deed for which Tyndale was eventually strangled, and afterward his body burned. But too late: His bible was so popular that less than a century later, King James I ordered a team of scholars to produce an English version in his own name, which became the King James Bible. In other words, 1500, by chance or not, was the center of the period that finally loosened the choke hold of Christian doctrine on the culture of Europe; just enough for the human gasp of the Renaissance to emerge.

What I wonder is how much perhaps we cared about the year 2000, maybe to some degree without even knowing it. We are superstitious, weird, worried, pattern-seeking creatures. Y2K was a little aperitif, and since then it has been more or less chaos in America, chaos without even starting in on the moral judgment attached to it: September 11th, two unending virtueless wars, the first black president, the legalization of gay marriage, the fucking coronavirus. Of course, it could have nothing to do with the year at all. A lot of those changes around 1500 can be attributed to the printing press. Then again, the printing press appeared on the eve of the year 1500. What appeared on the eve of the year 2000? The internet, by some distance the closest invention since Gutenberg to the press.

Maybe in this sense 2020 was the year we collectively realized it was the year 2000. We made it. We made it past the scary number. And one of the main convictions of last century, as Saul Bellow observed, that mankind had reached a terminal point, may at last have broken. Whatever comes next, that exact sense of twilight and stagnation is gone, that faded hope lingering from nuclear America into the age of 9/11. The neoliberal dam couldn't hold any more. The virus, Black Lives Matter, Trump, they were coterminal culminations of a system that could not survive its own internal fragilities.

We changed since the start of last year, and we left flesh and tendon behind to do it. No one even knows if things are better yet, just that they're different. Hundreds of thousands of people here died, some percentage of them unnecessarily. George Floyd was murdered. We saw the tenacity of the marches and the tenacity of the voters who wanted Donald Trump gone. Abroad, Navalny and the ongoing and courageous protests in Russia, the unfathomably large farm protests in India. If last century was the end of the world, maybe this one is a beginning. It's like how they say Aslan is on the move in *The Lion, the Witch, and the Wardrobe*. What if people could live fairly, you dare to think. What if immigrants got a handshake and a fair shot. What if we all had health care and food. What if *Hamilton* took over the world a few years ago because we were near the start of a revolution.

The educated medieval mind had an obsessive respect for symmetry. Even demons were often depicted in the churches, because their existence was thought to logically imply the existence of angels. Educated men believed that every animal on earth had an exact analogue in the sea, proof of God's divine construction of the world, and took specimens from fishermen and attempted to compare them to foxes, otters, and so forth. Much of the strangeness of their art derives from this symmetry, at least as I understand it. It makes a certain sense. They didn't know what Galileo was going to discover; the best science by their lights suggested that our planet was the center point of the universe, which immediately implies symmetry. So they built their churches around it, the most intricate symbolic codes, expressed in heraldry, art, and architecture.

After I learned all of this, and a great deal else I've forgotten, I visited a church once, and for a moment I stood there and I really saw it—how beautiful the symmetry and the ornate symbolism must have been to the medieval eyes, how beautiful and complete a dream it made. I saw in that moment the relief and wholeness of belief. I wonder if it's our turn, as a species, to turn toward some new belief now. Each other, ideally—our planet. Maybe that's high-minded nonsense. I personally feel that hieratic hush most often in nature, though innumerable people still find it in church, the feeling a physical space can give you of being close to something larger and full of love than you understand—the form, in John Ashbery's sad words, of some creator who has momentarily turned away.

January 4

The Georgia runoffs are today. I have felt almost from the moment of the election results—the narrow, grim, ground-out victories in Michigan and Wisconsin (Ben Wikler, hero!)—that Democrats might be about to flip the traditional wisdom on off-year elections. At least I've said it on Twitter. I think all those people turned out for Trump, I really do, not for the cadaver of the Republican Party. Trump's not on the ballot today, and there's been enough babbling for long enough on the right about fraud that there has to be some skepticism of all elections seeping in. We'll probably lose both seats by twenty points. But I can't help it. I think Warnock will win, and I think Ossoff has a chance. I Slack this. Everyone thinks Democrats will lose both seats. ("They're Democrats," says Rachel.) If I'm right, the Senate could pass the Green New Deal on January 21. Until we lose tomorrow it's not impossible.

January 5

We won.

January 6

A mob of Donald Trump supporters stormed and briefly seized the Capitol today. It's the first time it's been out of U.S. control since the War of 1812. We won that one at least! There were countless injuries and at least a few deaths, though the details are still emerging.

It happened as a lot of people across the country watched, tuning in to see if Mike Pence would "certify" the election. He had no choice—it's a procedural formality—but we all know coups are built on extremely flimsy legal pretexts that are immediately forgotten, and this was their shot, Pence's "certification," something Trump has been focused on with an unusual attention span for him. I wasn't worried enough, I see now. I don't think of Pence as a guy who wants to start a revolution. He wants to eat unsweetened apple pie and think about the prophet Elijah, or however his free time is occupied. Nor did I think McConnell would permit it, more significantly. He pretty clearly wants off the ride. But it turned out neither Pence nor McConnell's wishes were relevant in the cyclone of the day.

The sequence of events was straightforward. The President has been urging his supporters to gather near Congress on this date to protest the election, which he keeps saying was stolen from him, even though he's lost dozens of lawsuits arguing as much. (All this is the result of Trump declaring the election a fraud starting a year ago, because he knew he was probably going to lose and couldn't bear it. As with covid the competing sides are his ego vs. our lives.) Along with him, various politicians, including Josh Hawley of Missouri and Ted Cruz of Texas—two slick Harvard fellas, trying to game the rubes as they plot their 2024 campaigns, only to realize six hours later that they had inadvertently become terrorist organizers—built up support for the lie, giving it a sheen of senatorial support. Finally this morning they gathered, and after a series of increasingly incendiary speakers, Trump addressed them. It was the usual blood and soil stuff. He ended his speech by urging his followers to march over to the Capitol with him. Then he went home while they thundered in that direction, ultimately breaking down barricades and climbing steep walls to break down doors and windows into the Capitol, waving enormous MAGA banners and TRUMP flags as they flooded the few police officers guarding the entrances.

Trump being back in the White House staring at the carnage on TV is blackly funny, so in character; he has no interest in his supporters, probably no interest in being president any longer, he just needed a little nutrition pellet for his ego.

The assault itself actually seemed kind of funny too at the very start, for two reasons. First, in the earliest photos that started to emerge, it looked like just a couple dozen people, not the hundreds it became. They were in the Rotunda and the halls, taking pictures or livestreaming. Second, there was a guy (currently being called "the shaman") who looked as if he had come straight from Burning Man, in a headdress, fur vest, and leather pants, and he briefly occupied the internet's attention as we raced to generate the maximum number of jokes in the most efficient time possible, like good soldiers.

Of course, nothing about it was a joke, but those first impression have been hard to shake. Only as news has leaked out over the course of the day have people's tones modulated, as they realized how genuinely close we came to losing control of a building full of hundreds of elected officials and their staffs. The protesters had set up a gallows and were chanting "Hang Mike Pence!" Signs said the same—the siege seemed spontaneous, but appears to have involved a great deal of premeditation. (Trump is not speaking to Pence tonight, much less apologizing; he thinks Pence should have refused to certify the election.) There were protesters arrested carrying zip ties and bombs. Every moment the reality of how close we came to a more serious tragedy becomes clearer. Apparently, a group broke into the Senate chamber literally seconds after the last senators and staffers were evacuated by a side door. The first protester I've seen identified is not a "rural white," but the well-heeled CEO of a company in Schaumburg, Illinois, called Cogensia. "Transform your data into relationships," its benign website says. Well, that sums up the protest, in a way.

There was something strange in the faces of the rioters. The first protesters' chins were tilted up in at least a little awe at being inside the Capitol. More than anything, it looked like they were on the first day of the cruise they've been having to cancel all year, ever since the *Diamond Princess* lay anchored hopelessly off the coast of Yokohama. Of course, they regathered their wits pretty quickly, and a horde of them got into Nancy Pelosi's actual office within minutes, probably ready to murder her then and there after years of the mainstream right treating her like the devil incarnate. There were representatives throughout the crowd from the Proud Boys, the Three Percenters, the Oath Keepers, and other right-wing groups. Some wore t-shirts that said **6MWE,** an acronym that the anti-Semitically obsessive white nationalists use to identify each other in crowds and that stands for a pro-Holocaust catchphrase: "Six million wasn't enough."

January 8

Enough of the right rich and powerful people are sobered— politicians from Congress especially, as it's become clear they could easily have been killed two days ago—that the insurrection seems to be confined to the 6th. That's obviously not certain. Twelve days to last. But Trump made a halfheartedly contrite video, and even several Republican senators have been stirred to say they could listen to a hearing on his impeachment, apparently so incommoded by their near-deaths that they are kinda willing to stand up to the President. If he were impeached and convicted in the Senate it would take away his ability to run again in 2024, his family's Secret Service details, and a host of legal protections. Every indication is that he knows as much and would prefer to slink away in two weeks.

There are rising calls for Josh Hawley and Ted Cruz to resign from the Senate, and initial investigations into whether they and the Trumps could bear criminal responsibility for the insurrection. There is also likely to be an investigation into why Lauren Boebert, a QAnon-curious congresswoman from Colorado (where she owns Shooters Grill, a gun restaurant) was giving tours of the Capitol to the rioters two days before the attacks.

A man named Charles Johnson turned 88 two days ago. Johnson went to Yale and afterward took over his father's mutual fund with his brother. From rich beginnings, he grew inordinately rich. His current net worth is $5.5 billion, according to *Forbes*. Over the years he has donated a microscopic percentage of that fortune to Yale, and as a result Yale is home to Johnson Field, the Johnson Center for the Study of American Diplomacy, and the Brady-Johnson Program in Grand Strategy. Very fine-sounding stuff.

It was also Johnson who donated much of the money that paid for the two new residential colleges at Yale in 2016, the first new ones since the 70s. It was the subject of huge debate among students and alumni what they would be named, but he apparently bought his way into some of the rights in that debate. In the end, one college was named after Pauli Murray, the woman who saw John Henry Corniggin die in that field when she was six before becoming a civil rights icon.

The other was named after Benjamin Franklin. Franklin is the first person not associated with Yale to have a college named for him. He didn't go to Yale, didn't care about it in any way, and means nothing to its history or students. To boot he was a slaveholder.

But Franklin is Charles Johnson's hero and the namesake of the mutual fund his daddy gave him, and now Yale has a college named after Ben Franklin.

Gross, I figured when the colleges were named, but just how

things are. Then recently, Ben sent us a tweet. This same old Charles Johnson (happy birthday, hope you name something nice after yourself) maxed out in contributions not just for Donald Trump, it turns out, but also for Lauren Boebert and other candidates of the far, lunatic right. If you squint, morally, a donation to Donald Trump could be mere crass, acquisitive self-interest. But a donation to someone as unserious and vicious as Lauren Boebert— that takes real stupidity, and a snakelike meanness of heart and mind. Yale's big donor isn't just a selfish finance asshole, he's an idiot.

The tweet gets me incredibly down, the way sometimes things just can. I go for a long walk, grabbing a joint, unable not to get high, which gets me down too. It doesn't bother me for Yale, the Charles Johnson thing. I've accepted that Yale is for sale. It bothers me for Pauli Murray. She mattered too much to be the fig leaf for some racist billionaire's lazy desire to leave behind as much stuff named after himself as possible, himself or (since Yale has a policy that no college can be named for a living person) his hero (and no doubt the man he dully thinks he's just like, since all the rich people have picked avatars to convince themselves they are great, not lucky). Benjamin Franklin. How embarrassing. But much more, I hate that this Charles Johnson deigned, probably a little disgusted, to let a college be named after Pauli Murray so he could do it. He and Yale cut that deal. And I am implicated in that. Good PR at least, I'm sure he thought. But he might as well have been carrying zip ties into the Capitol the other day. That's who donated Pauli Murray College at Yale University. The honor demeans her.

Amazon owner Jeff Bezos's net worth may have grown by as much as $75 billion this year. To put that in context: If you agreed to earn a dollar a minute by going backward in time, it would take eight days to make a million dollars. To make what Bezos has added to his bank account since the pandemic began, by contrast, you would have to live every second in reverse until roughly the year 200 B.C. And it's not even close to his entire fortune. I wonder if even Jeff Bezos thinks that's a reasonable allocation of money.

In the spring I was thinking that having gone to Yale didn't mean anything to me any more because of people like Charles Johnson, because for all the good people who went there, there are hundreds of scumbags like him and Bezos skulking around every corner at Yale and Princeton and Harvard, thinking themselves fine for setting their names on things. I've been across tables from them. I know their faces.

But sitting outside this evening, I wonder if that shows too little sympathy for the person I used to be, maybe. Part of me knew that if I went to somewhere like Yale, from then on there would be something about me that nobody could say was bad. I don't even think I really had a plan after that. My plan was to do well in high school, do well at a good college, and then be a writer. It was an impulse of how not to get hurt by being alive, and I have lived a long time in obedience to it. But the debt is paid, it occurs to me. I never have to write again if I don't want to. Maybe I don't. Everything could be completely different—for me, for anyone. We could enact a 90% wealth tax on billionaires tomorrow and feed the world. And me, none of what I have done is permanent, either. That's the lesson of the pandemic, mutability. It's a scary and thrilling thing to learn. Another world is possible.

Our friend Mike, with the aerophone, is moving back to Pennsylvania after ten years in Los Angeles. Lots of people suddenly seem to be moving, actually, as if the new year was a benchmark. Even Wulf is thinking about trading out of the hacienda, though I'll believe it when I see it. My friend Jess, in Brooklyn, met someone. He's a personal assistant to a restaurateur, or something. "What are the odds?" she asks elatedly. I almost ask what she means, since the odds of that don't seem long, but realize she means, what are the odds that she should have met someone she likes so much, it had seemed impossible, actually impossible, and then it happened. She's the first person I know whose pandemic seems over.

January 9

It emerges that one woman "took a private jet to Washington to storm the Capitol." Meanwhile 3,777 people dead of covid yesterday, the numbers so high that while it's barely a news story, Nathan is back under incredible duress. A graphic goes around showing that the deadliest days in the history of America were Pearl Harbor, the Battle of Gettysburg, and last Tuesday, Wednesday, and Thursday. This butchery is the price Greg Abbott and Ron DeSantis decided to pay by opening everything. All of us try to cheer Nathan up, but it's clearly hellish. Seven patients on ventilators.

My grandmother was fascinated by polar exploration. Of the three famous explorers who tried to reach Antarctica first—Shackleton, Amundsen, and Scott—her favorite was Amundsen, whose hundreds of small decisions (to use dogs, not horses; to make his tents black, not white, for the relief of his men's eyes and to make them easy to find; etc., to the last detail) meant his expedition was the only successful one of the three. (Though everyone with a heart loves Shackleton. As the explorer Sir Raymond Priestley's great quote goes: "For scientific discovery, give me Scott; for speed and efficiency of travel give me Amundsen; but when disaster strikes and all hope is gone, get down on your knees and pray for Shackleton." Shackleton and P. G. Wodehouse went to the same high school, Dulwich College. I went there once to see the place that made them. It was lighter and less serious than the other public schools in England. You can still see Wodehouse's library preserved there, students in blazers racing by, ignoring it.)

Amundsen died in an airplane crash. It was many years after his famous expedition. A group from the Norwegian government came to him because a younger explorer had been lost, and they wanted his help. Amundsen died during the ensuing search.

What my grandmother loved about the story of his death was his reaction to the envoys. Amundsen was sitting in the garden of his house when they came to him, reading a book. He listened to their account, didn't ask a thing, and put his book facedown before standing up, ready to go. She loved that: the instant readiness, the instinctive courage of willingness to help without delay.

I thought about it today because that's how at some stage I started to think of the health-care workers we have here, as cases and deaths surge and hospitals are overwhelmed in dazed reprise, all the doctors, nurses, orderlies, techs, and so forth. Tributes to them have become rote, meaning we've stopped thinking about what they did. Covid came and hundreds of thousands of them flew to their stations, leaving their books facedown. Nearly 3,000 have died so far. Nathan would be so embarrassed if I told him to his face he was a hero, but he is. He's not *my* hero, which is Yankees slugger Don Mattingly, but he is *a* hero. Still pretty good.

January 10

We've made it past the coup attempt, for the moment. D.C. is being guarded as nervously as a winning lottery ticket by a variety of local and national forces. Joe Biden is somewhere safe. Mitch McConnell is feigning indignation about Trump's behavior. The House is moving to impeach. A few of the strongest Trump allies have wobbled slightly and perhaps more will come. As Shakespeare said, men shut their doors against a setting sun.

Trump has plans to fly dramatically to Mar-a-Lago just before Biden is sworn in. I still can't believe any of it as real. (**What Can I Say** asks James Comey in one of the best *Onion* headlines in the last four years, which sums up more about misogyny and male privilege than twenty online essays, **I'm Just a Catty Bitch from New Jersey and I Live for Drama**.) Trump's sudden silence after being banned from Twitter was bizarre at first, until it suddenly dawned on us that he had no backup strategy—everything depended on his being able to drop his caprices and plots into the minds of a hundred million people whenever he wanted. Everything. We thought social media was cute and fun in its early years, I remember. It turned out to be a great white shark, though—an apex predator.

Ha! Today, after dithering for a long time, I finally talked to a psychiatrist—an actual physician—who told me that my "cannabis use" (gross) sounds like "textbook medical treatment, in fact." Smoking is not distracting me; it's affecting my health positively; etc. etc., down a long list of red flags, and I pass the test on every question. Every one! I wish I hadn't designed my own test in my head so many times, given that I know nothing and am an idiot.

I could have saved myself so much guilt. "I do worry about your lungs," the doctor went on, but that sounds like modern faddishness. Ha! I am the picture of mental health!

January 19

400,000 deaths in the U.S.

January 20

Inauguration. It's a somber, cautiously optimistic event, with small clusters of people sitting at social distance on the dais. Bernie Sanders wins the day, in the same ratty coat he always wears, a drugstore surgical mask, and inexplicably enormous mittens made by a Vermont schoolteacher. The whole event is a curious mix of grief and relief. Earlier, Trump waved goodbye to a thin crowd at an airport in Maryland. At the end of his short address, he said, "Have a good life! See you soon!" Perfect last words. Now he's in Florida. The reporters are still tracking him, but I just have this feeling that if we wait long enough, he'll disappear. It'll go away. He'll go away.

The tone of Biden's speech and of the day in general reminded me what has been sometimes easy to forget in the excitement of winning the election, staving off the coup, and watching the Georgia runoffs, which is that he takes office after a year of historic grief. After the ceremony ends, I put on a light jacket and go for a walk in the gray afternoon.

Part of why I like watching the inauguration is that I like to see Washington, D.C. It's the city where my grandmother lived for the last forty years of her life. She and my mother are where my story begins. When I was growing up, the two of them were my two parents more or less. I couldn't have asked for better ones.

Since my grandmother died in 2004, though, I've rarely been back to Washington, so I like to see it up close during the inauguration. She was an artist named Anne Truitt, my grandmother. She was one of the earliest Minimalists. She was well known in her lifetime, but has become better known since she died, or since near the end of her life when the art historian James Meyer foregrounded her innovations in his defining history of Minimalism. She arrived at the artistic concept first chronologically, it's been argued, in fact, with a plain white sculpture called (fittingly) *First*. Soon after making it she began to show her work in New York and had success throughout the 60s, appearing in the seminal show *Primary Structures* and in 1973 becoming one of the first female artists to have a solo retrospective at the Whitney.

In the years that I knew her, some of that initial fame had faded. She still appeared in histories and memoirs, but the art world had iterated a dozen times since 1961, and the Minimalists who commanded outsized attention and money were (the usual story) compelling men, Donald Judd, Carl Andre, Ellsworth Kelly, and a half dozen others. When there was room for a woman, it was usually Agnes Martin, and after that my grandmother if there was a second. Usually not.

It didn't affect her work in the slightest. Every day I knew her she would make the short walk out to the studio in her backyard. "If I had fifteen minutes to work, I worked for fifteen minutes," she once told an interviewer, and I can verify it. For years the rewards were slim. Now you can see a painting, drawings, or sculpture by her in any first-rate museum. Of all the things I wish I could tell her, this would be one of the first, that people see her work. I get to see her sculpture *Morning Choice* when we visit Emily's parents in St. Louis and *Catawba* when I go to MoMA, and just after I moved here, LACMA finally bought its first sculpture by her, filling a gap in their collection. She and I spent thousands of hours in museums when I was little, and I don't think we ever saw one of her sculptures. A painting once, at the National Gallery. We saw more Ellsworth Kellys than you could count. I try to imagine how she would react. I think she would be happy, though not as happy as I'd like: "Good, I'm glad," she might say in her brisk way, and I would say "You can just be EXCITED!" and she would laugh and say "Oh Chooch."

Though she's best known for her sculpture, I grew up around her paintings. Like all the great Minimalists, she produced work which describes how much you can do with the very least means—in her case, sometimes astonishingly little, a single pencil mark on a field of white paint in her *Arundel* series, though more often she used color, colors she mixed herself and that are like pure titrations of feeling: the beautiful pink one by my mom's bed, a vast foggy ice shelf at daybreak; the brilliant yellow painting that was the only work of hers my grandmother kept in her own room, and which from my earliest memories I recall as being like a great pouring out of golden feeling, a sunny field in summer. I later recognized the same sensation of warmth in van Gogh.

As she pointed out to me, artists had been achieving these effects for a long time. When I was little, I would run through ten galleries while she looked at two or three paintings. Then she would make me come back and sit in front of a painting with her, and explain to me in her soft, sweet way, as unlike a formidable artist as you can imagine, to *me* at least, the way (for example) Degas flooded the lower third of a canvas of drinkers with nothing but pure color field moonlight, or how if you looked at parts of a Rembrandt the right way, it could blur so easily into a Rothko or a Mitchell.

Her patience in articulating it to a child is the reason I'm not one of the people who would look at a painting she made and say, what's that blue nothing, a kindergartener could have done it. I had seen the different things blue could mean. The yellow painting she kept—the one artwork in her bedroom—is in my room now. I look at it and see different shades and light each time, the very pale yellow horizontal interruption in the middle, which is easy to miss on first glance: these days, without the miracle of her own self here, it strikes me as a miracle of placement, perception, understanding, in other words a true fragment of her, my best friend. That was her radicalism as an artist: She saw one day that she could express everything she had been feeling much more simply—not twice as simply, but exponentially more so. And so a rectangle of yellow becomes the color of living.

She was a New England aristocrat by birth and bearing, though she did not subscribe to any notion of aristocracy in America; for instance, though she loved her ancestors, the doughty officers in the Revolution, the bookseller who corresponded with Emerson and Thoreau, her favorite was I think a man named Robert Williams (her mother was a Williams), a cordwainer who in the 1630s was also listed as both the "ditch-digger" and the very first "bell-ringer" of the small new city of Boston. Imaginatively she was one with him: a radical. He had crossed an ocean to follow his ambitions. When he had fifteen minutes to work, Robert Williams had worked. Within two generations his family was one of the most prominent in Boston.

Her parents raised her on the Eastern Shore of Maryland. Her father, Duncan Dean, was taken home by stagecoach after he was born, she once said to me, and lived to see Hiroshima. He was a small, dapper gentleman, deeply amiable by all acounts. He never worked. During the Depression, he kept gold dollars in his suit pocket and handed them out, though the Depression had taken a pretty good chunk of their money, too. My grandmother was educated by a governess, then at a French school, and finally at Katharine Hepburn–era Bryn Mawr. (She loved that college and would point out politely that Radcliffe, where her twin sisters went, had been more "social." The twins disputed this. Their own grandmother, Anna Palmer, was in the first graduating class of Smith College. The great female artists of the last century tended to come from families that had valued women and their education for at least a few generations.)

Her mother died while she was still in college. After she graduated, she became a nurse's aide on a casualty ward through the end of the war, then not long after married my grandfather, James Truitt. He was gone by the time I knew my grandmother, and she and I fell, from my earliest memories, into the most natural, companionable of friendships, as she has written about in her own books; a true compatibility of minds and hearts, both of us readers, both of us chatters and easy to laugh—at least, privately, for in public she was polite but very formal.

I don't know, she was a grandmother, she had straight soft white hair that I loved to bury my face in, she held my hand when I went into kindergarten. (There's a deep chaste physicality between grandparents and grandchildren, they furrow into each other, they breathe closely, the old and the young, love binding them.) She was great at being a grandmother. For twenty years of my life I thought that both she and I couldn't draw. Then I realized that while I actually can't draw, she meant in comparison to Fra Angelico or someone, one of her random favorites. I only learned this when she quickly drew something to entertain my sisters Julia and Isabelle. I accused her of being a liar (which I stand by) but anyhow that's the kind of grandmother she was. She kept little bottles of ginger ale on the landing down to the basement for when her grandchildren visited. When I got sick she drove through the night to get there. When I woke up at the hospital she had brought pizza, because she knew it was my favorite food, but she had received it at her hotel by the hospital and, I guess puzzled, cut it into slices like pita bread for me. I ate it cold not long after I got that first, decisive IV treatment. It tasted incredible.

She had true New England cleanliness, she, her practical well-made clothes, and her house. The house had few things in it, and all of them were therefore fascinating: art by Mary Meyer and James Lee Byars, an ancient and beautiful thin Japanese "door," no more than a driftwood plank with characters on it, portraits of her ancestors. Her favorite of these was a watercolor profile in an oval frame of Captain John Pulling, who was a revolutionary, childhood best friends with Paul Revere, and one of the two men on the famous night who hung the lanterns for Revere (one if the British were coming by land, two if by sea—it was two, some people don't know that). Captain Pulling survived a British raid on his house by hiding in a barrel of potatoes and lived to fight in the war and have the portrait on my grandmother's wall painted of him.

She had a Japanese sand garden on a side table, which I loved to play with (there was a tiny teak rake in it) and the side table itself was clattering-full of silver from her grandmothers and great-grandmothers, so dating, most of it, to the 1860s and 1870s. There were also lots of silver things all over her house, though never congregating together. This must be true of a lot of Wasps who are no longer part of whatever financial elite they once were; I myself have loads of them, the best a silver cigarette box from Cartier the size and weight of a brick, lined with cedar, which my great-grandfather Henry Finch received from his father on his wedding day, October 5, 1915. I store my weed in it, that's how much I love it. The cedar keeps it fresh. My guitar picks are in his wife's baby cup. The portrait of Captain John Pulling, which my grandmother left to me, is by our front door.

She would tell me these stories at night (when I asked), and I would go off sleepily to bed at some point. The next morning by the time I had woken up she would have put two coats on a new sculpture, each one a quintessence of color and light, a sensation unto itself, if you stood alone with it and actually paid attention for longer than a few seconds. I can't believe she left that behind. I can't believe she left me behind.

As the inauguration sinks in, I feel an enormous internal release. The awful heart-pounding vigilance of the last four years is over, really over. In its place is something new and circumspect and hard to name. It might be grief. Maybe that's why my grandmother is on my mind as I walk. It seems as if we've lost so much in the last four years, even more in the last nine months, without a second to stop and consider what because we were too busy fighting, phone banking, disinfecting our groceries.

When my grandmother died, it seemed like the natural order of things. She was a grandparent, so while her death was a surprise, after a very brief illness, it didn't seem tragic. Now I don't know. Sometimes, since her death, I've wondered whether perhaps the real genealogy of the world is not patrilineal or matrilineal, but a far finer tracery of family trees designed to include all the surrogate figures in children's lives, aunts, nannies, servants, grandparents, neighbors, most of them women, some of them men. They are as real as parents. I came to love my mother and grandmother so much when I was little—and, in time, to be wary of others—that I still draw on the feeling of their love if I ever feel really in trouble, though one's 3,000 miles away and the other's dead.

As I walk uphill past Los Feliz Boulevard, I cast my mind back to the weeks after my grandmother's death. When I went to cancel her cards at the library and the gas station, both the librarian and the gas station attendant I told got emotional, one cried, I remember that vividly. It sounds far-fetched, but it happened—I think because she believed down to her last cell in the idea of manners, and not manners as an artifice to smooth life, but the deeper good manners of caring about whatever person is in front of you, regardless of who they are, paying attention to them with your full self, treating them as real. (A means and not an ends, Kant would say.) That was what the gas station attendant was crying about. Imagine the power of the same kind of attention on a little boy.

She had so much time for me because she lived alone. She never remarried, and her routines were unvarying, work and family. She lived in a small comfortable house in a quiet neighborhood in Washington called Cleveland Park, where, especially after I started at boarding school, I took to going to stay with her for three weeks at a time, a month, most of every break.

Yet when I picture her as I walk today it's not there or at the National Gallery, but, Bill Evans's *Peace Piece* keeping me company on repeat, in rural New York. Every other year or so from the 70s onward, my grandmother went to an arts colony near Saratoga Springs called Yaddo. She was the acting director there for some time to help out a friend, and we spent Christmas there when I was five, throwing ice into the ponds and sledding by the studios on the empty campus.

Maybe it's because my visits to Yaddo were brief that I can picture her there so clearly. She always had on a green L.L.Bean barn coat, and in her studio (four coats on Christmas morning) would walk among the tables she'd set up of different paintings and drawings, adding or discarding, adding layers while I sat and we talked. I've heard frequently since she died about how she never let people in her studio while she was working, and feel a selfish little nod of internal validation; I was right, she cared about me most. Told you.

One of the last long times I spent with her was at Yaddo. She was 83, and I was 23. She was in excellent health, though as it happened she had almost no time left. We drove all over Saratoga and into the countryside, where we stopped to pick a few apples and have apple cider and donuts outside on a crisp autumn day, talking about her work, my own grandiose plans (I wonder now what they were), the same conversation we had been having more or less without stopping since the day I was born, my mother too when it was the three of us, and both subordinate to the hours they had been talking daily since my mother was one, in person or by phone. As we were walking back through the rows of apple trees toward the car, she needed a rest, as she often did, and we sat down on a bench. I remember her saying, "Chooch, when *you* have a grandson, you can remember how kind you were to me." I told her that was silly, of course it was nothing to stop. Only now that she's gone do I realize how many breadcrumbs she left like that one, to find in my mind after she was gone. I think she knew I would be sad without her.

After I had been there for a week, she drove me to the Amtrak station in Saratoga. It felt too soon to say goodbye for both of us, though I would be visiting her in Washington a few weeks later, planning to stay for two weeks before Christmas. We sat in her small hunter-green Subaru and chatted, half an hour early to the train, and then at last the train rounded the corner slowly toward us and it was time to say goodbye, and we hugged, and I smelled the good clean laundered smell of her, her skin. I jumped out of the car and grabbed my duffel bag and waved to her, walking over to the train. It had started to rain harder, and I turned back and waved one last time. She was standing by her door, having put on her yellow slicker, and maybe because we had both been feeling a little blue she stood there beaming at me and waved. I got on the train thinking that was it, we'd said goodbye, only to see, when I had finally chosen a seat, that she was still there, standing and smiling, occasionally putting a hand up and waving, watching the train. The thing I think about now is that she had no idea if I'd even sat on the side of the train where I could see her. But she stayed just in case, even as the train pulled away, so that I would see her and know she was there. That's the image I try to remember, as I walk these hills for the thousandth time since March and try to calm my nerves, try to last until the vaccine.

A right wing talking point that started immediately with covid was that at least most of the fatalities were among the elderly, those who have lived "full lives," were "already vulnerable," etc. And though it's not even the whole truth, people of all kinds are getting sick from this fucking thing right now, beyond which we don't even know its long term effects yet—besides all that, I think, even if every single one of the 400,000 people gone were old, it shouldn't matter if they were old, they were people. I knew an old person once.

As I near home, I call my mother (golden herself, my grandmother would have said) and we talk for a long time, until, after we hang up, I take down the correspondence box full of my grandmother's letters to me and open it for the first time in years. It's just too bad we can't talk, I think for the millionth time. I would love to catch up, that's it. Instead I talk to her more and more, though I know she can't hear me. But it's like the way she waved, I figure. It's only fair.

"Thousands of young men had died that things might go on," wrote Virginia Woolf after the war. I'm out in the yard, in the soft late light, reading her diaries again, when I come across a line that makes me laugh out loud in surprise: "Must order macaroni from London." Virginia, I know this feeling! A grin on my face, I hold my place in the book with a thumb and look up. A sudden loose fling of birds moves left to right across the orange-pink sky, a few palm trees jutting into it here and there, beautiful little incidents on the flat horizon. The birds wheel in a loose beautiful pattern made only of their senses, then disappear east, leaving behind the clean impersonal swept sky, scentless and seasonless and far. Inside I feel a yearning for something I have never understood, god probably, and I wonder the usual things, which is who we are, and why, and why it ends. I change the album, roll a neat joint, and watch as eventually the last light goes. And so the days glide forward, into a future we have to hope other people haven't already made for us.

Acknowledgments

This book owes so much to Reagan Arthur, such a graceful and smart editor that any amount of hassle would be worth working with her. Instead, she's amazing, funny, warm, and wonderful—without her friendship, I really don't know if I could have finished writing this. Reagan, thank you so much.

Reagan's assistant editor Annie Bishai was an invaluable voice in early readings of the manuscript, a constant source of welcome good cheer, and saved me from my own disorganization more times than I can count. Boris Kachka and Peter Schjeldahl both provided indispensable early feedback. Additionally, I'm very thankful to Erinn Hartman, Maria Massey, Lisa Montebello, Julianne Clancy, Janet Hansen, Demetris Papadimitropoulos, Isabel Meyers, and the other great people at Knopf. Cosmo Bjorkenheim did a superlative job of fact-checking the manuscript.

To the friends who got me through the pandemic, you accidentally also made it possible for me to write this book. So that's on your consciences. Nathan, Rebecca, Matteo, John, Matt, Rachel, Jared, Dan, Peter, Jess, Alice, Chris, Ben: thank you. I love you all.

Nobody has ever had a better mother than I do. Mom, thank

you for doing exactly what Rosie said—teaching me unconditional love. Henry, Julia, Rosie, Isabelle, I miss you all every second I'm not with you. I just love you all so much. Dennis, Linda, I love you both and feel so fortunate to have you. Your steadfastness during the pandemic was heroic. And finally, Emily, to borrow a line from one of our old trips—somewhere in my youth or childhood.